Developmental
Teacher
Evaluation

Developmental Teacher Evaluation

Ben M. Harris

University of Texas at Austin

ALLYN AND BACON, INC.

Boston   London   Sydney   Toronto

Library of Congress Cataloging in Publication Data

Harris, Ben M.
  Developmental teacher evaluation.

  Bibliography: p.
  Includes index.
  1. Teachers—United States—Rating of.   2. School
supervision—United States.   I. Title.
LB2838.H33   1986   371.1'44   85-28662
ISBN 0-205-08667-5

Printed in the United States of America

10   9   8   7   6   5   4   3   2   1   91   90   89   88   87   86

**Dedicated to
my children and grandchildren**

Contents

List of Exhibits

Preface

Teacher evaluation has long been viewed by school boards and administrators, and practiced by principals as an event—an act of making one or more value judgments. This primitive notion of evaluation has failed to make a meaningful contribution to efficient operation of schools and has been negatively related to the improvement of teaching. Modern evaluation theory and practice have developed to the point of making dramatically different kinds of teacher evaluation feasible. Demands of the society for more and better education are making such new approaches to teacher evaluation urgent.

This book presents both theoretically and practically a new way of approaching teacher evaluation in our schools. Evaluation is presented as a set of processes rather than as an event. As such, the processes are seen as requiring a systems approach to making teacher evaluation operationally effective. Two distinctly different kinds of evaluation are described—developmental and summative—and while needing to be linked together, the author makes a hopefully compelling argument for the separation of these two systems of evaluation and for giving developmental teacher evaluation the highest possible priority over the administrative decision-making processes. Finally, the practical problems of organizing, data gathering, and guiding the instructional improvement process are all given attention as part of the total system.

A unique feature of this book is the presentation of a specific design for a teacher evaluation system in a public school setting. This design gives detailed, concrete illustrations of the essential principles and guidelines presented. While many illustrations are provided throughout, the reader will soon become aware of frequent references to the DeTEK system. It is hoped that the advantages gained for the reader in finding illustrations of nearly all concrete suggestions will outweigh the overemphasis on a single system.

The current scene in the public and private schools of the United States is also rapidly shifting and developing. When this book was first planned, United States schools were moving rapidly toward *developmental teacher evaluation*. Much that is now being advocated, even mandated, is anything but developmental in nature. It is my contention that *developmental* efforts are more productive and also prerequisite to summative decision making. Practitioners are urged to view this book as a beacon in behalf of excellence. The current fads—merit pay and punitive attitudes toward school personnel—will surely soon pass.

Ben M. Harris

Acknowledgments

This book has been thirty years in the making. In 1954, as a personnel director for a rapidly growing suburban school district, I began struggling with the realities and problems of teacher evaluation. Those experiences have been followed over these decades by a constant quest for effective ways to assure the children and youth of our schools that they would have teachers who were growing, developing professionals. That takes more than teacher evaluation to accomplish, but cannot be realized without a guidance system.

I am indebted to an extensive array of fine educators for stimulation and help in developing the ideas in this book. Every graduate student group with whom I have worked in the past twenty-five years has had to help me try out new ideas about teacher development. Practitioners all across this nation and in several other countries have been more than candid in giving me "corrective feedback" as we conducted pilot efforts together. My colleagues in the Department of Educational Administration, in the Southwest Educational Development Laboratory, and in the Council of Professors of Instructional Supervision have always been helpful with encouragement and feedback.

My special professional thanks go to Kenneth E. McIntyre for getting me deeply committed and creatively involved in the business of developing observation techniques for the classroom. Ms. Jane Hill, as a long-time colleague, never failed to help me balance the ideal with the practical. Superintendents and their professional staffs in Alamo Heights, DeKalb, Montgomery, Baytown, Lufkin, Post, and many other communities gave so willingly of time, enthusiasm, and even funds to test the materials and procedures presented in this book. Without all of these assistants, few new ideas could be expected.

My personal thanks, of course, must go to Dolores Payton who typed impossible notes; to Mary Ellen Milbourne for loving attention to the artwork in Chapter 8; and to Mary Lee Harris for editing, proofing, and moral support.

1

Current Practices and Problems

The character of teacher evaluation in the elementary and secondary schools of the nation is primarily an outgrowth of the priorities and problems that have confronted school boards and administrators over the past forty years since World War II. College and university faculty evaluations have also been shaped heavily by the fast-changing events of those years, but colleges retain many practices that have their origins in older traditions dating back even to ancient times.

It would be a mistake to view teacher evaluation in current practice without due regard for the past. It is also unwise to ignore new technological developments and emergent programmatic needs. Teacher evaluation practices are now improving. But they generally fail to measure up to the current expectations of the society and will surely fall short of future needs unless changed in substantial ways. The knowledge base on which to build new teacher evaluation systems is more adequate than ever, but it is still largely underutilized (Webster, 1983).

NEEDS FOR TEACHER EVALUATION

The tacit assumption that teachers "need" to be evaluated is easily made but rarely considered thoughtfully. The presumptions about need shape the responses to its fulfillment. At least five quite different needs can be identified as giving both purpose and form to teacher evaluation:

1. The teacher, as the central figure in the school's operation, *needs* to be evaluated if, in fact, educational evaluation of any significant kind is to be undertaken (Costa, 1977).

2. Parents no longer have close personal contacts with the teachers of their children and youth, and those parents have a *need* for new assurances about teaching competence and the welfare of students (PDK, 1979).
3. Administrators and supervisors, in trying to maintain and improve the quality of the school program, are dealing with many highly autonomous operating units, which seem to defy coordination, development, and even simple adjustments. These instructional leaders are in *need* of detailed information about the teachers in charge of each of those classroom units (Madaus et al., 1979).
4. The classroom teacher or instructor tends to perceive himself with considerable uncertainty and ample distortion, and hence *needs* reliable feedback from external sources (Hardebeck, 1974).
5. The practice of personnel decision making regarding selection, contract renewal, promotions, reassignment, certification, new program staffing, retirements, leaves of absence, and in-service education *needs* objective information on teacher performance to guide these decisions (Cronback, 1963).

The five kinds of "needs" are elaborated below to provide a context for thinking about current practices and problems.

A Changing Technology

Teacher evaluation can be viewed as a problem demanding *basic changes* rather than minor modifications in procedures and revision of instruments. Teacher evaluation as a developing professional technology is comparable to air transportation at the start of the 20th century. To go aloft in hot air balloons was not uncommon practice then, but the basic nature of such air travel endowed it with very limited utility. The improvement of balloons and other such "aircraft" continued, but failed to satisfy man's need to fly with direction, speed, reliability, and safety. Only *basic changes* in the approach were capable of responding to such needs. A technological breakthrough occurred with the joint development of aerodynamic wing structures and internal combustion engines. The airplane, not the balloon, became the basic approach to air travel. The use and development of balloons continued, of course, and gave rise to the Zeppelins of the 1930s. Nonetheless, this persistence in an outmoded technology made little contribution to the need of man to span the regions of the earth.

The danger of using mechanistic analogies to help us think about educational problems is self-evident. Historical precedent can also be misleading. However, there are numerous situations in which such analogies and historical perspectives can be useful. In this instance, it seems appropriate to think of much, if not most, current practice in teacher evaluation as technically and historically analogous to the practices of the era of the hot air balloon in air travel. The technology did get man aloft. It provided some limited advantages over other forms of travel by land and water; however, the gas filled bags had overwhelming and persistent limitations. Currently, teacher evaluation is easily described in the same way. Current practices are useful in some limited ways, but the overriding need for a system that can give impetus and direction to instructional improvement in classrooms is simply not being satisfied (McIntyre, 1979).

The analogy above has value in focusing our attention on the relative merits of "modifying" the balloon versus abandoning it in favor of basically different forms (Tracy and MacNaughton, 1984). Teacher evaluation, we shall argue, will produce urgently needed results only as the old system is abandoned and entirely new ones perfected (Levin, 1979).

The Teacher as Central Figure

The importance of the teacher in the formal school setting has rarely been challenged. To be sure, other elements in the operation are clearly recognized as important, too. Buildings, materials, administrative leadership, curriculum, fiscal support, and public support all contribute to the quality of the instructional program influencing student learning. There have been sporadic efforts to discount the teacher. "Teacher-proof curricula" and "teaching machines" have had their advocates (Bolvin, 1967). However, little evidence is available to challenge the long-accepted notion that "the teacher makes the difference," at least as far as the formal learning processes are concerned, for which schools are generally organized and maintained (Good and Brophy, 1975; Kean, et al., 1979; Medley, D. M., 1979).

The most overwhelming evidence regarding the importance of the teacher as *central to instruction* include the budget allocation, the size of the teacher staff, and the reliance on teachers as the "workers" of the school. One could argue that these are the outgrowth of old traditions, and hence are misguided. Such arguments are heard occasionally, as in Ivan Illich's *DeSchooling Society* (1971). But with rare exceptions, proposals for improving instruction call for more people in teaching roles, not fewer.

The emphasis upon teachers as central figures in the school (and college) operation looms large as a rationale for giving teacher evaluation a high priority. Obviously, if teachers are important to learning, if resources are allocated primarily for their services, if schools cannot function without their work, then teacher evaluation is essential for understanding and improving the school operation. Without teacher evaluation, all other efforts at educational evaluation are relatively nonproductive.

This argument for teacher evaluation as the "heart and soul" of educational evaluation seems logical enough; strangely, it is often rejected or overlooked in practice. Student minimum competency testing, for instance, places the central focus of evaluation on pupil appraisal (NAESP, 1979).

EXHIBIT 1.1   What it's really all about in a cartoon

Cartoon by David Baker. Reprinted from *ASCD Update* with permission of Association for Supervision and Curriculum Development, Alexandra, VA.

Accreditation programs of the various states and accrediting associations give attention to many facets of school and college operations, but rarely focus with any rigor on faculty performance (Commission on Elementary School, 1970; NSSE, 1973). Popham (1971) is one of many who advocate paying attention to student achievement almost to the exclusion of concern for teacher evaluation. Federal projects and programs (Title I, Title III, P.L. 94-142, bilingual education, etc.) are replete with regulations and evaluation requirements that almost always neglect the question of the competence of the teacher (Block, 1978; Spady, 1977). The massive "study of schooling" directed by John Goodlad was curiously limited in its emphasis on *teaching,* giving preference to *schooling* (Goodlad, et al., Nov. 1979).

   Obviously, evaluation of educational programs should extend beyond teacher evaluation. More importantly, teacher evaluation can and should be seen as the most important facet of any meaningful program evaluation effort (Madaus, et al. 1979). Although the teacher is certainly not the only important concern of educational program evaluation there is no comparable focus that can become an alternative. The teacher is *central* to the teaching/learning process (Rossmiller, 1983).

The Concerns of Parents

Urban societies lose touch with their teachers as persons. The urban society provides for the rearing of its children and youth in a variety of ways— school, playground, church, scouts, little leagues, electronic games, television, street gangs, and movie houses all play a part. Much of the personal relationships tend to be lost and parents turn back to the school as the most promising source of assistance with child rearing. The teacher is no longer a neighbor, a friend, and a member of "the congregation." Parents often give up even trying to know the teacher. Schools are large and pupil assignments become impersonal. School organization has grown steadily more complex and segmented, so that students often are in a given school for only a few years and rarely with a single teacher for more than one year. Beyond the primary years, departmentalization is invoked, giving parents an often confusing array of individuals to relate to as "teachers." Desegregation and "crosstown bussing" illustrate with dramatic overtones some of the many parental concerns that grow out of the urbanization of schooling.

There have been educational gains from this urbanization of education, but the way society feels about its teachers has been seriously affected. Opinion polls report "teacher's lack of interest" and "getting good teachers" as among the top ten educational problems of the nation (PDK, 1979). Even when parents retain rather positive attitudes toward teachers and the school, these tend to be based on very little information and are less than fully consistent. Confidence in nearly all public and private institutions apparently is on the decline in recent years. Schools have not suffered as severly in this decline as has "government" or "corporations," but increasing uncertainty and even suspicion and hostility are signs of our times not to be ignored.

"Back to basics" and accountability compaigns seem to be recurrent phenomena supported by various segments of our society. In part, these campaigns gain support from parents as hoped-for ways of improving the "program." But instructional programs are controlled by teachers, and dissatisfaction, anxiety, or uncertainty about the educational program is consciously or unconscioulsy directed at the classroom teacher (Gallup, 1977). Administrators, "the system," the curriculum, the textbooks, the "methods," the grading system, and other targets of discontent must be seen as symptomatic of a society that does not know its teachers and does not understand their teaching.

Teacher evaluation can be a vehicle for helping restore confidence in the teacher as well as in the school and its program. The complexities of relating the evaluation of teachers to the image of the school are great. The feasibility problems are numerous, but the well-being of teachers as practitioners and of the public school as an institution require some such linkage. In the absence of well-established evaluation systems that give public assurances, there has developed a growing movement for state mandated and prescribed teacher evaluation (Popham, 1971), for teacher competency testing (Cole, 1979), and for stricter licensure. Whatever the merits of such efforts, they are hardly consistent with the essential character of the problem or the state of knowledge about improving personnel performance in schools (Carey, 1980).

Administrators and Supervisors Need to Know

The most neglected need for better teacher evaluation is that felt by administrators and supervisors—superintendent, directors, coordinators, principals, and department heads. The need for detailed information about teacher performance is essential to leadership presonnel who are planning, organizing, communicating, deciding, facilitating, and coordinating instructional programs. Every action of these officials is based on assumptions that they have relevant knowledge about the operations that teachers control.

In fact, most such leaders have only fragmentary and often fallacious information. The information most readily available to them tends to be least relevant and least reliable. The teacher lounge gossip, the friendly chats in the hall or office, the faculty meeting discussions, the complaints from parents, and the reactions of students are all events supplying a stream of information. But the information that is most urgently needed pertains to teacher performance—especially in-classroom performance—and it is largely unavailable.

The lack of information of crucially important kinds needs to be seen as a special problem of schools. The practice of compartmentalization of teaching, which places every teacher in a separate subject, with a separate room and a separate grade, produces bariers to free access to information. The barriers are both physical and psychological. The separateness of each teacher from others, and from principal, department chairman, and supervisors, is produced by walls and closed doors, but also by autonomous assignments. The teacher is indeed autonomous, not by reason of desire or competence, but because that's the way the school is organized, and teachers not willing or able to work that way do not survive or even make application for employment.

The lack of information for administrators and supervisors about teacher performance is perpetuated by several school traditions. The rural tradition of the "school master" who answers to no one but the chairman of the board or town committee persists. The school board and community have long since given up trying to evaluate the teacher directly. Instead there has emerged the teacher-held attitude that "I know my business, so if you don't like how I teach, get another teacher"; or "I'm a professional and I have the right to be left alone, to teach in my own way."

Even more widespread is the tradition that holds students responsible for learning, rather than the teacher or the school or the program. Again, this has its roots in the rural American faith that schools and teachers are "good," while students "are privileged to attend." It follows, then, that if students fail, students are at fault. More recently this same tradition is reflected in standardized testing programs and especially in recent student minimum competency testing programs. The effect of these traditions has been to focus hardly at all on the evaluation of teaching.

Teacher Feedback Needs

Much has been said and written about teacher evaluation to improve teaching, and this usually implies that feedback needs are given high priority. The autonomy and isolation of the solitary teacher in the classroom does, indeed, present a very difficult problem. Workers whose products are concrete and readily observable receive feedback by viewing that product. Those who work in teams—mechanics, surgeons, lawyers—are constantly observing, comparing, reacting to each other in ways that provide for corrective or reinforcing feedback. Industrial, shop, and office workers who are closely supervised by someone who is constantly close at hand and often working with them have a situation in which feedback can be immediate and specific. These are work conditions that prevail very rarely for teachers in schools or college settings. Athletic coaches are sometimes in situations where opportunities for feedback are provided, but only rarely do we offer useful feedback for the classroom teacher (Harris, et al. 1979).

This no-feedback circumstance that faces nearly all teachers has very predictable consequences. Lower levels of professional morale, higher levels of closed-mindedness, greater feelings of anxiety, slower growth rates, and distorted perceptions of one's own performance are all predictable consequences. It is this array of negative consequences from no-feedback situations that argues for teacher evaluation that is very heavily focused on feedback to the teacher *rather than on judgment making and reporting to authority figures!*

Unfortunately, teacher evaluation efforts currently in vogue do not respond well to teacher needs for feedback. To be valuable, feedback must be *immediately* related to performance. Evaluations which collect data for annual review purposes do not respond to needs. Feedback should be frequent, it must stress objectivity, and it cannot be threatening beyond the teacher's capacity to cope. Current practices rarely provide for such feedback, but the needs are urgent. Teachers, like other human beings, have a persistent need to know about themselves as seen through the eyes of others. A teacher evaluation system that can respond to such basic needs of those doing the work of the school will have an effect that should not be underestimated. The all-too-common failure of school officials to respond to such a fundamental human need has made teaching less humane and less effective than it might be.

Personnel Decision Making

The need to make personnel decisions based on teacher evaluation is commonly cited as important. The term *personnel decision* is often translated into *teacher dismissal.* However, a great variety of personnel decisions might be informed by evaluation data of appropriate kinds. McIntyre (Sept. 1979) cites "validating the teacher selection process" as one of several important reasons for teacher evaluation. Others include promotions, reassignments, and special recognition, as well as dismissals (Harris, et al., 1979).

The validation of prior selection procedures or techniques has not been a popular endeavor. In the long era of teacher shortages (1940–1975), there was little pretense at rigorous selection. In more recent years, even though shortages have been largely eliminated, selection procedures have continued to rely heavily on dubious data sources and techniques (Bolton, 1973; Harris, et al., 1979). Letters of recommendation, interviews, and inappropriate tests are but a few of the data sources that often are nearly worthless (McIntyre, 1979). But the process by which these and other kinds of data are utilized often makes selection decisions very much a game of chance. (Yelland, 1968). Even so, post-selection review is rarely undertaken in most school districts, for the teacher evaluation data are not suitable, and time and interest are often lacking. Nonetheless, as teacher evaluation procedures grow increasingly sophisticated, the resultant improved data can be utilized to improve the selection process.

The dismissal decision is among the most worrisome from the point of view of both classroom teachers and administrative or supervisory personnel. Teachers understandably fear the use of evaluation data when dismissal decisions are imminent. Their fear is often exaggerated, but much uncertainty is engendered when a teacher evaluation operation is subjective, unsystematic, and hence perceived as producing whimsical or unpredictable decisions. In fact, there is substantial reason to believe that only rarely does a direct connection exist between formal teacher evaluation and dismissal decisions. Finlayson (1979:69) discovered that as far as "incompetence" is concerned, only eleven ". . . teacher dismissal cases due to incompetence (were) appealed to the secretary of education . . ." in Pennsylvania from 1971–1976. Obviously, there are more dismissals than those reported by Finlayson, who writes, ". . . there are a few informal, out-of-court purges in some districts. These cases, of course, involve young, nontenured teachers" (1979:69).

But dismissal decisions do loom larger than the one study in Pennsylvania would suggest. The young teacher is often urged to "move on," a de facto dismissal that may or may not have been warranted by evaluation processes. Teachers who do not conform to someone's biases or community norms are often pressured to leave teaching or move on. Again, this is a de facto dismissal that may not be in the best interests of students. More common than dismissals of any kind, however, are the numerous instances of incompetence or marginal effectiveness that are not dealt with in any systematic way (AASA, 1979).

EVALUATION GAMES

At least some of the current practices in teacher evaluation can be better understood as the "games people play" rather than as formal evaluation. Much current practice is simply not defensible in terms of sound concepts of evaluation. Criteria are often not clearly specified. Irrelevant criteria are commonly employed. Data gathering is often superficial and objectivity neglected. Analytical procedures are largely lacking, in a formal sense, and in their place are global, judgmental, simplistic expressions of opinion.

Rather than just criticize such practices, it is useful to consider ways in which such unsound evaluation endeavors do, nonetheless, serve some useful purposes. Games often emerge as informal ways of handling otherwise perplexing problems. In some forms, these games may be nonproductive, but not harmful. Serious hidden consequences can result, however.

The No-Nonsense Game

Most common of all is a set of practices that provides a facade of straightforward, highly businesslike, objective, systematic evaluation. The principal is the lone, all-knowing evaluator. The teacher pretends to be docile and completely accepting. When the date for submitting the annual report arrives, the principal sits alone for a few minutes, completes his/her ratings, signs it with a flair of authoritativeness, and the job is done.

Teachers in this game play a very dependent role. In contacts with the principal before and after the "judgment day," the teacher makes clear his or her faith in the principal in numerous ways. The principal is invited to the room to see a new bulletin board. Students are sent to visit the office with "something to show." Cookies or cakes or flowers are brought from home for the faculty lounge. The principal's advice and permission are eagerly sought, even for only trivial matters of concern.

The principal remains aloof at all times, being cautious not to know too much. Observations are avoided, while brief drop-in visits are by invitation only or on special occasions. Complaints from parents, students, or other teachers are met with a firm response. After all, the principal must "protect his/her faculty" and the self-image of the principal must be maintained as the omniscient evaluator; "nonprofessional" influences are not tolerated!

This no-nonsense approach to the game of evaluation works only so long as the set of conditions described above can be maintained and a few simple rules are followed by both teacher and principal. The principal must enjoy playing the roles of judge, jury, and defender; gaining a sense of power and importance from the annual affair; and enjoying the illusion that teachers have unlimited faith in virtue of the judgments being made. Conversely, the teacher must find it enjoyable to act dependent, protected, and subservient to the judgment of the principal. An obvious source of comfort for the teacher comes from not having to be self-critical.

This game can be played only so long as *all* or *nearly all* judgments are harmless to the teacher. For all practical purposes, the ratings must be completely positive and nondiscriminating. Any slightly discriminating rating that deviates from those generally conferred are perceived as a threat. The price of omniscience which the principal must pay is complete acceptance of the teacher.

The Abdication Game

Many evaluators, usually principals, have serious difficulty in assuming any clearly professional role in the evaluation process. They recognize the complexities of evaluation, but fear damaging the interpersonal relationships they hope to build with teachers. Hence, a role reversal is arranged. The teacher becomes the evaluator and, mimicking the unsystematic practices widely in use, the opinions of the teacher are used as the basis for assigning ratings. The principal assumes a very dependent relationship to the teacher in this game. The principal's rationale is verbalized like this:

> Now, you [teacher] know so much more about your own teaching than I can ever know that I really must have your judgments. If I evaluated you, I'd probably overrate you on some things and underrate you on others. But you know your strengths and your weaknesses and I know you'll be professional and guide me in making out this report.

The process of substituting teacher opinion for principal opinion is useful in maintaining "peaceful" relations with a teacher, and it also drastically reduces the principal's work load related to data gathering. The teacher gains control over the situation, gets a sense of power and independence, and has only to admit some slight deficiency in exchange.

This game permits the principal to be the "good guy," fulfilling his/her strong desire to maintain "friendly" personal relationships. The principal must be willing, of course, to accept only passively involved in instructional leadership. He or she keeps busy facilitating, supporting, coordinating, but is not a dynamic, initiating supervisor of instruction.

The teacher can play this game as long as no real needs are perceived and the security gained is comforting. The principal must, of course, accept all teacher judments and proffer questions with great deference and caution. If the teacher's judgments are not fully accepted at face value—that is, as though they were indeed objectively data-based—then the entire structure of the game is destroyed. Hence, teachers push their advantage, making themselves look quite excellent while the principal glows with pride.

The Let's-Be-Accountable Game

This game is characterized by ritualized procedures that are seemingly very systematic, scientific, and objective. The game is played in two forms. The old form involves elaborate instrumentation, narrative reporting, assigning weights to ratings, and computing scores or preparing profiles. Sometimes, both teacher self-ratings and principal ratings are combined and differences resolved by negotiation and compromise.

The new form of the accountability game takes a management by objectives format (MBO). Instead of ratings, a ritual is developed for identifying a few objectives for improvement. The review of progess toward the "target" objectives becomes the process that leads to judgments of relative success.

The accountability game is one that involves the principal in very active endeavors in the old form, for he or she assumes responsibility for gathering information, doing much paper work, initiating the planning and review sessions, and finally submitting the completed report. In its newer form, the teacher's role is much more active and initiating, for it is the teacher who writes up the proposal, selecting objectives, and describing ways in which he or she proposes to make progress. In both of its forms, the game is time consuming but often not satisfying. Teachers gain little insight into their ways of performing because top priority is given to *showing* that we "measure up to expectations." The principal, too, tends to be concerned with *appearances* of progress and excellence in the staff rather than with problem finding or problem solving.

The Ineffectiveness of Such Practices

The three games described are, of course, stereotypes of real practices. They do not reflect the full array of approaches in current use. They also make the life of the evaluator seem too simple and evasive. Actually, approximate versions of each game are played in most school settings, but they vary with circumstances.

The games described are all somewhat productive in the sense that some personal and organizational needs can be met in each instance. They tend to have anxiety-reducing effects for both evaluator and evaluatee. They tend to offer some bases for interaction, and the consequences can be somewhat satisfying to both parties (Crone, 1980). What these games don't do is produce evaluations. In terms of the needs for evaluation described above, all of these games are nonproductive.

Counter-Productivity

Other common practices that need to be recognized include many that are essentially counter-productive. Evaluation efforts that are essentially punitive, creating anxieties and confusion for the sake of the evaluator's sense of authority, are not uncommon and should obviously be eliminated (Haefele, 1980). Situations in which evaluation efforts have no structure or substance, consisting simply of contract renewal decisions and a word of praise are actually nonevaluations. Evaluations that call for judgments or action decisions based on student test scores alone (Doyle, 1983), or rumors of malpractice, are of course not defensible either.

It may be that much of the current effort to develop elaborate statewide plans for summative evaluation will also prove to be counter-productive. Carey's (1980) analysis of an array of state-mandated efforts reveals nearly all of them to be far from "state of the art." In Chapter 10 this author reviews some examples of state-level efforts to either confuse or ignore the essential requirements for *both* summative and formative evaluation. Many of the state-mandated programs being initiated in the early 1980's are already being recognized as crude, clumsy, and expensive at best (Finn, 1985; English et al. 1985). The great probability is that highly summative, highly controlling, elaborate systems will fail in eliminating incompetence, rewarding the outstanding, and stimulating the reluctant. Developmental effects, are surely not to be derived from these systems. The danger is, that new games played on a state-wide basis will emerge in schools across the land.

SUMMARY

Teacher evaluation in current practice is full of problems and struggles for change. The importance of formal education to society and of teaching to schooling, gives urgency to improvements in teacher evaluation as demands for instructional accountability grow. Potentially, teacher evaluation can be much more than it is; more than a perfunctory checking to avoid crisis. Parents, administrators, students, and school officials all have a right to know that teaching is effective and improving. Teachers more than any other group need to know about their own teaching. They also have a right to expect that their colleagues know how to teach and are improving, too.

Because teacher evaluation is complex, threatening, and not well understood, much of current practice involves "games" rather than systematic professional evaluation. The games are nonproductive at best and counterproductive in some forms. To a large extent, these games and other problems inherent in current practices reflect an array of concepts of evaluation that conflict with promising practices. Evaluation as judging, punishing, rewarding, or controlling acts are simply inconsistent with the needs of all who are involved or concerned. Evaluation as a process for guiding the decisions for improving teaching requires concepts that focus on teaching, knowing, diagnosing, collaboration, and development of people. Current efforts to develop and impose state-wide systems on local schools are generally ignoring these concepts.

SELECTED STUDY SOURCES

American Association of School Administrators (1978). *Standards, Policies and Practices for School Personnel Administration*, 3rd ed. Seven Hills, OH: The Association.

   A detailed set of standards; includes explicit statements on developmental requirements as well as summative and legal practices.

Bloom, Benjamin S. (1980). "The New Direction in Educational Research: Alterable Variables," *Phi Delta Kappan* 61 (February):382–85.

An appeal for emphasis in research on those things that can be altered to improve education. A basic concept of developmental evaluation is carefully analyzed.

Bolton, Dale L. (1973). *Selection and Evaluation of Teachers*. Berkeley, CA: McCutchan Publishers.

Although old, this is still perhaps the outstanding book in this field. Bolton's emphasis on selection of teachers and his effort to contrast selection criteria with performance criteria is fundamental.

Borich, Gary D. and K. S. Fenton (1977). *The Appraisal of Teaching: Concepts and Process*. Reading, MA: Addison-Wesley Publishing Co.

A scholarly collection of papers on a broad array of topics, this work gives the reader excellent perspective on the problems, issues, and future technology for use in teacher evaluation.

Castetter, William B. (1971). *The Personnel Function in Educational Administration*. New York: The Macmillan Co.

A source of historical importance because of its emphasis on appraisal for essentially developmental purposes in Chapter 10.

Eisner, Elliot (1979). *The Educational Imagination*. New York: The MacMillan Co.

A scholarly work of advocacy for qualitative and "artistic" methods in evaluation of teaching.

Gage, N. L. (1978). *The Scientific Basis of the Art of Teaching*. New York: Teachers College Press, Columbia University.

A succinct summary of two decades of research, with prespective on what we know and how it can be better utilized. A classic.

Haefele, Donald L. (1980). "How to Evaluate Thee, Teacher—Let Me Count the Ways," *Phi Delta Kappan* 61(January, 1980): 349–52.

Critical review of many common practices that must be reformed. Describes twelve different "approaches" but criticizes all except MBO using regular observation and feedback.

Harris, Ben M. (1985). *Supervisory Behavior in Education*, 3rd Edition. Englewood Cliffs, NJ: Prentice-Hall, Inc.

Chapter 8 on "Evaluating Instructional Programs" deals with evaluation as a part of supervisory practice.

Joyce, Burce R. and Marsha Weil (1972). *Models Teaching*. Englewood Cliffs, NJ: Prentice-Hall, Inc.

Even now, this is one of the most useful sources for reviewing the whole spectrum of knowledge about teaching, its alternative forms, and above all its complexities. The authors conclude the *variety*, as distingushed from conformity, is the essence of teaching effectiveness.

McGee, Reece (1979). "Criteria Problems in Assessing Teaching Performance." A paper presented at the annual meeting of the American Sociological Association. ED 179 171

Discusses barriers to effective evaluation of teaching in colleges. Traces historical efforts. Emphasizes lack of any clear agreement on what is good teaching among academicians.

McGreal, Thomas L. (1982). "Effective Teacher Evaluation Systems", *Educational Leadership* 39 (January):303–306.

A systematic analysis of basic requirements for evaluation systems. The author makes a stong case for formative efforts.

Medley, Don M., Homer Coker, and Robert S. Soar (1984). *Measurement-Based Evaluation of Teacher Performance: An Empirical Approach.* New York: Longman, Inc.

A somewhat technical, comprehensive treatment of many aspects of teacher evaluation. These distinguished writers draw heavily on the research of recent decades.

Peterson, Penelope L. and H. J. Walberg, editors (1979). *Research on Teaching: Concepts, Findings and Implications.* Berkeley, CA: McCutchan Publishing Co.

One of the best recent efforts to bring the research on teaching together in summary form in a single volume. Medley's chapter on teacher effectiveness is especially useful.

Rodin, Miriam (1975). "Rating the Teachers," *Education Digest* (November).

A brief digest criticizing student ratings of teachers and use of test scores in judging teacher performance.

Rossmiller, Richard A. (1983). "Resource Allocation and Achievement: A Classroom Analysis," in *School Finance and School Improvement,* Allan Odden and L. Dean Webb, editors. Fourth Annual Yearbook, American Education Finance Association. Cambridge, MA: Ballinger Publishing Company.

Reports on studies of actual classrooms leads this distinguished researcher to conlude ". . . whether those resources are used effectively and efficiently will depend primarily on teachers and principals . . ." (p. 189).

Ryans, David G. (1960). *Characteristics of Teachers.* Washington, D.C.: American Council on Education.

A classic on the character of teaching in U.S. classrooms, this book was a summary of findings produced by a nation-wide study of 5,000 classroom teachers, K through 12. No such study has since been attempted. It's general conclusions remain surprisingly valid 25 years later.

Tracy, Saundra J. and Robert MacNaughton (1984). "New Wine for Old Bottles: Refurbishing an Existing System," *Thresholds in Education.* 10 (May):30–32. DeKalb, IL: Northern Illinois University.

The authors criticize national and state efforts to create new teacher evaluation systems. They argue instead for better training of administrators to implement current efforts more rigorously. This is a clear example of a position which seems highly unrealistic in not addressing fundamental issues.

2

Basic Concepts

INTRODUCTION

The needs for effective teacher evaluation described here are frustrated by all of the games and undesirable practices depicted. Concepts that can undergird effective evaluation practices can be delineated rather clearly, but confusing and inappropriate application of concepts are illustrated in the games being played so often.

Several concepts that are important to delineate include:

- judging as distinguished from knowing
- an act of evaluating as distinguished from a process of evaluation
- punishment and reward as distinguished from development of people
- the teacher as distinguished from teaching
- external locus of control as distinguished from collaboration
- decision making as distinguished from diagnosis
- delegation as distinguished from support.

EVALUATION CONCEPTS IN CONFLICT

All of these concepts are useful in developing and implementing teacher evaluation systems, but they tend to be confused with each other. They are often inappropriately applied to the evaluation of teaching and are used in ways that promote conflict, raise anxiety levels, and generate negative side effects.

Judging and Knowing

Evaluation involves making judgments (Raths and Preskill, 1982). Inevitably, someone must take the information available and apply a set of values to that information to make a judgment—"good," "OK," "needs improving," "terrible," "not important," "needs reconsideration," etc. But judging in the absence of information that is available and relevant perpetuates ignorance. Judging, when no judgment is needed, is to disrupt a productive process. For one to make judgments when another is better qualified corrupts the quality of evaluation. To make "holistic" judgments when only limited ones are needed creates counter-productive anxiety.

The concepts of judging and knowing are both important and need to be seen as related to each other in the evaluation process. They are sequentially related, in that knowledge needs to precede judging. They are situationally related, in that judgments of very different kinds may be needed. For instance, a "global" judgment regarding the entire teaching effort in a given classroom is rarely useful or necessary. Why seek a judgment such as "He's a weak teacher," if that serves no useful purpose? A global judgment, "He's an outstanding teacher," may be quite useful for individual ego building, but may be harmful if it is not fully verifiable—and may be harmful, anyway, to the moral of other teachers. But the judgment, "You've made plenty of progress in asking open-ended questions," may serve several useful purposes including building self-confidence, enthusiasm, and signalling the beginning of a new cycle of evaluation.

Judging needs to be related to knowing in terms of the person or persons most appropriately serving as "judge." The one with the best array of relevant information has some claim to the right to be the judge. However, the one who must assume responsibility for deciding and acting on the judgment also has a claim. Judging is very often most rational as a joint endeavor, because evaluator, evaluatee, and even third parties may *share* the requisite knowledge *and* responsibilities.

Act or Process

Evaluation as process has been mentioned in several places. This conflicts with the widely held view of evaluation as a single act of judging or giving an opinion or deciding. Evaluation as a process involving a whole series of acts is carefully reviewed later in this chapter (Stufflebeam, 1971). It is essential that specific evaluation acts—observing, recording, profiling, checking, etc.—not be confused with the total process of evaluation, regardless of the particular notions or approaches to evaluation that one prefers (Stufflebeam and Webster, 1980). Even the simplest approaches to evaluation involve a series of acts in some kind of sequence. Evaluation of teachers always involves acts on the part of more than one person. It is always a two-or-more person transaction. Accordingly, there are many actions involved.

Teacher and Teaching

The teacher is a person. Teaching is a complex domain of teacher behaviors. The teacher is a person who does much more than teach, so evaluation of teaching is never dealing with the whole person. However, the teaching person is not neatly separated from the person who is also mother, bus driver, citizen, church member, student, etc. If the person were neatly divisible, then distinguishing between teaching, teacher, and person would not be a concern. Teacher would equate with teaching, but that is not true. The teacher brings his or her biases, worries, aspirations, and interests into the school and into the classroom. Teaching as behavior related to producing student learning is the essential focus of teacher evaluation, but the interactions between teaching and other facets of a person's life cannot be ignored.* They are best recognized and given due consideration while not being confused with teaching as such.

Reward/Punishment and Development

Two of the three games described were concerned almost entirely with gaining rewards and avoiding punishment. Development or improvement in teaching is a distinctly different concern. Once again, evaluation of teaching can be designed for various purposes, but the system that punishes and rewards is not likely to be developmental in nature, nor will the converse be true. The distinctions between essentially summative and developmental evaluation systems will be addressed in detail in two later chapters. The concepts, however, need to be clear as evaluation processes are discussed.

Evaluation efforts that focus on reward and punishment must guide the making of sharply discriminating judgments. If punishments are severe, the quality of due process is of very great importance. If rewards are highly prized, due process is still very important. If the consequences of evaluative decisions are serious, the validity of the evaluative criteria must be very high and negative side effects must be carefully considered.

The concerns that are of importance in developmental evaluation efforts are quite different. Diagnostic judgments are needed and they need to be sharply discriminating among practices, techniques, skills, and knowledges, but not among individuals. Due process in a legal, procedural sense is not required in developmental evaluation, but substantive process within the context of good working relationships is still of great importance. These differences are elaborated in later chapters and the relating or linking of developmental and summative systems is analyzed. (See Chapter 10).

---

*Two useful ways of conceptualizing teaching and distinguishing teaching behaviors from other professional endeavors are found in: Ben M. Harris, *Supervisory Behavior in Education*, 2nd ed. (Prentice-Hall, Inc, 1975); California Teachers Association, *Six Areas of Teacher Competence.* (Burlingame, CA: California Teachers Association, 1964).

External Control and Collaboration

Many aspects of teacher evaluation involve external controls, in the sense that neither evaluators nor evaluatees have freedom of choice or even freedom to adapt or modify procedures. Other aspects of evaluation may be subject to collaborative efforts. Evaluation efforts that are equitable and also rigorous in guiding the improvement of instruction will include both controlled and collaborative elements. Instruments may be externally controlled, even though collaborative efforts are employed in their development. Procedures for gathering and recording observation data, or administering student inventories, may be rigorously controlled by the use of standardized directions. However, the interpretation of these data and the weighted values ascribed to them are more appropriately determined via collaboration.

Control and collaboration are not antithetical to each other. They are both essential concepts to apply in planning and implementing a program of teacher evaluation. The issues to be resolved in considering these concepts have to do with appropriate uses of control and the quality of collaborative endeavors (Wise and Darling-Hammond, 1984).

A well-designed evaluation plan will be structured to assure uniform procedures where these are essential while allowing for flexibility in the way such procedures are applied to individuals. A set of carefully defined performance criteria is essential to any well-designed system of teacher evaluation. However, job descriptions for individual teachers may vary substantially, drawing heavily on some criteria while giving little attention to others. Such variations in criteria emphasis may well be determined collaboratively with teacher, principal, and instructional specialist reaching concensus (see Chapter 9).

Decision Making and Diagnosis

All evaluation efforts are presumably concerned with decisions of one kind or another. It is important, however, to be clear on both the *kinds* of decisions involved and the *timing* or *sequencing* of decisions. Decisions may be large or small, unilateral, bilateral, or participative; they may be summative, formative, or diagnostic. If evaluation processes are to guide decision making, then those processes must be relevant and appropriate in various ways. Chapters 7 and 8 relate the observation and analysis of data processes to this concept. The observational requirements for diagnostic analysis and related decisions about improvement process are dramatically different than the requirements for dismissal or merit pay decisions (see Chapter 10).

Sequencing of decisions is also of great importance in the evaluation of teaching. When decisions are made first and evaluation later undertaken to support those decisions, a corrupt effort emerges. Yet this is precisely what often happens in many summative instances. (It also appears very common in political circles as well.) The normal sequence for decision making is that which clearly follows analysis, interpretation, and valuing, as shown in Exhibit 2.1.

Timing of decisions may involve still other considerations. Time is often required for individuals—evaluator and evaluatee—to think through and give value-laden meaning to the findings, even after interpretations are made at an intellectual or rational level. Furthermore, it takes time to resolve differences when value differences emerge in a collaborative evaluation process. Finally, there are needs for prioritizations. An array of diagnosed needs may be subjected to decisions over time as circumstances dictate.

Delegation and Support

The need to delegate responsibilities for various aspects of the evaluation process seem constantly in conflict with the need for a well-structured support system to make it work. Some of these conflicts are reflected most dramatically in renewed state-level efforts to utilize teacher evaluation for educational quality control. Evaluation procedures will inevitably be delagated to principals or supervisors in 100,000 school buildings across the U.S. But nearly three million teachers must also be intimately involved, especially if effects are to be developmental and positive. Yet this complex undertaking also dictates a support system capable of following through on decisions that emerge, and few states have yet to discover a satisfactory way of balancing such needs.* Somehow, the emerging systems are always woefully deficient.

EVALUATION AS PROCESS

There are essentially eight distinct steps in evaluation as a process, as the term is utilized in professional circles. There are several somewhat different definitions commonly employed by specialists in the field of evaluation (Scriven, 1967; Stufflebeam, 1971; Cronbach, 1963). The definitions vary, largely in their emphasis on purpose and technique (Wolf, 1979). There is a great deal of agreement on the specific elements of evaluation process and even some agreement on procedures (Johnson, 1979; Stake, 1967; Stufflebeam 1979). Strong disagreements are registered by some scholars who emphasize qualitative (Eisner, 1977) or highly product-centered approaches (Popham, 1971). Raths and Preskill (1982) even question the use of the term "evaluation" when summative, holistic judgments are not being made.

---

*It is interesting to note how a study of 21 state policies on teacher evaluation revealed many of the same concerns expressed in this chapter. Carey (1980:14) reports a comparison of state policies with Stufflebeam's (1979) "standards for evaluation." Carey summarizes to the effect that ". . . quantitative information was not accounted for by any of the 21 states. . . . Eleven of the 29 standards were referenced by 5 or fewer states."

Definition

In this book, evaluation is viewed as a process for studying an operation to more clearly understand it, in order to guide changes, while retaining and supporting those components of the operation which are judged to be desirable. This definition clearly places the focus of evaluation on a specific operation such as teaching. The emphasis is on understanding or knowing about teaching rather than on judging the teacher. Unlike research, however, evaluation is concerned with understandings that can guide decisions toward change or maintenance of practices (Alkin, et al., 1974).

Evaluation models of numerous kinds are able to function within the framework of this definition (Stake, 1967; Stufflebeam and Webster, 1980). This writer draws upon systems analysis models in analyzing and presenting teacher evaluation programs.

Formative, Summative, and Relational Approaches

Formative and summative evaluation efforts have been contrasted rather widely in both theory and practice. Bloom, Hastings, and Maudaus (1971) gave prominence to these terms in the title and contents of a compendium on evaluating student learning. In effect, Bloom and his colleagues clearly differentiated three types of evaluation as: (1) diagnostic, (2) formative, and (3) summative. While the characterization of these different forms of evaluation referred to student learning, the forms do apply to some degree to teacher evaluation as well:

> "... formative (evaluation) ... is to determine the degree of mastery of a given ... task and to pinpoint the part of the task not mastered." (Bloom, et al., 1971, p. 61)

> "... summative evaluation is directed toward a much more general assessment of the degree to which the larger outcomes have been attained ..." (Bloom, et al., 1971, p. 61)

> "Diagnostic evaluation ... has as its primary function determining the underlying circumstances or causes of ... deficiencies ..." (Bloom, et al., 1971, p. 87).

Borich and Fenton (1977) grapple with the problem of several kinds of evaluation by proposing "stages" in a large complex process. Their stages are described as "pre-operational," "immediate process," "intermediate process," and "product." They suggest different instruments as well as different purposes to be served at each stage. Such a four stage view of evaluation adds to our thinking about process evaluation, but also to our concern for precursors or pre-operational characteristics of the teacher (or the situation).

Stake (1977:157) suggests that "operative evaluation is perhaps some blend of formative and summative evaluation . . . ," but he argues for viewing it as a kind of "monitoring, trouble shooting, . . . the alleviation of problems that arise. . . ." As such, he adds new dimensions and perhaps some confusion as well.

What various scholars and practitioners seem to be revealing, aside from the fact that they too are groping for answers, is that evaluation of teaching inevitably has diverse forms, dictated by purposes and situations. The Stufflebeam CIPP Model (1971) provides what may be the best single way of viewing any and all evaluation efforts in the contexts of formal organizations. This model gives attention to the complexities of organizations, emphasizes attending to four different kinds of factors or forces in any given situation, and suggests evaluation approaches that will vary, depending on which factors are most important to the purpose to be served. The CIPP acronym stands for factors as follows:

C = context factors
I = input factors
P = process factors
P = product factors

These are not unlike the four "stages" of evaluation proposed by Borish and Fenton. Formative evaluation tends to be closely related to input and process, while summative evaluation is more concerned with product. Diagnostic evaluation is formative evaluation that focuses on process factors with greatest specificity.

The unique contribution of the CIPP model is not the distinctions drawn among the four sets of factors, but the relationships among them that reflect organizational reality, yet guide evaluation efforts. Hence, developmental evaluation as that term is used in this book refers to development as purpose, and hence stresses actions directed toward changes in processes, inputs, or their relationships.

Context factors are those forces, events, or influences outside the organization which nevertheless have a bearing on inputs, processes, and products. In teacher evaluation, the curriculum in use is an input that may influence teaching practices, having been influenced (if not controlled) by social forces promoting or prohibiting certain curricular content. The social forces—pressure groups, business interests, political advocates, special interest groups, or just defenders of traditions—represent the context factors.

Input factors are those resources, guidelines, and regulations, that very directly influence operations. Money, students, materials, staff, transportation, equipment, and facilities are obvious inputs. Curriculum guides, scope and sequence charts, textbooks, and what teachers, parents, and students bring to school as expectations are all very direct input factors influencing individual teaching performance.

Process factors depict what people do with inputs to promote learning.

Teacher behaviors and students reactions are the key elements in instructional process. We often use the term "teaching/learning process." Certainly, interactions between teacher and student are enormously important process factors—so are questions, answers, directions, elaborations, wait-time, and time-on-task. However, teacher behavior and that of students may be related to materials in ways that also relate to learning. Planning, organizing, studying, reading, analyzing, grading are but a few action verbs that suggest process factors to be considered in teacher evaluation.

Product factors are outcomes. Instructional outcomes are usually too narrowly considered as "gain scores" on a pencil and paper test. However, attitudes, skills, commitments, decisions and habits may be products. The CIPP model gives attention to products presumably directly associated with processes. Nearly all evaluation plans make such assumptions. Negative outcomes are all too often ignored in product evaluation. Similarly, unanticipated outcomes of desirable kinds—simultaneous learnings—are not uncommon but do tend to be neglected.

Developmental teacher evaluation, is one type of evaluation that is primarily focused on *process*. The teacher is the primary agent of instruction. Schools are instructional organizations that subject students to experiences to *produce* learnings. As such, instruction is the process and the teacher is most directly and responsibly involved. In fact, the teacher is in control of the teaching-learning process or it is out of control.

The emphasis on instruction in teacher evaluation, and the process emphasis demanded, does not eliminate our need to recognize alternative approaches. The operation being evaluated can be thought of as an ongoing flow of events of context factors influencing inputs, which in turn influence processes and products. Evaluation modes simply select different portions of the total operation as the focus for data gathering and analysis.

An Eight-Step Process

The eight steps that comprise the evaluation process start with the specification of criteria and proceed to instrumentation, data gathering, analysis, interpreting, valuing, decision making, and action. The first five of these steps shown in Exhibit 2.1 have long been recognized as essential. The latter three, while sometimes questioned regarding the evaluators' responsibilities, are the essential steps that give evaluation its distinctiveness regarding the improvement of instructional operations.

1. *Criteria* are carefully specified as an essential first step in evaluating teaching. Clear understanding is essential regarding the specific teaching behaviors, events, or related elements that are to be the focus of later valuing, deciding, and action. Those who argue that teaching is best analyzed in terms of its outcomes (Popham, 1971), such as student learning, must then specify these criteria very explicitly, if actions are to follow. But those who give emphasis to teacher verbal interactions (Bailey, 1974), or

EXHIBIT 2.1   Eight steps in the evaluation process*

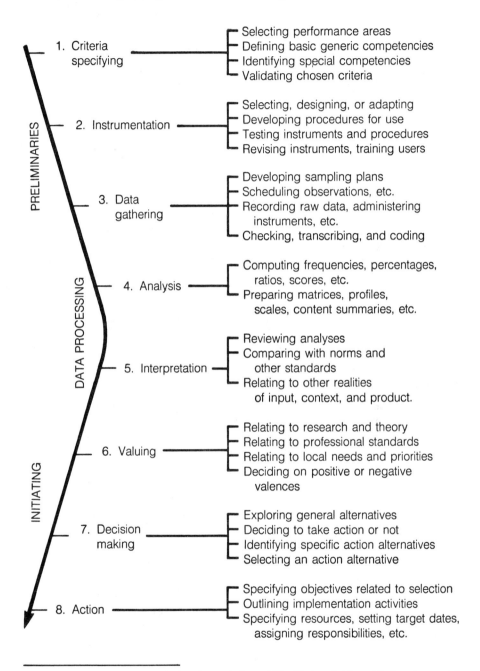

*Adapted from Ben M. Harris and Jane Hill, "Trainers' Manual," *Developmental Teacher Evaluation Kit*. Austin, TX: Southwest Educational Development Laboratory, 1982.

questioning strategies, or any other teacher behavior, must initiate such evaluating by explicitly defining these criteria. See Chapter 4 for suggestions on criteria specification, sources, and uses.

2. *Instrumentation* for data gathering involves developing materials and procedures for systematically observing and recording data that clearly relate to the specified criteria. Since criteria which are specified in step 1 are necessarily limited in number and variety, so too the instrumentation and procedures developed will be strictly limited. In fact, instrumentation often is as much concerned with excluding data as it is with making sure relevant data are both observed and recorded. Instruments include tests, questionnaires, observation guides, and interview schedules (see Chapter 6).

3. *Data gathering* is the step that involves utilizing appropriate procedures with instrumentation to produce date—raw evidence related to the specific selected criteria. The training of those who will observe and record is an essential part of this step. Sampling in a systematic and unbiased way is also involved since there is often too much to be observed, and recording all evidence may not be possible. Creating conditions that both facilitate data gathering and prevent undue contamination of the situation is still another important part of the data gathering process.

Data recording will take different forms determined by the instrumentation developed. Tests are simply administered while interviews involve careful questioning and recording of responses. Observations in classrooms with various instruments (guides) may involve tallying, checking, describing, or coding. Mechanical, electronic, or photographic recording mechanisms may supplement that of the human agent.

4. *Analysis* is a step that involves manipulations of data in one or more ways to reduce, simplify, categorize, compare, contrast, or visualize it in forms that can better inform the users. Coded data is sometimes analyzed using a matrix, as developed for Flanders' interaction analysis. Raw descriptions of events are sometimes scaled by comparing descriptions of observed events with a set of descriptors. Scaled scores may then be displayed in the form of a profile using bar-graph techniques. Sound recordings may be content analyzed generating frequency distributions of types of content by categories. Photographic or video recordings, too, may be analyzed using any of these techniques (see Chapters 7 and 8).

5. *Interpretation* of analyzed data is sometimes referred to as "deriving" the findings. Data as analyzed have to be related to a larger set of operational realities to give them meaning. A profile of frequencies of types of questions asked by a teacher gains meaning via interpretation that gives attention to the objectives of the lesson, the ages and abilities of the students, the complexity of the subject content, etc. Interpretations do not bring values into play, but do draw conclusions based on insights revealed in the analyses as illuminated by relevant other realities. Hence, 80 percent recognition and recall type questions with few demonstrations

of skill or analysis, or opinion questions asked by the teacher seems quite normal or expected for a test review on subraction facts. It would not seem normal for a discussion of current events related to SALT II talks in Geneva.

6. *Valuing findings* as interpreted is a step that is essential, even though often misplaced and overemphasized. When analysis and interpretations are completed so that both evaluator and evaluatees have substantial understanding about the objective reality being assessed, then and only then are values properly applied. Using the simple illustration of teacher questioning, one valuing drill and memorization in teaching will assign positive supportive valences to the recitation of subtraction facts. One who values concrete experiences in teaching abstract number concepts will assign negative valences to the same lesson. One who values both kinds of teaching, or has no particular value orientation in this instance, will tend to assign neutral valences.

Valuing is crucial as a distinct step when values held by various persons involved differ widely. If the same set of data as interpreted were identically valued by all persons, this step would not need such careful attention. However, values do vary and hence it is important to seek agreement through understanding on the realities, so that value differences or agreements can be dealt with realistically, as opinions, points of view, values, etc.

7. and 8. *Decision making and acting* on those decisions follow from having assigned values. If values are in agreement, decisions for action can be readily, cooperatively derived. Agreements that are positive suggest decisions to reward, reinforce, and sustain. Agreements that are negative can lead directly to discussions of alternatives for action that would be corrective in some way. Disagreements over values still face the challenge of decision making. Decision alternatives may include arbitration, turning to additional sources of data, pursuing alternative analyses, or even delaying action until value differences can be resolved.

Decision making and follow through actions are not necessarily integrated steps in the valuation process. These steps are essential, of course, if evaluation efforts are not to be wasted, but they can be operationally separated from the other steps in the process. In the case of teacher evaluation, where values and decisions are so closely intertwined, these steps should be integrated, not separated.

Illustrations of Process Applications

A case report of a teacher and supervisor working together in a formal evaluation sequence is presented to illustrate the eight-step evaluation process introduced above. Obviously, this illustration pertains to only a single approach to teacher evaluation. The specific form of each step would vary as different approaches are used.

Step 1: Criteria Specifying   The teacher (Helen) and her supervisor conferred with each other, reviewing the overall plan for using the particular evaluation system (DeTEK). While Helen ". . . was confused about the mechanics of the system," the supervisor tried to reassure her by going over the self-report instrument. A carefully detailed description of all performances to be utilized was handed to Helen so that she could study them and proceed to participate with understanding. These performance specifications had been provided to all faculty members in a previous meeting, so that Helen was not unfamiliar with them (see Appendix B).

While the criteria in this system were already carefully specified, the teacher and supervisor both made use of them in their collaborative evaluation efforts. The teacher has actually used these criteria as her frame of reference in describing her own teaching when completing DeTEK Instrument I—Teacher Self-Analysis Survey. Now the supervisor and teacher are conferring to decide which criteria will be utilized for further diagnostic purposes (see Appendix C).

Step 2: Instrumentation   In the DeTEK system, a full array of instruments has already been developed and directions for their use carefully developed as well. However, the supervisor reviews these instruments with Helen as they discuss procedures for diagnostic analysis of one or two selected behaviors.

Step 3: Data Gathering   The data gathering began in this illustration with the teacher self-report. Helen has responded to both a forced-choice and a free-response set of items in describing herself.

"I left her alone to do the self-report. . . . When I returned she had not finished—in about 15 minutes. I reassured her that there were no 'right' answers. . . . She went ahead and finished it promptly."

The supervisor also gathered observation data using a comprehensive descriptive instrument in Helen's classroom earlier in the day. Later, diagnostic data gathering was pursued by both Helen and her supervisor. Once a behavior had been selected for analysis, three kinds of data were gathered: (1) Helen completed another self-report, describing her teaching in more detail, focusing only on the few behaviors previously selected. (2) The supervisor observed in Helen's classroom again, focusing on the same behaviors previously selected. (3) Students were asked to describe Helen's teaching, using simplified checklists, keeping the same focus used by teacher and supervisor (see Appendix C-5).

Step 4: Analysis   One kind of analysis involved the simple development of a profile, using the self-report data originally provided by the teacher.

"When the self-report had been completed we prepared the profile together. I showed her the profile form of the observation report; we discussed similarities and differences between the two. She was quite pleased with the balance shown. . . . We seemed to agree on most items of performance."

Profile preparation involves re-ordering responses and clustering them for easy enumeration and comparison. No computations or technical manipulations are called for in this particular system; however, plotting, graphing, computing, and weighting are sometimes useful.

Further data analysis was undertaken by both Helen and her supervisor as they brought the three additional kinds of data to a follow-up conference.

"Helen and I worked together to summarize the Classroom Observation Report. We discussed what had been recorded and which indicators were most clearly in evidence . . . The result was considerable consensus. . . . Then we took the self-report and the student checklists and transferred all of this data to the diagnostic worksheet. This made it easy for us to see agreements and disagreements, similarities and differences; we weren't arguing!"

Step 5: Interpretations   The diagnostic analysis step in the DeTEK system is a simple procedure involving both analysis and interpretations. For each performance indicator, the three sources are compared. Agreement and disagreements are objectively recorded. Where agreements are positive they are designated as "accomplishments." Where they are negative, they are designated as "needs for improvement" (see Appendix C-6).

Step 6: Valuing   Once accomplishments and needs for improvements are diagnosed, they must be put into perspective. In fact, one of Helen's accomplishments may be nothing new, a confirmation of well-known practices. Still another, however, may be cause for celebration as something that resulted from hard work and conscious efforts.

In a similar way, agreements on "needs" may be interpreted quite differently. Helen reacts to one need: "That's always showing up as something that needs attention, but I still can't see it as important as this other one. Let's ignore it for now!" To this there may be general agreement. But other values may be considered too: "You know Helen, I've heard you say that before. You really don't seem to attach much importance to that kind of teaching practice. I wonder if you don't need to rethink that view. Most of our profession would argue that such practices are more worthy than you are willing to acknowledge."

Steps 7 and 8: Decision Making and Action   What actions should we expect to emerge from the previous six steps? When values have been adequately considered it is time for decisions. This often takes the form of assigning priorities to an array of diagnosed needs.

Helen: "I'm willing to review my thinking on this indicator, but let's postpone it until summer. I'm going to take some classes at the University. I'll make that one of my goals."

With this decision, other needs are prioritized, a growth plan is developed for working on one of two improvements, and dates set for review of progress (see Exhibit 9.2).

TEACHING AS ART, SCIENCE, AND TECHNOLOGY

Most of this chapter has focused on current practices and problems from the evaluator's perspective. Such a perspective assumes that scientific methods of evaluation are appropriate for use in dealing with problems of teaching and learning. This is not an acceptable assumption to some scholars. Eisner (1977) and many others argue for the methodologies of the humanities, such as "connoisseurship," in preference to systematic data gathering and analysis. Still other objections to scientific objectivity in teacher evaluation rely on less philosophical positions; not that teaching is essentially an art, but rather that it is still too primitive a science.

If teaching is an art, then the methods of the humanities should indeed be more extensively employed in designing teacher evaluation systems. If teaching is not yet a clearly understood applied science, as is pharmacy, dentistry, or mechanical engineering, then only limited use can be made of research and theory in the evaluation process. This author views teaching as potentially among the most complex of all human endeavors. As such, evaluation of teaching is indeed full of artistry, craftsmanship, science, trial and error, and sheer stimulus-response mechanisms. But such complexities do not preclude the utility of systematic evaluation procedures. On the contrary, more complex phenomena call for more systematic efforts, and a greater variety of evaluation procedures.

Teaching must be viewed as complex, not simple. However, it does little good to view such complexity with despair. Myths about teachers' sensibilities, the magic of rating scales, and the omniscience of the building principal add to the difficulties encountered in making teacher evaluation serve to improve teaching and learning. The enormous complexity of teaching makes clear the limitations in knowledge that evaluators must constantly acknowledge. Yet, much is known about teaching (Gage, 1976; and Shulman, 1977). A professional knowledge base has been well established, using a combination of "practitioner wisdom, educational research, and teaching-learning theory." Educators are too inclined to overlook the accumulated wisdom of centuries of teaching endeavors. Research in recent years, while terribly fragmented, has nonetheless been instructive when properly synthesized (Gage, 1984). Teaching theory too has made enormous contributions to the practical understanding of the teaching-learning process.*

---

*Two especially instructive books emphasizing synthesis of theory of teaching and learning are: Bloom, Benjamin S. *Human Characteristics and School Learning* (1976); Joyce, Bruce R. and Marsha Weil, *Models of Teaching* (1972).

Teacher Characteristics

The massive study of teaching by David Ryans (1958) was one of the first efforts to synthesize and empirically verify the characteristics of teachers in the United States. This *Teacher Characteristics Study* involved some five thousand elementary and secondary school teachers. To date, it is the only study of its kind. Its findings continue to be useful in guiding teacher evaluation.

Three "patterns" of teaching were identified in Ryans' work:

Pattern X_o Friendly, understanding, sympathetic, vs. Aloof, egocentric, restricted.

Pattern Y_o Responsible, systematic, businesslike, vs. Unplanned, slipshod, haphazard.

Pattern Z_o Stimulating, imaginative, surgent, vs. Dull, routine.

A broad array of "characteristics" was clustered together to form each of the three patterns. Using factor analytic techniques on classroom observation, interview, and questionnaire data, Ryans concluded that these three patterns were those that most clearly characterized and differentiated teachers at all levels and in all subject fields.

No effort was made to relate these patterns or characteristics to criteria of effectiveness in the Ryans' study. However, numerous studies, before and since, provide enormous support for this generic core of three patterns of behavior. They can be regarded as factors of importance any time we are concerned with general teaching competence.

Individualization

Studies of human growth provide extensive evidence for adding individualization to the three factors identified by Ryans. An enormous variety of specific teaching practices, ranging from tutoring to diagnostic analysis to small group activity to independent study to programmed instruction, have been included in research and development efforts related to capitalizing on teaching for individual differences (Shulman, 1976). Bloom's (1976) mastery of learning theory illustrates one significant effort to synthesize many related research studies and points to teaching practices most likely to be effective. Dunn (1977) and others have approached the problem from the perspective of differentiated learning styles, diagnosis, and prescription.

The specific practices for individualizing instruction that assure success in learning are still not fully understood. However, the realities regarding significant differences in learner characteristics are such that any view of teaching competence will give importance to individualization as a pattern. In all probability, teaching will be more effective when at least five kinds of teaching for individualization are emphasized:

1. Groups are organized in varying sizes, and students are assigned to such groups on the basis of assessment of differences among learners.
2. Learning tasks are structured, presented, and differentiated on the basis of differences among learners.
3. Media and experiences for learning are differentiated for individuals and groups, even when common learning outcomes are desired.
4. Time and sequence are differentially utilized by teachers in guiding student learning.
5. Interpersonal interactions between teacher, student, other students, parents, and others are utilized in highly individual ways to support student learning efforts, both emotionally and intellectually.

Obviously, teacher evaluation that includes a concern for competence in individualizing instruction is made still more complex. The evidence supporting this as another pattern of teacher behavior in the generic core is compelling, even though the specific "characteristics, behaviors, or practices" are yet to be fully documented.

SUMMARY

Teacher evaluation in current practice is full of problems and struggles for change. The importance of formal education to the society, and of teaching to schooling, gives urgency to improvements in teacher evalution as demands for instructional accountability grow. Teacher evaluation can be much more than it is— more than a perfunctory checking to avoid crises. Parents, administrators, students, and school officials all have a right to know that teaching is effective and improving. Teachers more than any other group need to know about their own teaching. They also have a right to expect that their colleagues know how to teach and are improving.

Because teacher evaluation is complex, threatening, and not well understood, much of current practice involves "games" rather than systematic professional evaluation. The games are nonproductive, at best, and counter-productive in some forms. To a large extent these games and other problems inherent in current practices reflect an array of concepts of evaluation that conflict with promising practices. Evaluation as judging, punishing or rewarding, and controlling are simply inconsistent with the needs of all who are involved or concerned. Evaluation as a process for guiding decisions for improving teaching requires concepts that focus on teaching, knowing, diagnosing, collaborating, and developing people.

Evaluation of teaching that builds on these latter concepts is still fraught with many complex problems. The focus on teaching, and especially on the teaching-learning process, allows for few simple approaches.

However, the science and art of teaching has a substantial knowledge base on which better evaluation systems can now be developed.

SELECTED STUDY SOURCES

Alkin, Marvin C., Richard Daillak and Peter White (1979). *Using Evaluations: Does Evaluation Make a Difference?*, vol. 76, Sage Library of Social Research. Beverly Hills, CA: Sage Publications, Inc.

Several case studies in Part II give the reader interesting insight into how evaluation operates in schools and the numerous problems it encounters.

Anderson, Scarvia B. and Samuel Ball (1979). *The Profession and Practice of Program Evaluation.* San Francisco: Jossey-Bass, Publishers.

This book is directed primarily to the educational evaluation profession. However, Part I, *Evaluation Practices,* gives perspective; Chapter 2 on evaluation purposes is especially useful.

Cronbach, Lee J. (1980). *Toward Reform of Program Evaluation: Aims, Methods, and Institutional Arrangements.* San Francisco: Jossey-Bass Pulishers.

A stimulating, broad-gauge review of evaluation of education as a field or professional practice. Chapter 1 reviews the past efforts. Chapter 3 is especially valuable in dealing with basic processes in evaluation. A unique listing of "our 95 theses" introduces this volume.

Harris, Ben M., Kenneth E. McIntyre, Vance C. Littleton, Jr., and Daniel F. Long (1985). *Personnel Administration in Education.* Boston, MA: Allyn and Bacon, Inc.

Chapter 11 focuses on personnel evaluation, giving special attention to purposes, use of competencies, and problems with rating scales.

Millman, Jason, editor (1981). *Handbook of Teacher Evaluation.* National Council on Measurement in Education. Beverly Hills, CA: Sage Publications, Inc.

A collection of papers that ranges widely over the subject and has special merit in chapters on context/environment effects and political realities.

Rivlin, Alice M. (1971). *Systematic Thinking for Social Action.* The 1970 H. Rowan Gaither Lectures of the University of California at Berkeley. Washington, D.C.: The Brookings Institute.

Rivlin explores the dilemma of guiding public policy, especially social policy, in rational, systematic ways. Two chapters are especially pertinent. Chapter5—"Can we find out what works?"—argues for more systematic procedures. Chapter 6, on accountability, raises serious questions about decentralization and community control.

Trang, Myron L. and Owen L. Caskey (1981). *Improving Instructor Effectiveness Through Videotape Recall.* Palo Alto, CA: R and E Research Associates, Inc.

In addition to reviewing video-tape methods for improving teaching skills, these authors emphasize the danger of narrowing our view of teaching too sharply.

Weiss, Carol H. (1972). *Evaluation Research: Methods for Assessing Program Effectiveness.* Englewood Cliffs, NJ: Prentice-Hall, Inc.

Although a bit old, this small book is still significant as a way of viewing research related to evaluation. Chapters on purposes and action programs and personnel relationships are especially useful.

Wise, Arthur E. and Lindarling-Hammond (1984). "Teacher Evaluation and Teacher Professionalism," *Educational Leadership* 42 (December/January):28–33.

A critical review of many current practices is based on a study of four school districts. The authors emphasize the "bureaucratic" nature of many evaluation practices. They criticize uniformity in procedures and criteria as well as reliance on the principal as evaluator.

3

Operational Models

INTRODUCTION

A variety of existing teacher evaluation practices were discussed in the preceding chapter, giving emphasis to evaluation as process. In this chapter basic principles and guidelines for the design of teacher evaluation systems will be presented. Several actual operations will be described as "models" in the sense that each is strikingly different from many others. Advantages and limitation of each model will be identified.

Current practice across the country appears extremely uniform in several ways. Most schools' teacher evaluation efforts are not truly evaluative. They tend to involve ad hoc procedures, emphasize simple judgmental ratings, involve only a single evaluator, and provide for little data gathering, feedback, or follow-up action (Grabinski, 1977). However, there are increasing numbers of school districts that are attempting to design evaluation systems that depart from past practices. (Stipnieks, 1981). Carefully detailed performance specifications are being developed cooperatively in many districts and on a state-wide basis in Georgia (1983). Classroom observations with pre- and post-conferences are being required in more and more school districts.

Objective data gathering that precedes judging is also becoming more common. Furthermore, some plan of action for guiding improvement processes is quite often prescribed in these newer efforts at teacher evaluation system building (Haefele, 1980).

Growing Consensus

In addition to the increasing efforts to design and operationalize genuine systems for teacher evaluation, there is also apparently a growing consensus on a number of basic principles and purposes. Stipnieks (1981) found that nearly all the districts that had made recent revisions in their teacher evaluation efforts focused primarily on "improving the performance of the individual teacher." Virtually no other purpose—formative or summative— was given a high priority. Still another strikingly recurrent feature of many new teacher evaluation systems is some mechanism for clearly separating formative and summative procedures (Georgia Dept. of Ed., 1985; Stake, 1977; Raths and Preskill, 1982).

Castetter (1971) makes this distinction semantically using the term "appraisal" instead of evaluation. But few writers or practitioners distinguish "assessing," "appraising," and "evaluating." They do, however, give increasing attention to evaluation of teachers and teaching as necessarily formative or developmental in many essential ways (Rose, 1964; 1981).

Grasha (1977: 115) contends that traditional procedures focusing on summative ratings are ". . . an empty system . . . Development must be an issue from the beginning to ensure the long term survival of the evaluation [process]. . . ." Haefele describes an array of twelve different "approaches" to teacher evaluation and argues against them all with the exception of the one emphasizing goal-setting and development along the lines of Redfern's models (1980). Medley emphasizes a research basis for developmental purposes in teacher evaluation:

> Nobody really feels that the effective teachers presently in the schools, . . . are effective enough; it is the state of the art of teaching itself that is in need of improvement. (1979:26)

Other trends also need to be recognized. Teacher evaluation in some quarters is reviving an older emphasis on self-evaluation (Dunn and Dunn, 1977; Simpson, 1966). Thompson (1972) reports, for example, on a teacher self-evaluation program in Sonoma County (California) schools. Several Texas schools report implementing programs relying heavily on self-analysis.* Harris and Hill (1982) make extensive use of self-analysis in their DeTEK system. These uses of self-analysis are generally supplementary to other procedures and data sources. Borich (1977), Dunn and Dunn (1977), Harris et al. (1979), and many others give emphasis to various sources of evaluation data, including peers and students as well as supervisor and self.

George Redfern (1980) has been a most influential long-term advocate of using "management by objectives" (MBO) techniques for personnel evaluation. His emphasis has been less on evaluation and more on follow-up activities. It has captured the interests of many educators and is widely

---

*Carrollton-Farmers Branch School District, Carrollton, Texas; Highland Park High School, Dallas, Texas; VESS Project Schools, Texas Catholic Conference, Austin, Texas; Abilene Schools, Abilene, Texas; Ector County Schools, Odessa, Texas.

utilized. Curiously, the work of Cogan (1973) and others in promoting "clinical supervision" as a systematic improvement process has many similarities to MBO systems, including the emphasis on follow-up activities with only limited concern for instrumentation, data gathering, and analysis techniques.

Divergent Notions

Evaluation operations that take quite different approaches include those that are clearly more summative (Raths and Preskill, 1982), and those that focus on programs (Rossi, Freeman and Wright, 1979), rather than focusing on teachers and teaching. Popham (1971:3) is among those who emphasizes " . . . assessing student progress . . . as a way of evaluating teaching." Such product-oriented evaluation systems often emphasize "instructional effectiveness" or "teacher incompetence" (Munnelly, 1979). However, emphasis on program (Clift and Imrie, 1981), students evaluations (Veldman, 1970), and "accountability" (Burlingame, 1978) are not gaining widespread professional support, even though these efforts have political appeal. Rutman expresses the major problem:

> Too often evaluation . . . focuses solely on outcomes . . . it is impossible to account for the results." (1977:16)

This severe limitation of product-oriented evaluation of any kind is accentuated for teacher evaluation because of the great diversity of teaching styles and variables involved (Dunn and Dunn, 1977; Centra and Potter, 1980; Center on Evaluation, Development and Research, 1980).

Another divergent view emphasizes teaching/learning style concordance. This has been made popular in the work of Ken and Rita Dunn (1977). Special educators have been persistent in their efforts to make learning "modalities" a key focus of teaching. Federal legislation—Senate Bill 94-142—requiring individualized plans (IEPs) gives emphasis also to teacher evaluation focusing upon response to learning needs.

Still another divergent view is expressed by Eisner (1972) and Sergiovanni (1977), among others, who worry about overly scientific, mechanistic approaches to evaluation. Eisner (1979) seeks evaluation models borrowed from the fine arts. He argues for more subjective, qualitative techniques patterned after the work of the art critique and "connoiseur." Sergiovanni (1977) is less severe in not rejecting objectivity, but he suggests less emphasis on measurement with more attention to "naturalistic" data, borrowing from the field of anthropology.

Wise and Darling-Hammond (1984) are among those critical of much of current practice, using the term "bureaucratic evaluation." They support, apparently, many of the proposals for more collaborative endeavors in teacher evaluation, but add an emphasis on the use of "expert teachers."

THREE FACTORS FOR DESIGN

In one way or another, each operating teacher evaluation system can be viewed as reflecting three distinctly different factors. These are orientation toward change, emphasis on purposes, and the type of implementing process. *Orientation* relates to the underlying assumptions about the utility of engaging in evaluations. *Purpose* relates to the consequences assumed to follow from the evaluations. *Process* relates to tactical or procedural elements selected for use. Obviously, these three factors are each complex and highly intererelated.

Orientation

Orientation toward change can be viewed on a scale from dynamic, innovative, redesigning, or restructuring to tractive, resisting, enforcing, or codifying (Harris, 1985). Applying this scale to teacher evaluation systems focuses on the features of the operation that promote or restrict change in teaching. Both formative and summative efforts can be dynamic in nature. However, summative systems that focus on "ideals," "innovations," or "best practices" are more clearly change oriented than those stressing "minimum competencies," dismissal, remediation, and compliance with rules and norms. Change-oriented evaluation systems will stress growth expectations for all, not just those with deficiencies (Houston ISD, 1977; Thomas, 1984). Tractively oriented systems will stress documentation without too much concern for feedback and follow-up support, or will provide feedback in terms of simply affirming that standards are not being ignored.

Purpose

Purposes to be served by the findings of a teacher evaluation system vary widely and influence the character of the design. Both summative and formative evaluation systems can be as developmental in purpose. Both can serve to improve teaching and hence learning. However, the strategies for improvement must be carefully considered. Evaluations tend to provide guides to action or they are not truly evaluation systems (Stufflebeam, 1980). However, what kind of actions are presumed to follow?

1. The teacher may be replaced (dismissal or nonrenewal of contract).
2. The teacher may be reassigned (a new location, subject, grade, type of student, etc.).
3. The teacher may be improved (new skills, knowledge, reinforcements, incentives, services, etc.).

Exhibit 3.1 attempts to show these three kinds of action alternatives as related to basic design and evaluation processes. These three types of

EXHIBIT 3.1 Relating evaluation sequence to process orientation and purpose factors

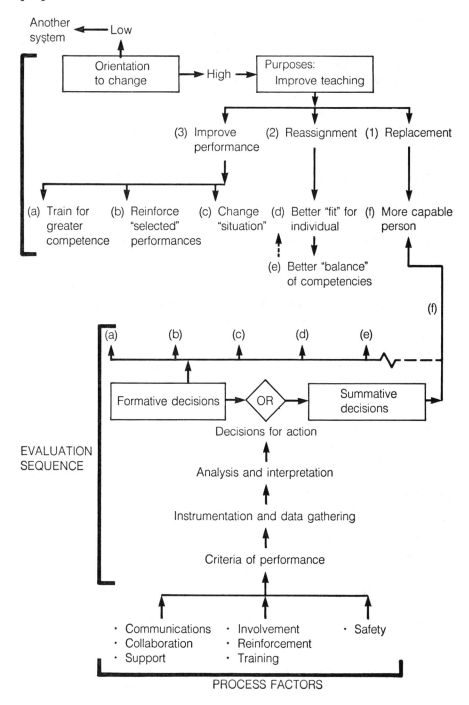

purpose (Harris, Bessent and McIntyre, 1969) call for substantially different evaluations, even though each has a commonness of purpose in improving teaching.

Replacement calls for comprehensive assessment and due process that measures up to legal requirements (Munnelly, 1979). This purpose is also fraught with special concerns for morale, ethics, and labor market conditions.

Reassignments are hardly such drastic actions; however, they require more attention to situational variables, including openings, staff balance, and transportation costs. (Harris et al., 1979).

Improving individual teacher performance is still different from replacement and reassignment in calling for an evaluation design. In fact, the focus on the individual teacher requires still further analysis as to purpose (Mager and Pipes, 1970). Such improvements occur by helping the individual teacher gain new skills, knowledges, and attitudes. This calls for actions involving in-service education and other interventions. However, improved performance also derives from creating conditions which facilitate or enhance the fuller use of already existing knowledge and skills. Hence, quite different actions need to be stimulated by evaluation efforts in these instances (Harris, 1980). To improve skills requires highly individualized, diagnostic evaluation techniques. Such diagnostic techniques may not be so crucial, however, if conditions influencing teaching are to be the focus for action. Knowledge deficiencies are more readily diagnosed in testing or interview situations while skills need to be analyzed in real or simulated settings. The absence of incentives or the presence of constraints may well be evaluated using questionnaires or in-depth interviews.

Process Factor

The technical process of evaluation as a series of steps—criteria specification, instrumentation, data gathering, analysis, interpretation, decision making, and action—was carefully detailed in Chapter 1. Here, we are looking at those same basic steps, but also considering the change orientation and purpose factors that influence the character of the system.

The overarching processes utilized for the operationalization of the teacher evaluation system need special attention. Some processes seem to be crucial, regardless of the specific step in the evaluation sequence or purposes to be served. Some of these process factors include the following:

1. *Clarity of communications.* The extent to which the entire system for teacher evaluation is clearly understood by all persons involved, especially by teacher evaluatees.
2. *Direct involvement.* The extent to which personnel engaged in operating the system have been directly involved in initiating it, have opportunities to be involved in the operation of the system, and sense the possibility for changing the system as inequities arise.

3. *Collaboration.* The extent to which opportunities are provided for the evaluatee to share as fully as possible in each step of the evaluation sequence.
4. *Reinforcement.* The extent to which the procedures and instruments assure that present teaching performance will be positively reinforced in meaningful ways.
5. *Safety.* The extent to which procedures offer evaluatees maximum protection against punitive or embarrassing consequences of being evaluated.
6. *Support.* The extent to which policy, procedures, and resource allocations clearly offer supporting services to the evaluatee in response to evaluation findings.
7. *Training.* The extent to which learning experiences of high quality and relevance are provided.

These seven process factors are related to the steps in evaluation and the design of the system, but they seem even more crucial to the successful implementation and continued operation of any teacher evaluation system, so long as there is an orientation toward change and the purposes are developmental to some degree. Obviously, these process factors are most crucial to the success of formative evaluation operations (McGreal, 1982). They become nearly impossible to maintain in the most sensitive summative efforts. For these reasons, this educator places heavy emphasis throughout this book on developmental (formative and diagnostic) teacher evaluation as that which is feasible and certainly most profitable. However, even teacher dismissal and nonrenewal of contract decisions are more readily implemented with proper attention to basic processes of evaluation.

PRINCIPLES AND GUIDELINES

A set of principles and guidelines for teacher evaluation was developed by the Texas Cooperative Committee on Teacher Evaluation (1979). Representatives of seven different educational associations ranging from school board members to classroom teachers worked through a set of agreements regarding the guidelines for use by local districts in reviewing their evaluation systems. Exhibit 3.2 lists the eight principles on which these educators were able to reach substantial consensus. Sets of "guidelines" were specified by this committee under each of these "principles." (See Appendix A for a complete list of guidelines for local evaluation systems.)

These principles and guidelines were promulgated on the premise that developmental or formative teacher evaluation was of foremost value in any school setting. The need for summative evaluation efforts was not ignored or rejected. But the Committee quickly decided, despite many

EXHIBIT 3.2   Eight principles for teacher evaluation*

A teacher evaluation operation at the local school and district levels must be a developmental system if it is to serve effectively to stimulate and guide the improvement of teaching and learning. Eight basic principles define what is meant by a developmental system. These are presented briefly below.

A. *Preconditions for Teacher Evaluation*
   The conditions surrounding the instructional efforts of the teacher must be conducive to effective teaching and student learning.

B. *General Principles*
   The total educational enterprise must be supportive of the teacher evaluation system with clearly defined purposes, enabling policies, and genuine commitment to professional quality evaluation efforts.

C. *Sources and Uses of Data*
   Systematic and selective data gathering that directly serves the purpose of improving teaching and learning must be the central focus of the teacher evaluation system.

D. *Instrumentation*
   The instruments utilized in gathering and analyzing data must be highly reliable and valid, but they also must be selected, developed, or adapted to serve local needs.

E. *Collaboration*
   All aspects of the teacher evaluation process must seek to maximize collaboration among those who have an interest in teacher evaluation outcomes.

F. *Training in Evaluation*
   Only those who have both the technical and conceptual skills required shall be delegated specific responsibility for teacher evaluation.

G. *Due Process*
   Individuals whose lives and futures are directly affected by the outcomes from teacher evaluation must be assured that a full set of procedural safeguards are provided to prevent abuses and promote development.

H. *Improvement Activities*
   Teacher evaluation efforts must be directly linked to opportunities for teacher improvement of truly substantial and important kinds.

Source: Principles and Guidelines for Teacher Evaluation Systems by the Texas Cooperative Committee. Austin, TX: Texas Classroom Teachers' Association, 1979.

disagreements, that formative evaluation should predominate in any system and should nearly always precede summative efforts.

While these principles speak most explicitly to formative evaluation systems they also have substantial relevance to summative evaluation. Principle A refers to pre-conditions that make sense regardless of evaluation type or form. Principle B also applies without modification to any evaluation effort. Principle C needs modification to apply to many summative purposes. Principle D is widely applicable to all situations, as are F and G. Principles E and H are those that are really uniquely important to teacher evaluation if formative, developmental purposes are to be well served.

In the cases that follow, these principles and the three sets of design factors will be utilized to suggest strengths and weaknesses in the models presented. Unlike the "games" depicted in Chapter 1 to illustrate common malpractices, these cases are selected to reflect promising practices. Each case is distinctly different from the others in a variety of ways. That this author regards them as promising is not a sign that they should be adopted by others. These are times when new possibilities for design are being recognized. Hence, teacher evaluation systems should emerge in the 1980s that are far superior to those of the past. Furthermore, if evaluation is a local affair, as it properly should be, then systems should be developed locally or those developed elsewhere should be systematically adapted to meet local needs.

The American Association of School Personnel Administrators formulated a set of "Standards for School Personnel Administration" in 1972 and revised them again in 1978. The earlier standards were procedural and summative in character, stressing "grievances," "suspensions," "terminations," and "notification." A much more developmental approach is reflected in the 1980 standards. These standards reflect concern for "the continuing professional development of personnel," with "cooperative (evaluation) process designed . . . to improve the quality of teaching" (Harris, et al. 1985: 274–275).

In the cases presented in the following sections of this chapter, many of the "principles" are shown to be operationally realistic. Yet all of these case descriptions are less than perfect. They illustrate forward movement toward effective teacher evaluation, but they also remind us of the creative development work still to be done.

CASE #1: THE ASSESSMENT TEAM*

As an outgrowth of legislation requiring new teachers to "demonstrate classroom skills," one large, rapidly growing urban/suburban school system launched a "supportive supervision" program of competency assessment and related competency development. A set of twenty performance statements was adopted. A staff of instructional and evaluation specialists developed a diagnostic analysis system calling for observations, interviews,

---

*This case and others in the chapter are based on actual operations. However, descriptions presented are necessarily simplified. In some instances, the practices described were found in separate schools but are combined here to illustrate a more complete system. In doing so, the identity of the school district is fully disguised.

tests and self-report inventories to be used with all new teachers in the fall semester of their first year on the job.

The plan called for involving principal, central staff supervisors, peer teachers, and evaluatee in the process of gathering a full array of data, utilizing the wide assortment of instruments. Once all data were gathered, evaluation specialists analyzed it and prepared the competency profile and diagnostic reports. These assessment reports went to the principal who, in turn, convened a "support team" to review the analyses and raw data.

The support team consisted of principal, supervisor, a peer teacher, and the evaluatee. Together they identified growth targets, planned improvement activities, and implemented them, with each member carrying out certain specific responsibilities.

Annual narrative reports of progress were drafted by the support team and these were submitted to the Assistant Superintendent for Instruction in lieu of any summative annual evaluation report. After two or more years (normally not more than three years), a complete re-assessment was undertaken using the same procedures described previously. These procedures produced comparisons with both earlier profiles and the norms for acceptable performance that were emerging within the school system. On the basis of these comparisons, a recommendation regarding re-employment and state certification was made by the principle following a review by the "leader" of the assessment team.

Analysis

This case clearly reflects a departure from the one person evaluation systems generally in common practice. It is one of many models that is primarily developmental, even though a summative phase is included. It might be thought of as a *diagnostic, prescriptive model,* with the diagnostic or assessment features being carefully separated from the supportive efforts. In fact, every effort was made to have assessment and support teams for each teacher composed of different staff members. As much as possible, only the principal served on both teams. Involvement and collaboration were best reflected in the support team operation. Change was obviously stressed in this system. Improvement activities planned by a separate team gave assurance that real support would be provided.

Strengths   The commitment of the entire school system to this evaluation effort was clearly evidenced by an adopted set of procedures and instruments and by a staff clearly assigned to team responsibilities. A wide variety of types and sources of data were utilized. Instruments were developed by specialists, field tested, and checked for reliability and validity. Collaboration was exemplified primarily in the inclusion of the new teacher on the support team. Further evidence of collaboration was evidenced in the use of a variety of staff personnel on both assessment and support teams. Substantial training was provided to all personnel serving on assessment teams. Due process was assured to some extent in carefully separating team assignments and clearly designating a whole set of events prior to any summative decision making. Furthermore, the evaluatee presumably was privy to all instruments, reports, and team meetings. Improvement activities were, of course, the whole focus of the support team operation.

Weaknesses   Due process for the teacher was provided in this system in only a limited fashion. It was true that the teacher would normally be allowed two or three years to demonstrate "competence," but the details for handling difficulties that might arise were not clearly a part of the system.

The improvement activities provided were clearly linked to diagnosed needs and to district expectations; however, their quality tended to depend heavily upon the particular "support team." When the team functioned well, the teacher was served well. But, these teams were composed of very busy people who could not always provide the support needed.

An element of collaboration was missing to some extent in this system. The principal tended to share responsibility with a team of individuals who were often assigned to other schools and programs. This tended to complicate a truly collaborative effort. In fact, a single member of the support team often took major responsibility.

The most severe weaknesses in this system derived from what might seem to be a strength. The distinct separation of the assessment process and the supportive interventions seem logical. In fact, this design feature seems to have been the source of serious deficiencies. Those gathering the data and those using it were different staff members; hence, they tended to have less confidence in its validity, understand it less intimately, and used it only superficially. The process of data gathering and analysis was needlessly complex and time consuming, so support teams did not wait for the assessment report before going ahead to help the evaluatee with "problems" yet to be diagnosed. This led to ignoring the assessment reports when they were finally received.

The use of assessment and support teams as separate entities looked promising, but may have been too complex, too costly, too difficult to coordinate, and too disruptive of school-level operations.

CASE #2: THE TARGETING PLAN

A carefully developed set of policies and procedures has been adopted in this district to guide three evaluation program "tracks." Staff development, dismissal, and tenure are structured to be separate, but related efforts. Performance criteria have been developed for each position. Criteria were field tested and revised in use over a five year period. A Staff Development Committee with representatives from teaching, administration, community and Board levels guided implementation of the program including relating in-service training to individual needs as evaluated.

The evaluation system follows a model that is focused on "targets for growth." A five stage process or cycle was utilized.

1. *Preview:* All procedures are reviewed. A team is selected to include a supervisor (principal or other), a peer, and one or more other professionals. Responsibilities for implementing the various activities are agreed upon in team planning sessions. A pre-assessment observation of the evaluatee is scheduled as a team operation, providing each member of the team with a preliminary view of the teacher at work.

2. *Assessment:* Each team member completes an independent assessment of the teacher, using the approved performance criteria. These assessments are based on a second observation, one or more conferences with the teacher, plus a review of lesson plans, students' work, materials in the classroom, test data, etc. No formal instrumentation is utilized for the various data gathering processes, but the performance criteria are the required frame of reference that all team members most use. Team members make extensive notes of their assessment procedures and the evidence obtained.

Each team member submits a report in the form of a summary analysis of the extent to which each performance is clearly in evidence. These are objective summary estimates ranging from "clearly in evidence as a high quality performance" to "clearly not in evidence." "No evidence" is also a reporting option for each performance. Each team member submits his/her report along with abbreviated notations on procedures and sources of information.

The final step in assessment involves the principal (or other designated supervisor) conferring with the teacher, using all team member reports. The reports are not identifiable as to which team member was involved. Hence, the principal and teacher study the 3 to 5 sets of summary estimates of performance. Similarities and differences are analyzed. Consistently reported "high quality" performances are noted and reinforced verbally. Consistently reported "low quality" or nonevident performances are noted for further attention.

3. *Growth targeting:* This third phase may be a continuation of phase 2, but is generally scheduled a few days to a week later. The principal may work with the teacher on selecting and planning growth activities or may delegate this to another team member.

The specific performances reported as not clearly of high quality are the focus of the supervisor and teacher in this conference. One or more performances are selected for "targeting" for improvement. Then specific objectives for improvement are agreed upon and put into written form. Finally, time lines are established, indicating first, second, and third level priorities for various objectives, and completion dates set for each one.

4. *Growth plan implementation:* This phase is largely the responsibility of the individual teacher. However, each team member who receives a copy of the growth plan is expected to assist as needed. Monitoring visits

are scheduled as classroom observations. These are guided by established target dates. On request, the principal, team members, or others provide materials, demonstrate, arrange for intervisitation, or assist with guided practice in the classroom. Special workshops may also be planned around targets that are common to a group of teachers. Conferences may also be scheduled by either the principal or the teacher to permit discussion of problems, procedures, or plans.

5. *Review:* This last phase in the cycle brings the team back together with the teacher. The teacher and principal or other supervisor report to the team on the efforts to accomplish targeted objectives. Team members ask questions for elaboration, clarification, and verification. They add their own information to the discussion. Three sets of conclusions are reached and reported.

1. Extent of accomplishment of objectives.
2. Further growth activities needed.
3. Suggested next steps (recycle or return to phase 3).

Analysis

This is a data-based management by objectives model. It uses a set of carefully formulated performance criteria as the unifying framework for operating an otherwise rather flexible system (see Exhibit 3.3). Instrumentation is limited to a summary report form, but a variety of data sources and data gatherers are involved. The teacher is heavily involved in selecting growth targets and also in making use of summary report data in analyzing and interpreting estimates of various evaluators. Support is provided in the form of conferences, a resource team, and an in-service training program that can respond to individual needs.

Strengths The plan is highly systematic, sequenced, and unequivocally developmental in nature. Multiple data sources, including observations by several team members, are utilized. Data are systematically reviewed as the basis for diagnosing and projecting needs for improvement. Support services are provided to assure the opportunity to demonstrate improvements.

Weaknesses The use of a team for many phases of this plan in operation involves difficulties. Multiple observations by a team results in costs for training and continuing costs in staff time. Similarly, team planning in phase 1 and team participation in phase 4 means much staff time allocated to the individual teacher. The need for coordination of the diverse team activities poses still additional problems. This plan, with well formulated performance criteria, does not have a standardized diagnostic process. While one might emerge, the use of so many diverse data sources makes diagnosis a rather unsystematic process.

EXHIBIT 3.3   Five phases of the targeting plan

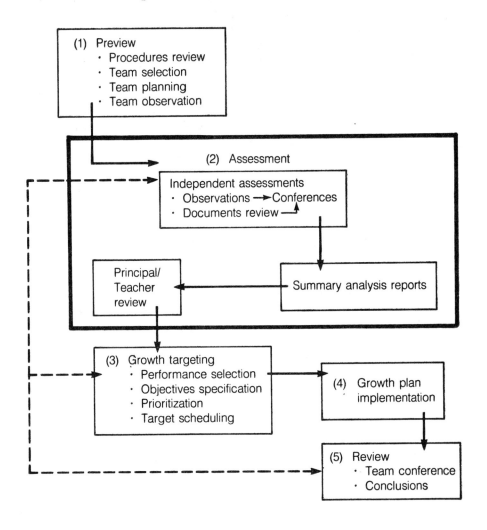

(1) Preview
  · Procedures review
  · Team selection
  · Team planning
  · Team observation

(2) Assessment

Independent assessments
  · Observations →Conferences
  · Documents review

Principal/
Teacher
review

Summary analysis reports

(3) Growth targeting
  · Performance selection
  · Objectives specification
  · Prioritization
  · Target scheduling

(4) Growth plan
    implementation

(5) Review
  · Team conference
  · Conclusions

CASE #3: THE COLLABORATIVE
DIAGNOSTIC PLAN (*DeTEK*)

The DeTEK system is being employed in a medium-sized school system
with about 700 teachers. As a structured "kit" the procedures tend to vary
more with individual teachers than with schools. This teacher evaluation

system is characterized by rather elaborate instrumentation. A set of performance criteria are specified in considerable detail, at three levels of specificity. Six teaching "styles" are described—"business like," "individual oriented," etc. Each style is specified as a set of three or four behaviors, and each of these behaviors is further explicated by a set of "indicators." The focus of all criteria is primarily on the teacher and on classroom practices; hence, only incidental attention is given to student behavior, physical environment, or out-of-classroom behavior.

The system calls for the use of carefully developed sets of instruments in a ten-step sequence. The purpose is clearly and consistently developmental, with growth planning and reinforcing procedures focused on improvement of specific practices. An evaluator's guide carefully details the procedures to be followed. Illustrations and guided practice activities have been provided in the guide to assure that principals, assistants, supervisors, and department heads are fully able to make the system operate. In addition, materials are listed in an annotated resource guide, and some of these materials—reprints, books, films, games, etc.—have been secured from professional libraries and are available in a central office collection.

The system operates using a continuous schedule but is clearly separated into three phases and ten steps. (See Exhibit 3.4)

Phase I: Pre-Diagnostic Survey

1. *Teacher self-analysis* is completed, using an instrument that surveys all 22 behaviors. A profile or overall teacher performance is produced.
2. A *classroom observation* is completed by the principal (or a designated assistant). Again, the observer records observable evidence related to each of 22 behaviors. A profile is generated when this data is analyzed.
3. A *conference* is held between teacher and observer. At this time, their respective profiled data are discussed and compared, and interpretations are drawn concerning "strengths," "need" for further diagnosis, and "other" for future consideration. The conferees are urged to strive for consensus based on existing data. No efforts to generalize beyond the data are attempted. Only three decisions are considered:
   a. Are there strengths clearly supported by data that need recognition?
   b. Are there behaviors (one, two, or three only) that seem likely areas for improvement efforts?
   c. Are there inconsistencies in the two profiles of performance that may need to be reconsidered at a later date?

On the basis of answers to these questions a diagnostic assessment phase is initiated.

EXHIBIT 3.4 Systems diagram of DeTEK in operations: a ten-step sequence

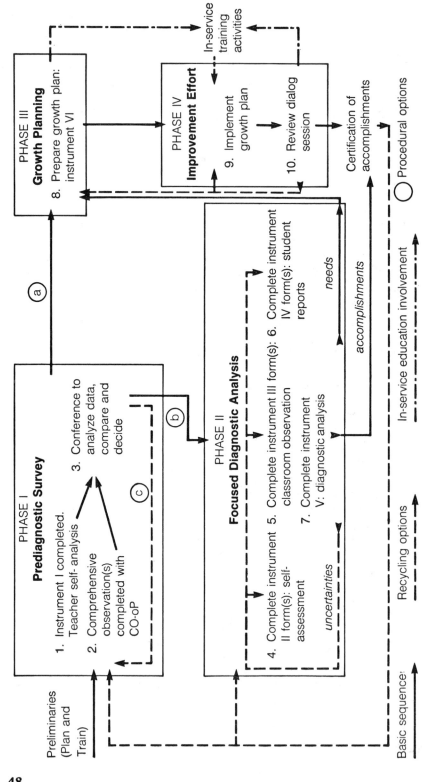

*Adapted from Ben M. Harris and Jane Hill "Trainers' Manual," *Developmental Teacher Evaluation Kit.* Austin, TX: Southwest Educational Development Laboratory, 1982.

Phase II: Focused Diagnostic Analysis

Phase II calls for focused data gathering and diagnostic analysis, using four additional instruments and steps as follows:

4. The teacher completes self-assessment instruments for only those behaviors identified above.
5. An observer completes a focused observation using only the selected behaviors as his or her focus.
6. Students complete inventories asking only for factual descriptions of what they observe the teacher doing in the classroom. (Primary level children do not use these instruments unless teacher and observer wish to take time to read the items to the children for their responses.)
7. A diagnostic analysis conference is scheduled. The teacher and principal or other supervisor compile the data from steps 4, 5 and 6, and use rather structured procedures for identifying "accomplishments," "needs," and "uncertainties."

Phase III: Growth Planning and Improvement

On the basis of needs clearly identified in step 7, growth planning is undertaken as step 8. A formal plan is adopted by mutual consent. Step 9 involves implementing the plan. Step 10 is called the "review dialog" session. In this last step, progress is reviewed, more planning is undertaken if necessary, and new "accomplishments" are recognized. Recycling of some kind follows so there is a continuous system in operation. Recycling back to step 8 or step 9 for continued efforts to improve are sometimes called for. However, more frequently, new accomplishments are certified; recycling then involves returning to steps 4, 5, 6 and 7 to pick-up another behavior for diagnostic analysis. Recycling may, on the other hand, involve returning to initial steps with further teacher self-analysis and classroom observations.

Accomplishments are not only recognized in this program, they are also "certified." Record keeping in this system provides for an individual teacher record. Both needs and accomplishments are recorded following completion of each ten-step sequence. When a behavior has been transformed from a need to an accomplishment, the record reflects that and certificates of accomplishment are issued annually to all teachers demonstrating such growth in teaching performance.

In-service training plans are gradually being linked to needs as diagnosed for individual teachers in this school district. Growth plans are being submitted to the central office responsible for coordinating in-service education plans for the district. A microcomputer file for each teacher and school is maintained to reflect both the accomplishments and the needs of each teacher. Common needs are identified and special workshops planned whenever a group of reasonable size emerges. Teachers with certified accomplishments are invited to assist in planning and conducting such work-shops. It is anticipated that consultants will gradually be making fuller use of the microcomputer as a tool for planning their work with individual teachers. Furthermore, future plans call for periodic reports to principals on the names and locations of teachers with accomplishments so they can make better use of these "experts" in planning intervisitations or demonstrations for teachers in need.

Reports to the superintendent and to the School Board are evolving in both form and substance. To date only growth plans are being submitted. However, the principals are now being asked to submit a "School Summary Report" annually. This report simply lists each teacher and shows needs identified and accomplishments certified; it leaves all other behavior designations blank. This report permits the assistant superintendent to report on strengths in schools, grades, and program. Furthermore, the number of needs embraced by growth plans can be reported and progress from previous years becomes concrete information.

The superintendent schedules an evaluation conference with each principal each year for purposes of reviewing needs identified, growth plans being implemented, new accomplishments certified, and problems, if any, that are in evidence. Hence, the total system is under review and the accountability of the principal becomes, it is believed, a reality.

Analysis

The system known as DeTEK: *Developmental Teacher Evaluation Kit* (Harris and Hill, 1982), is used for illustrative purposes in numerous places in this book. The author has, of course, a biased view of this plan for developmental teacher evaluation. DeTEK was developed in an organized effort to demonstrate and model the principles in Exhibit 3.2 and Appendix A. It does seem to be a promising system, one that will guide and stimulate developmental efforts, one that is highly collaborative, data-based, flexible, and clearly not summative.

Strengths   The greatest strength in this plan is that the system is completely "self-contained." All materials needed for implementation are included in the kit. Other strengths have been mentioned—collaboration, data-based, flexible, etc. However, the structure of the system is such that consistent use of procedures detailed in *The DeTEK Handbook* make for a rather sophisticated process of survey, diagnosis, and growth without elaborate teams, and with reasonable amounts of staff time (5 to 6 hours per teacher). Other strengths include a resource file, a training manual, and record keeping materials ready for use.

Weaknesses   The DeTEK plan demands high quality classroom observations with inter-observer reliabilities at 0.75 and higher. Without objective observations, the diagnostic analysis process may be weakened.

EXHIBIT 3.5 Comparisons of three cases on various system characteristics

	Case #1	Case #2	Case #3
Technical Evaluation (Steps)			
Criteria	+	+	+
Instrumentation	+	−	+
Data gathering	+	0	+
Analysis	+	−	+
Interpretation	0	+	+
Valuing	0	+	0
Decision making	+	+	+
Action	+	0	+
Design Factors			
Change Orientation Purposes	+	+	+
• Replacement	+	+	0
• Reassignment, fit	−	−	0
• Reassignment, balance	−	−	0
• Individual	−	+	+
• Individual, reinforce	0	0	+
• Individual, training	+	+	+
Process			
• Communication	+	+	+
• Involvement	0	+	+
• Collaboration	0	+	+
• Reinforcement	0	0	+
• Safety	0	+	+
• Support	+	+	0
• Training	+	+	+
Principles			
A. Preconditions	0	0	0
B. General policy	+	+	0
C. Sources/uses of data	+	+	+
D. Instrumentation	+	−	+
E. Collaboration	0	+	+
F. Training in evaluation	+	−	+
G. Due process	0	0	+
H. Improvement	+	+	+
Summary of comparisons	17	18	23

Key: + = system conforms clearly
      0 = system not clearly conforming
      − = system lacks characteristics

The last step in the sequence is less rigorous and systematic than all others. The momentum of collaborative involvement and growth are relied upon to make Step 10, the review dialog session, work. Since procedures for this session are general and a variety of decision alternatives are available, the quality of actions are likely to vary widely.

CASE COMPARISONS

The discussion of these three cases reveals more similarities than differences. They all reflect sound efforts at truly effective developmental evaluation. Exhibit 3.5 attempts to summarize comparisons among the three. The strengths of each are shown with a symbol (+). None is strong in every possible way, of course.

SUMMARY

As genuine systems of teacher evaluation begin to develop, replacing the practices of the past, a variety of operational models are available for study. Many divergent notions still prevail in the literature as well as in field practice, but much more unity regarding promising alternatives is also emerging. The orientations and purposes of various systems are becoming clearer. Essential process factors, especially in developmental evaluation have become more sharply recognized. Even the politically inspired, clumsy efforts of some state legislatures (see Chapter 10) to turn the clock back to summative dominated teacher evaluation, are being influenced by professional realities.

The principles and guidelines for good practice that are being widely accepted by scholars and practitioners alike do seem to be guiding better operational models. The three cases presented here are a limited sample of many real and exciting efforts to make developmental teacher evaluation a new influence for quality in education.

SELECTED STUDY SOURCES

Gitlin, Andrew and R. T. Ogawa (1983/84). "A Congruent Evaluation Structure and Process: Peer-Peer Review and Horizontal Evaluation," *National Forum of Educational Administration and Supervision* 1: 21–32.

   The authors report on a test of peer evaluation emphasizing the analysis of intents as related to observed practice. The emphasis is on understanding rather than change in practices per se.

Georgia Department of Education (1983). *Guidelines for the Implementation of Performance-Based Certification by the Georgia Department of Education, Regional Assess-*

ment Centers and Local School Systems. Division of Staff Development. Atlanta, GA. mimeographed.

A description via guidelines is provided of an elaborate new teacher evaluation system. This is one of the few systems designed to separate summative and developmental efforts. It is also one of the few efforts to date, on a state-wide basis, to implement a complete system as distinguished from fragments and edicts.

Harris, Ben M. and Jane Hill (1982). *The Developmental Teacher Evaluation Kit (DeTEK).* Austin, TX: Southwest Educational Development Laboratory.

A kit designed for use in full-scale implementation of the system depicted as Case #3. The kit includes the Handbook, Training Manual, Reproduction Masters, and a Resource File.

Mager, Robert F. and Peter Pipes (1970). *Analyzing Performance Problems or "You Really Oughta Wanna."* Palo Alto, CA: Fearon Publishers.

An interesting, detailed set of procedures for systematically analyzing performance deficiencies. The authors' unique contribution is in suggesting a diagnostic sequence for determining causes of deficiencies.

Manatt, Richard P. (1979). *Teacher Performance Evaluation,* National Curriculum Study Institute, 3rd ed. Alexandria, VA: Association for Supervision and Curriculum Development. (See also Manatt, Palmer and Hildebaugh (1976), *NASSP Bulletin,* 60:21–24.)

While stressing instrumentation and procedures, this author presents an array of ideas about comprehensive evaluation.

McConnell, John H. (1971). "The Assessment Center: A Flexible Program for Supervisors," *Personnel* 48 (Sept./Oct.): 34–40.

A review of essential features of the assessment center with emphasis on its use beyond simple selection process. (See also Merritt (1973), *Peabody Journal of Education* 50 (July): 309–12.)

McGreal, Thomas L. (1982). "Effective Teacher Evaluation Systems," *Educational Leadership* 39 (January): 303–06.

A variety of models are reviewed, illustrated, and discussed.

Popham, William James (1971). *Designing Teacher Evaluation Systems.* Los Angeles, CA: The Instructional Objectives Exchange.

A document of historical value, this is one of the early efforts to view evaluation in systems terms. The emphasis is on outcome evaluation. (See also Popham, W. J. (1975), *Educational Evaluation,* Prentice-Hall, Inc.)

Redfern, George B. (1980). *Evaluating Teachers and Administrators: A Performance Objectives Approach.* Boulder, CO: Westview Press.

A comprehensive review is presented of the main ideas that Redfern has presented over the years. His model is essentially MBO. He develops specific procedures and forms for implementation.

Sergiovanni, Thomas J. (1977). "Reforming Teacher Evaluation: Naturalistic Alternatives," *Educational Leadership* 34 (May): 602–07.

A critical view is presented of overemphasis on measurement and quantification in teacher evaluation. The author suggests alternative kinds of data and procedures to be considered.

Stulac, Josef F. et al. (1981). *Assessment of Performance in Teaching: Field Study Instrument.* Columbia, SC: South Carolina Educator Improvement Task Force.

An interesting example of efforts to design a state-wide system utilizing descriptive observation techniques.

Wise, Arthur E. et al. (1984). *Case Studies for Teacher Evaluation (N-2133-NIE).* Santa Monica: The Rand Corporation.

Studies of teacher evaluation as practiced in Salt Lake City, Lake Washington, Greenwich, and Toledo are presented as part of a larger survey of 32 school districts with fairly well developed systems.

4

Teaching Criteria

Any evaluation process, regardless of the specifics of system design or purpose begins with defining or selecting criteria. When the focus is on teacher evaluation, as distinguished from other evaluation purposes, then criteria of teaching performance must be among those given consideration. However, there are various alternative ways of selecting teaching criteria. The teacher as a person has often been the basis for selecting teaching criteria (Borich, 1977). Still another alternative stresses student outcome criteria as indicators of teaching effectiveness (Millman, 1981; Popham 1971, 1975). The interactions among teacher, student, and the material of the lesson has also been a criterion for evaluating teaching (Dunn and Dunn, 1977). The extensive research indicating that the teacher may be the primary influence on student learning within the school has placed much emphasis on teaching acts as criteria for evaluation (Bloom, 1976; Rosenshine, 1971; Gage, 1978; Good, et al., 1975; Dunkin and Biddle, 1974; Medley, 1977).

In addition to various views on the appropriate criteria for teacher evaluation, the scope of responsibilities to be evaluated is also a concern. Teaching defined in rather limited ways may attend almost entirely to the classroom and the actual processes of guiding, directing, and stimulating student learning (Harris, 1975). However, nonclassroom responsibilities are often included in job descriptions (Bolton, 1973; Redfern, 1980), and the "roles of the teacher" may be specified to extend well beyond even local job responsibilities to those of "professional" commitment (CTA 1964). Accordingly, criteria selected from several different domains of performance are often included in teacher evaluation systems.

Still further complexities are introduced when teaching is viewed as a function rather than as a job (Harris et al., 1979). Teaching teams such as teacher/aide/parent volunteer teams and librarian/teacher/resource teacher teams are two of the numerous ways of viewing teaching as a team function. These argue for selecting criteria somewhat differently, but also applying them in rather dramatically different ways.

Dunn and Dunn (1977) offer a complication in considering criteria as they argue for "matching" teaching acts to the "learning styles" of individual students.

In this chapter, these various views of teaching and teacher will be analyzed briefly to make explicit the differences that logically follow in criteria selection. However, much of this chapter will focus on a review of teacher effectiveness criteria as they are best reflected in both research and professional practice. The latter portion of the chapter then deals with the practical problems of formulating criteria in ways that guide instrumentation, data gathering, and analysis.

TEACHING DEFINITIONS AND FOCUS

Teaching as a function is one thing; teaching as a job description for an individual may be slightly different. As a set of processes for relating directly to one or more students, teaching may be still quite a different phenomenon. In every instance, however, there is one or more persons—teachers—to give focus to our definition of teaching. But people are complex and the narrowing of attention from teaching to teacher still leaves questions to be answered. Are we concerned with predictive criteria? Capacities? Knowledge? Attitudes? Acts? All might be useful, of course, but the field needs limitations.

Teacher As Person

If teaching is defined as what teachers do, we have a tautology. Furthermore, "teacher" needs to be defined in a rational and useful way to discriminate among personnel who are and are not included. Similarly, what teachers do (or are) must be differentially recognized as relating to learning or not (Millman, 1981).

Exhibits 4.1 and 4.2 illustrate two ways of viewing teaching, each starting from a different definition and frame of reference. In Exhibit 4.1, teaching is defined functionally as a broad array of "organized efforts" to help students learn. In starting with this functional frame of reference it follows that many individuals share responsibilities for fully implementing the function. The classroom teacher becomes, then, only one of a wide variety of persons who are teachers in one sense or another.

When this functional frame of reference is used, differentiating the criteria for evaluating either the person or the function becomes crucial. Obviously, there are common categories of criteria for evaluating teaching performance (White, 1981), but they are very broad criteria and would be

EXHIBIT 4.1 Functional/personal definition of teaching and related criteria

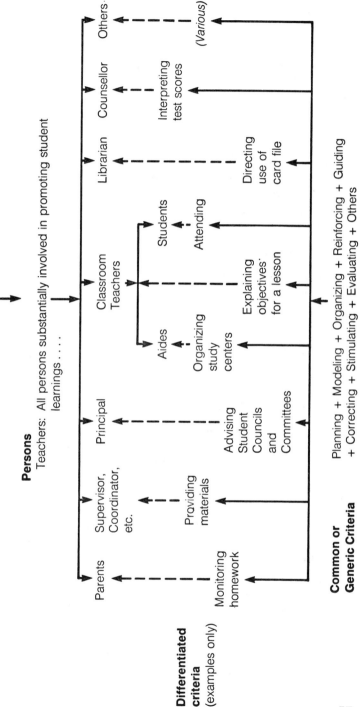

Function

Teaching: All organized efforts to promote student learnings related to the formal curriculum.

Persons

Teachers: All persons substantially involved in promoting student learnings . . . .

quite differently applied to the various persons involved. For instance, the planning, organizing, modeling, evaluating, and stimulating acts of principals, classroom teacher, and counselor would be distinct in many ways, even though reinforcing might be quite similar for all persons. On the other hand, differentiated criteria applying to the performance of various persons would be numerous and related only by function.

In Exhibit 4.2, a rather different definition of teaching is illustrated. Starting with a job-related frame of reference—classroom teacher—three major sets of duties or responsibilities are defined. "Teaching" is one set identified as largely generic performances that directly influence student learning. Those acts that support teaching in fairly direct ways are categorized as "instructional planning." The "other" category embraces a variety of criteria that are not very directly related to teaching or learning and yet are widely accepted as important to the job of the "classroom teacher."

Teaching Criteria

In both Exhibit 4.1 and 4.2, the teacher as a person (or set of persons) can be identified and so criteria for evaluating such persons can be rationally selected. This focus on persons calls attention to various kinds of criteria:

1. *Antecedent criteria:* Experience, degrees, grades, test scores, recommendations, etc.
2. *Personal characteristics criteria:* Knowledge, attitudes, goals, motives, intelligence, etc.
3. *Performance criteria:* Skills, techniques, behaviors, acts, events, etc.

These three kinds of criteria are not mutually exclusive, but they do tend to focus on rather different sources of evidence. The antecedent criteria tend to be focused on the person in the past. What evidence from the past can be secured for present and future use? The personal characteristics criteria tend to be focused on past, present, and the future. What do we know about this person as a person that might be useful now and in the future? Both antecendent and personal characteristics criteria presume a predictive use for such data or evidence. That is, past experience data is presumed to be useful in predicting present and future events. Similarly, intelligence measures or competency test scores are presumed to predict present and future performance. Both personal characteristics and antecedents are presumed to have rather long-term validity, especially in their predictive capability. More often than not, they are illusory, or limited at best.

Performance criteria, too, are presumed to be predictive. Techniques displayed in the present are presumed to be relatively stable and are not expected to disappear in the short-term future. However, the long-term validity of such predictions also must be questioned. Mager and Pipes (1970) make a convincing case that performances come and go with more or less reinforcement. Harris (1985) argues that cost/benefit analyses by teachers may extin-

EXHIBIT 4.2 Job related definition of teaching

Classroom Teacher: Any individual assigned to a specific grade, level and/or curriculum area with one or more regularly assigned student groups

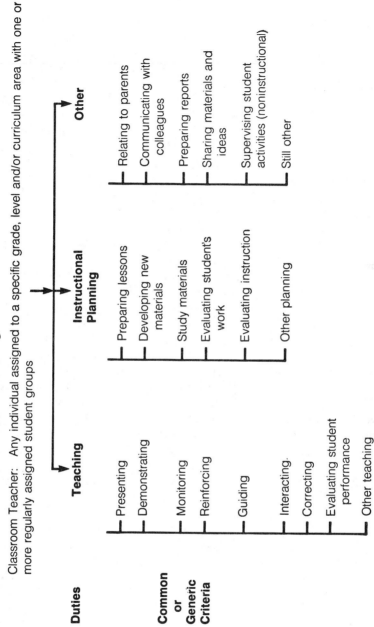

Duties	Teaching	Instructional Planning	Other
Common or Generic Criteria	Presenting	Preparing lessons	Relating to parents
	Demonstrating	Developing new materials	Communicating with colleagues
	Monitoring	Study materials	Preparing reports
	Reinforcing	Evaluating student's work	Sharing materials and ideas
	Guiding	Evaluating instruction	Supervising student activities (noninstructional)
	Interacting	Other planning	Still other
	Correcting		
	Evaluating student performance		
	Other teaching		

guish innovative practices if the costs are excessive in time, energy, and "abuse" in relation to benefits perceived. However, the stability of internalized performance is logically recognized as substantial, and both research and professional practice lend support to the use of this kind of criteria. Not only are performance criteria useful in that they predict reasonably well, but they also have greater face validity for gaining acceptance and guiding the improvement processes. Finally, the great advantage of performance criteria is their modification ability. They can be changed, and without this plastic characteristic any criterion is relatively weak for formative purposes.

"Face validity" refers to the rather obvious, logical relationships between a criterion, related data, and the thing being evaluated. For instance, consider the following set of linkages in Exhibit 4.3.

The three illustrations show criteria related to evaluation data or evidence. Illustration (a) suggests that there is a suitable "fit" between the criterion and the evidence (a1, a2, a3). However, neither the evidence nor the criterion is nicely related to the object of evaluation—that which we wish to know about. This suggests a limited possibility of validity. Such antecedent criteria are often rather limited in these ways; namely, the data generated, no matter how accurate or reliable, simply don't inform us well about the important questions to be answered.

Illustration (b) shows a personal characteristic's criterion related to the same object of evaluation. Here, too, the evidence is clearly related to the criterion and strongly indicates that the teacher may be highly knowledgeable of ". . . a variety of methods of instruction." However, knowledge is only a single factor relating to skill in teaching. Hence, this criterion and its data provide only very limited service in this evaluation effort.

Illustration (c) shows the potential for well-selected performance criteria to be useful. The criteria define various elements of the object of evaluation and the data are related to both in clear and explicit ways. Hence, face validity is more likely.

A variety of criteria could be advocated as producing even a better "fit" with the object of evaluation (Medley, 1973). This is often the case. However, a broader array of criteria calls for a greater variety of instruments and/or data. Hence, each criterion employed should be selected with maximum concern for its logical relationship to the evaluation object. Weak relationships should be avoided if possible.

Teams As Evaluatees

Sets or teams of people are sometimes influencing the student almost simultaneously. This is true in traditionally departmentalized instructional programs as much as in team teaching situations. Even in "self-contained" classrooms, there is usually a variety of adult "teachers" directly influencing learning in various ways—librarian, aide, principal, counselor, resource teacher, nurse, coach, etc. These influences for learning are not usually

EXHIBIT 4.3   Relating criteria and evidence to practical evaluation

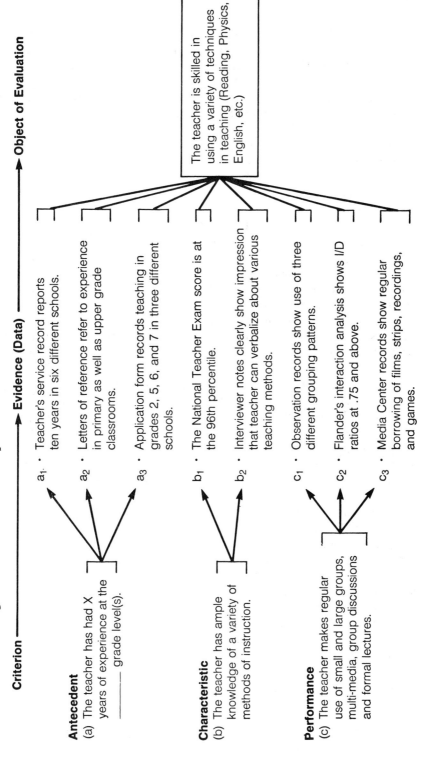

simultaneous in the minute-by-minute sense, of the word; however, unless we view the teaching/learning process as one in which learning occurs almost instantaneously with the acts of teaching, then the effects of multiple "teachers" on the student within a five hour school day must not be ignored. Curiously, little thought has been given to this reality as it relates to teacher evaluation. Curriculum specialists have long advocated attention to the obvious deficiencies of departmentalization, advocating correlated studies, team planning (English, 1969), core courses, and interdisciplinary studies (Siu, 1957; White, 1981). Most of these proposals have been ignored or vociferously rejected.

Whatever the reasons for fragmentation of the teaching function it is a wide-spread reality (Harris, et al., 1985). Accordingly, personalized criteria will always be somewhat limited in guiding comprehensive and summative evaluation efforts. A particular criterion of individual performance, such as "organizes each class group in such a manner that each student will know what is expected of him," may or may not be useful in evaluating a given teacher. A given teacher who acts in accordance with this criterion, may be "teaming" with five other teachers failing to do so, and this can influence the students in ways that nullify any positive effects. Conversely, one teacher who fails to act in ways that help students "know what is expected" may not have any overall negative effects if all others are very helpful to students in perceiving their learning tasks.

Team teaching situations have some clear advantages over fragmented departmentalized instructional programs if they offer well-coordinated, integrated, differentiated teacher/pupil relationships (English, 1969). Under conditions suggested by these terms, unified goals and objectives and highly inter-related content elements could be expected to compensate substantially for deficiencies in individual teacher performances while enriching student school experiences with a broad variety of teaching influences (Dunn and Dunn, 1977).

Recognizing the multiple influences for learning on nearly all students at all times does not render individual teacher evaluation useless, but does suggest cautions. When more than one influence for learning is present, the source of the learning outcome tends to be in doubt. However, if our performance criteria have validity in the sense that research and professional wisdom support them, then their use for formative evaluation purposes to reinforce best practices and guide improvement activities is clearly appropriate (Thomas, 1979). It is the *summative use* of such criteria that is clearly weakened by the realities of multiple influences in teaching and learning (Millman, 1981).

Classroom and Beyond

Performance criteria that focus upon teaching acts within the classroom are clearly of high priority. However, nonclassroom criteria are important, too, as suggested in Exhibit 4.2. The three sets of criteria all focus on the person called teacher, but even within this limitation the acts or events given attention range from very direct interpersonal attention to the learning process, to the preparation of an attendance report, to attending a faculty meeting.

School districts vary widely in the emphasis given to this array of nonclassroom categories of events in identifying performance criteria. Summative evaluation tends to emphasize nonclassroom performance, while formative systems are more classroom oriented (Dameroll, 1981). This is a curious reality, since one might logically expect that serious summative decisions would be most fully informed by instructional evaluation. In fact, various surveys clearly show the tendency for summative decisions to be based on noninstructional if not nonclassroom events (Damerall, 1981; Stipnieks, 1980; Ceballos, 1981).

Instructional performance criteria focus on classroom events as well as nonclassroom events, as shown in Exhibit 4.2 under both "Teaching" and "Instructional Planning." By contrast, the "Other" category of events tends to be less directly related to instruction. However, these useful distinctions are not without limitations. For instance, "Relating to Parents" may be highly instruction-related when parents are working with the teacher as volunteer aides planning a field trip for students. However, relating to parents via serving on the P.T.A. committee on "Membership" seems hardly instructional in nature.

Exhibit 4.4 provides illustrations of teacher performance criteria focused on different "Locale" and levels of "Instruction-Relatedness." While these are only illustrations of performance criteria, they do suggest a way of analyzing any criterion in terms of these two dimensions. Obviously, criteria of teacher performance that are highly instruction-related and close to the individual student in being both in-classroom and individual in locale are likely to deserve high priorities. Conversely, those criteria that are low or remote on instruction-relatedness and far from the student in locale must bear lower priority or be given special justification.

Various roles of the classroom teacher have been suggested by numerous studies. The California Teachers' Association (1964) produced a set of specifications for defining teaching as "roles" within which behaviors and specific indicators were defined. Six roles suggested in this study included:

1. Director of learning
2. Counselor
3. Mediator of culture
4. Community link
5. Staff member
6. Member of profession

EXHIBIT 4.4 Illustrations of teacher performance criteria by instructional relatedness and locale

Locale	Instructional Relatedness		
	Direct (a)	Indirect (b)	Remote (c)
Classroom "X" Direct, individual pupil/teacher interactions	Teacher accepts students ideas and utilizes them as a basis for developing the lesson.	Teacher advises Students on plans for SAT or other testing programs.	Teacher discusses personal and family problems with students seeking a friendly counselor.
Classroom "Y" Less direct, group/teacher interactions	Teacher moves about the room observing student activities and offering praise and assistance.	Teacher discusses rules, expectations, and procedures for operating the classroom with student cooperation	Teacher arranges for students to make announcements and plans for social and extra curricular activities.
Classroom "Z" Indirect or non-student related teacher acts.	Teacher arranges interest centers for student use as independent study activities.	Teacher organizes files, sets up displays, prepares bulletin boards, and makes other arrangements that generally relate to the subject-matter or teaching strategy.	Teacher cleans chalkboards, waters plants, and makes room attractive in various ways.
Outside Classroom Student/teacher interactions on individual or small group basis	Teacher meets with students who need extra help in completing assignments.	Teacher meets with Student Council, club, or hobby groups to advise and assist.	Teacher directs students in athletic, community or other activities that are not part of regular school program e.g., Red Cross, United Fund, Little League.
Outside Classroom Indirect or non-student related teacher acts.	Teacher participates in Teacher Center or local district workshops to develop skills.	Teacher serves on committees, advisory councils, or study teams developing school policies.	Teacher participates in association or union activities related to contract negotiations, grievance procedures, etc.

Unfortunately, clustering behaviors by roles that are very broadly defined tends to obscure rather than add clarity in some ways. Instructional criteria tend to be mixed with noninstructional criteria under such roles as "transmitter of culture." Colbert (1978) also identified a variety of roles of functions but focused primarily on only two, stressing the classroom behaviors of the "instructional facilitator" and the "instructional manager."

In a very recent review, Pearson (1980) identified over three hundred teaching criteria cited in the literature of recent years. Only eighty of these were validated, and they tended to cluster around eight styles or patterns of behavior as follows:

1. Variability
2. Task-oriented
3. Interpersonal
4. Clarity
5. Indirectness
6. Questioning
7. Enthusiasm
8. Opportunity to Learn

With one or two exceptions, these criteria tend to be classroom related. Pearson's work is a reminder of the thousands of "teacher competencies" identified by Dodl (1973) and published as the *Florida Catalog*. These were much more inclusive of the various classroom and nonclassroom categories that may be utilized. McKenna (1981) identifies an array of "performance component(s)" as follows: (1) subject matter knowledge, (2) cognitive strategies, (3) affective strategies, (4) psychomotor strategies, (5) planning, (6) evaluating, and (7) community relations. This seems to be an effort to relate a personal characteristic (knowledge), a set of roles, and a set of styles. As such it tends to create problems in specifying criteria within "components."

Nonclassroom evaluative criteria seem fairly well covered by the following categories:
Performances that

1. Relate to parents and community
2. Relate to school staff and program coordination
3. Relate to students outside classroom
4. Relate to in-service growth and development
5. Relate to professional activities beyond job assignments
6. Relate to other activities

This set of categories extends the boundaries of the individual teacher's world as practitioner even beyond what would ordinarily be required in any job description. However, criteria in any and all of these categories might be useful in some evaluation efforts. Summative evaluations are certainly likely to include many of these categories.

Specific criteria of performance in nonclassroom categories need to be carefully considered for their instruction-relatedness (Harris, 1985). Work with parents and others in the community is often instructional in nature. Work with students outside the classroom may also be instructional in some instances but not in others. The degree of relationship between a performance and its impact on the instructional program will surely effect how evaluator and evaluatees use the evidence. Procedures for giving differential weights to criteria of performance are often based on estimates of the extent to which a performance is or is not highly instruction-related.

Student Behavior Criteria

Student behaviors are nearly always included as criteria for evaluating teaching. The manner in which student behaviors enter into the criteria is crucial and controversial, however. Students are often referred to in instruction-related criteria that focus on the classroom. However, students are usually *objects* of teacher behavior in such criteria, which emphasize the unique responsibilities of the teacher as the agent for stimulating, guiding, and facilitating learning. This same recognition of the uniqueness of the teacher in the teaching/learning process leads many evaluation specialists to argue for criteria of "teacher effect" that describe student behaviors but virtually ignore teacher behaviors (Popham, 1971). Still others focus on student behaviors primarily as *learning process.* Such criteria emphasize learning style (Dunn, 1977) and learning theory in selecting criteria related to content, sequence, academic learning time, student attitudes and abilities, learning rates, prerequisite skills, attention span, reading difficulty level of materials, etc. (Bloom, 1980; Hunkins, 1980).

Student focused evaluative criteria are substantially different when that focus is on the student only as distinguished from focusing on the student in relation to teacher performance. If student learning outcomes are selected for emphasis in a teacher evaluation system, then criteria may be expressed as illustrated below:

> Maintains the interest, cooperation and respect of the students (Indicator 009-3. Ector County Schools, 1981).

The teacher is the subject, but the focus of the performance is on what students are doing, not what the teacher does. The word "maintains" tells us little about teacher behavior.

Student outcome criteria are those most "accountability" advocates stress. The use of outcome criteria for evaluating teacher performance allows test items of one kind or another to become the criteria. The interpretation of test scores of student "achievement" in terms of teacher performance is, however, a complex matter. Barro (1970) proposes an elaborate analytical scheme for estimating "the gains in performance made by pupils while in her (teacher's) class." McNeil and Popham (1973) advocate "performance tests" in which teachers are given one or more identical objectives and only the ends are given; the means are up to the instructor.

Criteria of student learning process are still different from those illustrated above. They tend to be more explicit behaviors, focus on events in the classroom, and imply a lesson context, instructional arrangements, a lesson, and a teacher. Some examples include the following:

"Work Involvement: pupils engage in assigned academic work." (Kounin, 1970).

Children select groups and seats part of the time (Stallings, 1977:110).

Peer teaching: students help other students instructionally . . . (Tikunoff, et al., 1975).

Student responses in the context of the lesson include:

(a) Individual Designation. Responding only when designated to do so, to the exclusion of any other student candidate.
(b) Group Designation: Responding as designated by the teacher from among a variety of other student candidates.
(c) Non-Designation: Responding as an individual without being designated by the teacher.
(d) Spontaneous: Verbalizing without a cue from the teacher to make it a response, in essence a student initiated response (Harris and Bessent, 1969: 158–161).

. . . . pupils take part in planning the work and in developing assignments (Harris, 1975: 368).

Stimulates students to participate in class discussions and activities (Redfern, 1980: 21).

Promotes students' self-discipline and responsibility. Independent effort, desire for investigation, self-discipline, and responsibility (West Des Moines Teacher Performance Evaluation Instrument, Form 74E. Reported by Manatt, no date).

All of these quoted illustrations use student behaviors as the object of some teaching act. They imply teacher performance criteria that are not explicit in most instances. To be most useful, the relationship between teacher behavior and student behavior needs to be explicit. They differ sharply from student outcome criteria and should not be confused with the latter.

Student learning criteria that specify outcomes are not particularly useful in evaluating individual teacher performance. It is not practical in most situations to isolate the contribution of the individual teacher in producing specified learning outcomes. Such criteria also are not very useful in the evaluation of teachers for developmental purposes. Whether student learning outcomes are or are not generated in association with any given teacher or teacher group, the findings offer little assistance in making decisions for either reinforcing or changing teaching practices.

As a general rule, student criteria should be used, if at all, only in ways that clearly relate them to explicit teacher behavior. Student behaviors can usefully be included in these teacher behavior criteria but should clarify the teaching acts under consideration, not replace the description of teacher behavior with that of students. To illustrate these important differences, consider the performance criteria presented below:

There is evidence that:

Students make steady progress in learning to read with high level comprehension.

This criterion defines, in general terms, a learning outcome that might readily be assessed using a series of appropriate tests of reading comprehension and other components of skill in reading. It is a student outcome criterion. However, it says nothing about the teacher or teaching behavior. It also says nothing about the learning process. In fact, such learning could be assessed in the absence of school, classroom, teacher, and schooling. But even in the school context, assessing such a learning outcome can lead only to conclusions about the student and not to conclusions about teaching or learning process.

A revision of the performance criterion above could focus on the learning process:

Students engage in a variety of activities to stimulate improved reading comprehension. These activities include . . .

Such a performance criterion still focuses only on student behavior, but it now specifies processes rather than outcomes. As such, assessment of such student behaviors could lead to conclusions about the extent to which the learning process matches the criterion of expectation. However, only inferences can be drawn from such an assessment about teacher behavior, since the teaching acts are only implied.

A further revision of the criterion stated above might read as follows:

The teacher arranges for a variety of activities to stimulate improved reading comprehension. These activities include using a variety of materials, previewing new vocabulary, discussing related concepts . . .

Such a statement of performance is a criterion of teacher/student relationships. This behavior can be assessed to draw conclusions regarding the extent to which activities were arranged for by the teacher according to specified expectations.

A still further revision of this criterion involves explicating the teachers' behavior as it relates to both the teaching and learning processes. Assuming that teaching is an interactive process, it makes sense to specify performance criteria to embrace a variety of aspects of the process desired. However, since the criterion is to guide the evaluation of teaching, the learning side of the process must remain the object of the acts of teaching. For example:

> *The teacher arranges for a variety of activities, stimulating improved reading comprehension by assigning a variety of reading materials, previewing new vocabulary with students, discussing related concepts,* etc. Students read silently, ask questions, listen to teacher explanations, and reflect interest and enthusiasm for reading activities.

These last statements add to the criterion of teaching a set of specifications for concomitant student behavior. Both aspects of the teaching/learning process are reflected in such a statement of performance. The advantages in such detailed explication are found in the vivid and realistic way the behaviors (both student and teacher) are described and related to each other, presuming causal relationships. However, the complexity of such performance descriptions also presents problems of precise measurement. Furthermore, simple rating scales are rarely useful in reporting on such complex behaviors. (See Chapter 6 for details on scaling evidence.)

TEACHER EFFECTIVENESS

Research theory and professional wisdom can be combined to guide the selection of performance criteria for use in teacher evaluation. Several practical realities need to be considered. (1) Teaching, however defined, is very complex. (2) All aspects of teaching could not regularly be evaluated, even if desirable to do so. (3) Some aspects of teaching practice are likely to be more crucial than others. (4) Only so much data can be utilized at any point in time. These practical considerations argue for being very clear about what aspects of practice are to be evaluated. Evaluation efforts must be selectively focused to avoid superficiality. Hence, a key question is: What specific teaching practices are most likely to produce more (or less) student learning?

Research

Teacher effectiveness research has been accumulating rapidly in the past two decades. While fragmented studies have created problems for practitioners, it is now possible to select performance criteria with considerable certainty. Some practices do give students better chances for learning while others do not. There are practices, of course, that we cannot clearly designate as either effective or ineffective. However, many practices have been thoroughly validated by research, have theoretical bases, and are supported by the professional judgment of teachers and supervisors who work most closely with the teaching/learning process. Curiously, most recent research findings are highly consistent with the most widely recognized "good" practices in actual classroom application. For instance, the extended controversy among practitioners as to whether teachers should be "kind" or "harsh" has generally been resolved in favor of the former. Few experienced, well-educated teachers would advocate harsh relationships with students (Ryans, 1960). The accumulated weight of research on teacher effectiveness also supports kind, friendly, empathetic, relationships with students; not just to be nice or to be liked, but because most students learn more under such teachers (Flanders, 1969; Gage, 1978; Medley, 1977; Stallings and Kaskowitz, 1974).

Caution needs to be exercised in thinking about teacher effectiveness. While it is necessary to specify performance criteria in explicit ways to clearly communicate about expectations, it is not realistic to expect "bits" of teacher behavior to be directly related to learning outcomes. Instead, it makes more sense to be looking for patterns of practice (Gage, 1978). Early studies of teacher questioning illustrate this concern. Studies of "open vs. closed" questions do not show consistent results. We cannot conclude that using more open-ended or less closed questions will produce more learning. However, studies that focus on "questioning strategies" looking at effects on learning derived from the utilization of more complex and systematic questioning sequences provide evidence that questioning behaviors of teachers facilitate certain kinds of learning (Taba, 1972; Hunkins, 1980; Carthel, 1977).

Ryans Patterns

Three major patterns of teaching behavior were identified in the 1950s in a massive study directed by David G. Ryans (1960). While this was not a study of effects, it did characterize teaching practices in ways that clearly differentiated one teacher from another. Subsequent studies have tended to support most of Ryan's teacher characteristics as related to effectiveness. The three patterns identified were: X_o—warm, friendly, empathetic; Y_o—organized, businesslike, systematic; and Z_o—stimulating, creative, imaginative.

Support for specific practices related to each of these three patterns can be found in reviewing the research on teacher effectiveness over the past thirty years. Many lists of such performances have been published. Some thirty to forty practices are widely accepted and utilized. Exhibit 4.5 shows Ryans' patterns with abbreviated statements of specific performances recognized by various scholars as having strong research support.

EXHIBIT 4.5   Selected practices supported by research on teacher effectiveness

Ryan's Teacher Characteristic Patterns	Selected Practices*	Scholarly Support[†]
X_0—Warm, friendly, empathetic	1. Interacts with students in positive ways	(1)(4)(3) (7)
	2. Expresses interest in students	(2)(3)
	3. Reflects empathy, concern	(7)(3)
	4. Demonstrates interest	(3)
	5. Encourages and guides students	(1)(4)
	6. Participates with students	
	7. Interacts with individuals	(4)
Y_0—Organized, systematic, businesslike	8. Organizes classroom activities	(2)(3)
	9. Informs students of	
	10. Delegates responsibilities	(2)(4)
	11. Paces activities	(3)
	12. Communicates clearly	(3)(1)
	13. Collects, organizes diagnostic data	(3)
	14. Plans to meet unique individual needs ...	(3)
Z_0—Stimulating, creative, imaginative	15. Expresses interest in subject	(3)
	16. Presents subject matter in	(1)
	17. Draws on student interests	(1)
	18. Utilizes a variety of questions	(1)
	19. Responds spontaneously	
	20. Uses audio-visual manipulative aids	(2)
	21. Involves students in multi-sensory ways ..	
	22. Directs instruction to unique needs	

*Abbreviated statements from *Developmental Teacher Evaluation Kit* (1982).
[†](1)=Gagne, 1978; (2)=Rosenshine, 1970; (3)=Medley, 1972, 1977, 1979; (4)=Stalling and Kaskowitz, 1974; (5)=Dunkin and Biddle, 1974; (7)=Flanders

Widely Accepted Practices

Practices of teachers as performance specifications are given support by acceptance in the field as well as by research and theory documentation. Teacher evaluation instruments in use in some 16,000 school districts reflect much variety, but also have some similarities. Stipniek's (1980) study of nearly 100 school district evaluation systems revealed that many such districts have been carefully revising their performance criteria in ways that reflect some degree of professional concern.

A comparison of evaluative criteria utilized in seven school districts with those in the Harris-Hill DeTEK System (1982) revealed surprising similarities. While the 22 behaviors listed in Exhibit 4.5 were selected primarily on the basis of a careful review of the literature, local school districts in diverse parts of the U.S. were using very similar performance criteria.* In

*Selected comparison districts were Austin, Texas; Bellevue, Washington; Arlington Heights, Illinois; Houston, Texas; South Euclid-Lyndhurst City, Ohio; Portland, Oregon; and Region 13 Education Service Center, Texas.

fact, the percent of agreement with the 22 behaviors selected by Harris and Hill range from 70 to 100, with all but two of the seven districts in nearly perfect agreement on these classroom focused performance expectations.

Erroneously Supported Practices

Performance specifications are not always supported by research and theory, even when widely incorporated into school district instruments. In fact, schools that have failed to utilize rigorous study processes in formulating their performance statements often perpetuate the use of criteria that are of doubtful validity. Damerall's (1981) survey of a stratified, random sample of school districts in Texas reveals widespread use of performance descriptors such as: "good appearance," "punctuality," "physical stamina," "good character," and "self-confidence." Any of these may be nice to promote among teachers but their relationship to teaching effectiveness cannot be assumed.

Some performance criteria that seem logically related to effectiveness are also commonly utilized, but must be questioned in the face of research evidence to the contrary. "Quality of voice" seems a worthy criterion, but is not supportable. Even knowledge of subject matter is reported in research studies as not significantly related to either teaching performance or to learning outcomes.

Innovations

Many teaching practices are appropriately utilized as performance expectations or evaluative criteria because they reflect promising innovative efforts to improved teaching and learning. In such instances, supporting research may be very limited. It is difficult to research practices until they have, in fact, become well installed in a variety of classroom settings.

Reports from some research are negative on the effects of "indirect" teacher behaviors in the absence of a well-structured learning environment. However, there is ample theoretical support for promoting such practices as "accepting and using students ideas," as suggested in Flanders' system of interaction analysis. Similarly, various individualized efforts to differentiate assignments, promote independent study, and increase small group activity are not clearly supported by all research, but still seem worthy of use as teaching practices, based on both theory and professional wisdom.

Team teaching practices reflect innovations which simply cannot be evaluated without further experience. In the meanwhile, team teaching remains a logical step in the improvement of teaching, and including performance criteria of these kinds in a teacher evaluation system could be readily justified. The school library represents a teaching/learning resource that is simply not fully utilized by the vast majority of teachers. Its potential seems great, but research support is limited. Again, it seems reasonable to specify teaching performances that relate to the use of the library, based on professional wisdom.

Peer tutoring represents one of a number of innovations that has been fairly well supported by research, but tends not to be accepted in common practice. Parental involvement in classroom activities, the use of community resource persons, the use of field trips, continuous progress curricula, and planned involvement in extra curricular activities all enjoy substantial research support and are theoretically sound. However, they are also rather widely neglected when teacher performance expectations are being specified.

SUMMARY

Meaningful evaluation of teaching demands careful attention to how we define teaching, the focus given emphasis, and the criteria of effectiveness to be used. Teaching can be defined narrowly or broadly, to include only intraclassroom events or extend beyond the classroom to include a broad array of professional pursuits of social and political kinds. Teaching needs some kind of limited definition or evaluation is not feasible. The emphasis for institutional purposes is appropriately on the teacher within the context of the school, with major emphasis on classroom practices.

The focus for evaluation remains at issue among evaluation specialists. Traditionally the focus has been on inputs—training, attitudes, character, experience, etc. Growing emphasis on testing and accountability have focused evaluation on student behaviors as indicators of quality teaching. However, strong interests in formative and diagnostic teacher evaluation (developmental evaluation) tends toward a focus on teacher performance.

Teacher effectiveness is a central topic of concern in selecting either a focus or specific performance criteria. Research theory and professional wisdom all contribute to the current state of knowledge about what makes teachers effective (or not). The research is adequate to clearly indicate certain teaching performance patterns as desirable. Theoretical bases add substantially to the decision-making processes when research is limited or unenlightening. Innovative practices are often given support in theoretical formulations rather than in research findings. Professional wisdom is well reflected in the consensus often found in the thoughtful opinions and carefully selected practices of our most experienced and well-educated practitioners. It is reassuring that high levels of concurrence are usually found between the best research, theory, and practice.

Tradition-bound concepts of teaching combine with a flood of fragmented research reports and a preoccupation with fads and political pressures to sustain the wide-spread use of erroneous practices in teacher evaluation. Hence, there is a continuing need to cross-validate teaching criteria in local use against external sources of professional expertise.

SELECTED STUDY SOURCES

Amidon, Edmund, and Michael Giammatteo (1965). "The Verbal Behavior of Superior Teachers," *The Elementary School Journal* 65 (February):283–85.

One of many early studies of verbal teaching influences.

Biddle, Bruce J. and Ellena, W. J., editors (1964). *Contemporary Research on Teacher Effectiveness.* New York: Holt, Rinehart and Winston.

One of the early efforts to synthesize research on teaching with a focus on effectiveness. Conclusions drawn are somewhat pessimistic compared to similar syntheses of later years.

Denton, William T. (1982). "Time on Task: What Does Research Say About Promoting Student Learning," *TASCD Newsletter* 18 (Spring):7, 10.

A summary of 14 major studies of beginning teachers in California reflects emphasis on academic learning time and task completion rates.

Dunkin, M. J. and Z. J. Biddle (1974). *The Study of Teaching.* New York: Holt, Rinehart and Winston.

Perhaps the most authoritative synthesis of research on teaching and teacher effectiveness. Reviews a much broader array of studies than most volumes of this kind. Rigorous efforts of synthesis reported.

Gage, N. L. (1978). *The Scientific Basis of the Art of Teaching.* New York: Teachers College Press, Columbia University.

A brief but very pointed critique of research regarding teacher effectiveness. Argues for more meta-analyses of fragmented studies. Concludes that there is even now a scientific basis for teaching.

Gupta, Nina (1979). *Some School and Classroom Antecedents of Student Achievement.* Austin, TX: Southwest Educational Developmental Laboratory.

A down to earth review of many studies of factors related to learning. Attends more to inputs than teaching practices. Summarizes findings with practical policy implication.

Joyce, Bruce R. and M. Weil (1972). *Models of Teaching.* Englewood Cliffs, NJ: Prentice-Hall, Inc.

A systematic review of research and theory related to teaching and learning. Defines seven distinct "models." Compares and contrasts them. Argues for diversity not selectivity.

Kerlinger, Fred N., editor (1973, 1975). *Review of Research in Education.* Volumes 1 and 2. Itasca, IL: F. E. Peacock Publishers.

Includes well-synthesized chapters on teacher effectiveness research by McKeachie and Kulik in volume 2. Gagne and Berlinger summarize research on trait-treatment interactions in volume 1.

Medley, Donald M. (1977). *Teacher Competence and Teacher Effectiveness: A Review of Process-Product Research.* Washington, D.C.: American Association of Colleges for Teacher Education.

Like several other volumes, this work attempts to synthesize the state of knowledge about teacher effectiveness. It is unique, however, in that the author brings a perspective that few researchers can match. Medley has been involved in research and development work on classroom observation and analysis of teaching for many years.

Peterson, P. L. and H. J. Walberg, editors (1979). *Research on Teaching*. Berkely, CA: McCutcheon Publishing Co.

One of an array of reviews of research on teaching. Draws heavily on recent studies of federally sponsored programs and projects. Needs to be recognized as having a rather narrow perspective.

Reyes, Donald J. and Gloria T. Alter (1984). "Research on Learning and Teacher Effectiveness: Implications for Instructional Supervision," *Thresholds in Education* 10 (May):17–20. Northern Illinois University, DeKalb, IL.

A systematic, brief review of studies with an excellent bibliography!

Zumwalt, Karen K. (1982). "Research on Teaching: Policy Implications for Teacher Education," in *Policy Making in Education*, Part I, 81st Yearbook of the National Society for the Study of Education. Ann Lieberman and M. W. McLaughlin, editors. Chicago, IL: The University of Chicago Press.

A critical review of research that has dominated the 1970s. Suggest values and limits inherent in much research that is narrowly quantified.

5

Selecting and Specifying Performances

The previous chapter gave careful attention to the need for limiting the focus of any teacher evaluation effort, in order to evaluate with rigor and still conform to the realities of local concern and need. Three ways of narrowing teacher evaluation efforts without losing rigor were suggested. (1) Focus on instructional processes only. (2) Specify criteria only in terms of teacher performance. And (3) select only those performances that clearly relate to learning outcomes.

Local school personnel involved in the evaluation process must understand the rationale for using criteria that offer such limited scope. They must accept the specific performance criteria selected in order to utilize them effectively (PDK, 1982). This chapter attends to the process of selecting performance areas and specifying descriptions of performance in sufficient detail that they communicate clearly, relate to practice, and can be objectively observed and used diagnostically.

Competency Controversy

Perhaps we should acknowledge some of the persistent disagreements about the nature of teaching and make explicit the assumptions that underlie the procedures proposed here. Some academicians still argue that teaching is not a definable set of performances or behaviors. This argument usually comes in three forms. (1) Teaching is too complex; hence evaluation must focus only on results, not on teaching itself (Klein and Aiken, 1972). (2) Teaching is an art and must be viewed as a creative effort, highly individual in form and style. Thus "connoisseurship" and highly qualitative (subjective?) evaluation is required (Eisner, 1979). (3) Teaching is the transmission of subject matter knowledge by a specialist in a field of study. Testing for knowledge is evaluation! (Price, 1974).

Each of these positions has some support among scholars of teaching and learning. The enormous complexities of teaching are widely recognized by instructional supervisors who work closely with teachers in classroom settings seeking better learning. N. L. Gage recognizes the artistry of teaching in the title of his book, *The Scientific Basis of the Art of Teaching* (1978). Supporting research and theory is, surprisingly, extremely limited in findings on the subject-matter-mastery view of teaching (Borich and Fenton, 1977). Yet the sheer logic of the argument demands some attention (Harris, 1981).

A philosopher's summary view offers some cautions in referring to geography, reading, art appreciation, and the rest: "But surely no one knows many of them; . . . Still there is this tendency to view teaching as "gadgetized . . . mechanized . . . (with all) the sacred vestments of efficiency!" (Price, 1974: 8).

A Solid Foundation

Both research and theory of teaching and learning are well along the road to making good sense out of teacher performance. "At long last we are beginning to know what is actually going on in the classroom, as well as what produces results. . . ." (Dunkin and Biddle, 1974: 418).

We know teachers can make a difference in both what is learned and how well. We know teachers can obstruct learning. We have teaching models worthy of consideration, and while no one model seems adequate (Joyce and Weil, 1980), the models used are not a hodge-podge of unrelated alternatives. In fact, each of the known models of teaching share some common elements of teaching practices with others.

We have teaching models worthy of use because in practice they promote levels of learning well beyond the scope of modern testing programs (Bloom, 1980). There appear to be performance patterns that are relatively effective in the sense that most students, facing most learning tasks, under most conditions, will learn more than they would otherwise. There also seems to be only a few, if any, highly specialized forms of teaching that are effective only with certain subjects or grade levels, or special student characteristics (Medley, 1977). On the other hand, certain teaching patterns may indeed be differentially effective with different types of learning tasks—cognitive, affective, convergent, divergent, creative, psycho-motor, etc. Unfortunately, these relationships have not been adequately researched (Soar, 1976).

In the midst of all this controversy, uncertainty, and complexity the researchers and theoreticians argue, pursue new hypotheses, and design further studies. Practitioners have quite different work to do. They cannot wait for more research and a better theory. They must make decisions now based on the best knowledge available (Medley, 1977). Hence the following assumptions:

1. Teaching is behavior that can be studied.
2. Teaching behavior tends to be patterned, not random or erratic.
3. Patterns of teaching behavior should be selected for guiding the evaluation and improvement processes.
4. Selected patterns of behavior should reflect theory, research, and professional wisdom.
5. Detailed explication of these selected patterns of behaviors should be systematically undertaken to communicate and provide foci for observation and diagnostic and improvement efforts.

SELECTING PERFORMANCE AREAS

The description of the several performance areas or patterns of performance to be included in any teacher evaluation system is a difficult task. It is a selective process because all possible aspects of performance cannot be included. The rationale for selection can be a theoretical model, a research-based synthesis, or an empirically derived set of operational categories.

Regardless of approach, the resulting categories (performances, patterns, behaviors, clusters, competencies) must be defensible. They should not ignore either research, theory, or operational realities.

Theoretical Models

A stimulus-response theory of learning, as reflected in the concepts of B. F. Skinner (Hill, 1964), R. M. Gagne (1976), and others, calls for teaching performance categories that stress student response modes, sequencing responses, reinforcement techniques, and testing for behavioral outcomes. A sharply different set of performance categories would be selected if cognitive field, social interaction, or Gestalt theory were drawn upon (McNergney and Carrier, 1981). In such cases, the performance categories would clearly include involvement of students, student-centered cooperation, problem structuring, simulation, and role-playing techniques, plus questioning strategies (Taba, 1972).

Steel and Stone (1973) drew upon the work of Guthrie, Piaget, Maslow, and Skinner, in formulating their "learning process model." It specifies five "competency clusters" with learning process "elements" identified within each cluster. The five clusters of competencies were labeled as follows:

1. *Situational* competencies: manages learning.
2. *Readiness* competencies: relates to students.
3. *Ideational* competencies: aids students to see.
4. *Task* competencies: guides student application and transfer.
5. *Feedback* competencies: provides positive reinforcement and corrective feedback.

More explicit process elements were designated for each competency cluster and specific teaching competencies designated for each element. For instance:

Situational competency #4—*stimuli:* "New stimuli are combined with old."

Feedback competency #12—*affective:* "Negative affect is replaced by nonreinforcement whenever possible. Reinforcements are offered with declining frequency once learning is accomplished."

Each of these illustrations clearly reflects the influence of theory, but also the use of learning process for teaching practice.

Research-Based Categories

Ryans' (1960) study of teacher characteristics is one of several that provides very useful categories for specifying teacher performances patterns. Ryan identified three major performance patterns in a massive investigation of classroom characteristics of thousands of teachers. The "classroom behavior patterns" he designated as most discriminating were:

X_o *Empathetic (warm, responsive, kindly)*
Y_o *Systematic (systematic, businesslike, organized)*
Z_o *Stimulating (stimulating, original, imaginative)*

These patterns were more precisely characterized by scales describing contrasting behaviors. While no theoretical model was utilized in the Ryans study, the finding that only three distinct patterns of behavior clearly distinguish teaching practice has been very useful. Each pattern has been clearly supported by research on teacher effectiveness to some extent in subsequent years. Numerous school systems have utilized these patterns because they are so clearly evident and are supportive by professional wisdom.

Other efforts to select and define a set of performance categories involve syntheses of research. O'Neill (1977) developed a set of "target areas/teacher exiting competencies" to guide Teacher Corps training and evaluation efforts. Twelve target areas were defined. With a few exceptions each of these areas could be supported by limited research findings. One illustration is given full description below:

Motivation and challenge: The teacher—
(a) shows enthusiasm
(b) demonstrates interest in activities
(c) involves students in active ways
(d) participation is differentiated for various students
(e) praise, encouragement, and recognition are verbalized
(f) nonverbal behaviors reveal acceptance, encouragement, attentiveness

It is probably not accidental that four of these six teacher behaviors relate to Ryans' X_0 pattern.

DeKalb County Schools (1975) in Georgia utilized a set of twenty performance areas as the general framework for a system of new teacher evaluation. The twenty performances were selected in part on the basis of research, but they also reflect a model of teaching:

Diagnosis I. Preliminary diagnosis. II. Diagnose specific needs. III. Prescribe objective.

Planning IV. Develop instructional plans. V. Utilize resource materials. VI. Utilize a variety of methods and techniques. VII. Utilize time effectively.

Implementation IX. Modify instruction on the basis of feedback. X. Maintain control. XI. Maintain a physical environment. XII. Exhibit enthusiasm. XIII. Facilitate comfortable feelings. XIV. Build harmonious relations. XV. Communicate with students.

Follow-through XVI. Evaluate pupil progress and effectiveness of teaching. XVII. Communicate with parents, administrators, and other teachers. XVIII. Maintain accurate records.

Miscellaneous (Other) XVIII. Demonstrate in-depth knowledge of subject matter taught. XIX. Demonstrate skills related to subject matter. XX. Demonstrate professional, ethical traits.

The model reflects diagnostic-prescriptive notions about teaching and learning, but also emphasizes social interaction theory. The last category, however, reflects common sense notions about teaching practice.

Theory, research, and operational concerns are often combined in selecting and defining major performance patterns or categories of performance. Just as the DeKalb County evaluation criteria were only partially research- and theory-based, some districts have been highly eclectic in the performance selection process. Bethany College (Kansas) selected and defined six performance areas ranging from "intellectual" and "personality" to "teaching skills" (Manatt et al., 1976). Many districts make no real effort to cluster or pattern their performance criteria. As a result, long lists of twenty or more performance patterns are sometimes generated and accepted even though they seem unrelated to each other or reflect little thought about research, theory, and local philosophy.

Multi-Dimensional Models

Several ways of selecting and organizing performances were suggested in Chapter 4. Exhibit 4.1 suggests a set of common or generic criteria which could be utilized if the "other" category were fully specified. Exhibit 4.2 suggests three major domains, including performances inside and outside of the classroom.

A multi-dimensional framework for selecting and organizing performances is given considerable structure in Exhibit 4.4. Five domains are defined by combining the locale (inside or outside of classrooms) with the student-relatedness dimension. Fifteen rather different performance categories are defined by using three levels of instruction-relatedness for each of the five domains.

A slightly different form of this multi-dimensional framework is presented here in Exhibit 5.1. The examples of performances in each domain category illustrate the three levels of instruction-relatedness. These examples have been selected from among the enormous number and variety that might fit these fifteen categories.

This particular way of organizing and categorizing performances has several advantages. By clearly identifying a full array of domains, the full range of responsibilities is made clear. By using both pupil and instruction-relatedness in defining the categories, the full complexity of teaching is reflected. Hence, the number and variety of performances selected for each domain help to give perspective on the importance of instruction-related performance. Performances organized by domain also facilitate the data gathering and analysis processes in clearly indicating the locale in which different performances are to be observed.

A somewhat different model was developed by the California Teachers Association (1964) in which "roles" rather than domains were utilized as the organizing framework for describing teaching performance. Unfortunately, such role categories had the effect of not clearly differentiating instructional and noninstructional performances. Furthermore, roles tend to cut across domains in ways that are confusing to data gathers. For example:

> Role 2: Counselor or Guidance Worker.
> 2.1 Utilizes effective procedures for collecting information.
> 2.2 Uses diagnostic and remedial procedures.
> 2.3 Helps the pupil understand himself.
> 2.4 Works effectively with specialized services. (California Teachers Association, 1964:18–26)

These four performance areas are all included in a single role and are observable in a wide variety of places—classroom, home, office, etc. Furthermore, some roles are clearly instructional in nature while others may not be.

EXHIBIT 5.1 Five domains of performance with examples at three levels of instruction relatedness

1. *Classroom Domain "X"*
   The teacher works directly with individual students to facilitate learning.
   Examples:
   - Keeps the difficulty level of assignments appropriate for each individual (Manatt, et al., 1976).
   - Advises individual students about entrance exam and careers.
   - Provides, career, health and financial counseling (Lessinger, 1979).

2. *Classroom Domain "Y"*
   The teacher works directly with groups of students to guide and direct learning.
   Examples:
   - Observes student activities moving from group to group and among individuals (Dunn, & Dunn, 1977).
   - Presentations are clear, cohesive, sequenced and employ examples and analogies (Armes, 1980).
   - Assists students in announcing and planning for extra curricular activities.

3. *Classroom Domain "Z"*
   The teacher works to make arrangements for student learning activities.
   Examples:
   - Develops instructional plans (DeKalb, 1975).
   - Designs instructional areas for different group needs (Dunn and Dunn, 1977).
   - Collects fees, distributes texts, maintains accurate and timely records (Montgomery Schools, (1982).

4. *Outside Classroom Domain "0–1"*
   The teacher works directly with students outside the classroom to enhance learning.
   Examples:
   - Assists students in library, study hall, or elsewhere, in ways that are consistent with goals of the school.
   - Advises student council or club groups.
   - Directs student athletic activity.

5. *Outside Classroom Domain "0–2"*
   The teacher works outside the classroom, but not directly with students, in enhancing the school's operation.
   Examples:
   - Develops print and other media for use in classroom (Lessinger, 1979).
   - Communicates with parents, adminstrators, and other teachers (DeKalb, 1975).
   - Participates in professional activities, supports the school's programs, avoids unnecessary absenteeism and tardiness (DeKalb, 1975).
   - Contributes to the development of professional standards (California Teachers Association, 1964).

Similar problems can emerge in any effort to select and organize an array of performances that are fairly broad. Redfern (1980) proposes seven major categories of teacher "responsibility" for use in the evaluation process. These include planning and organizing, motivating learners, relationships with students, utilizing resources, and instructional techniques. The categories seem logical enough, but actually have no natural sequence, no theoretical structure, and are highly overlapping. For instance, teacher performances under motivating learners will surely involve use of resources and both will likely be instructional techniques. The frameworks proposed by Lessinger (1979) have similar problems.

Categories are in the minds of men, not in the nature of the phenomena. The perfect category system with impeccable logic is yet to be found. But we should strive to organize performances in ways that serve evaluation purposes well and minimize overlapping and other logical inconsistencies. Smith (1980) presents a 280-cell grid built on five generic competencies, four levels of schooling, and fourteen subject areas. This is probably too complex for practical use and goes beyond current research support.

A multi-dimensional grid may be a useful way of organizing performances to reflect a diversity of kinds of logic. In Exhibit 5.2, the forty-cell grid attempts to allow for categorizing any performance on the basis of basic processes involved, the locale where the events occur, the instruction-relatedness of the practice, and the student-relatedness.

An application of this scheme to a variety of selected competencies is shown in Exhibit 5.3. It is obvious that each basic process is called upon

EXHIBIT 5.2   A forty-cell grid for analyzing teaching performances

Basic Processes	Instruction Relatedness	Locale			
		Classroom		Nonclassroom	
		Student	Nonstudent	Student	Nonstudent
Planning	Direct				
	Instruction	a	c	e	g
	Noninstruction	b	d	f	h
Organizing	Direct				
	Instruction	i	k	m	o
	Noninstruction	j	l	n	p
Presenting	Direct				
	Instruction	q	s	u	w
	Noninstruction	r	t	v	x
Facilitating	Direct				
	Instruction	y	aa	cc	ee
	Noninstruction	z	bb	dd	ff
Evaluating	Direct				
	Instruction	gg	ii	kk	mm
	Noninstruction	hh	jj	ll	nn

and more than one process is often implied in a single competency statement. Some competencies are more specific in that they "fit" only a few of the categories. Other more broadly defined competencies fit more than one process and various other cells as well. An analysis of a complete set of competencies using a format similar to that shown in Exhibit 5.3 would indicate the relative emphasis on the instruction-related vs. noninstructional performances and would also alert evaluation planners to possible needs for further refinement in their specifications. Classroom performances would be expected to be emphasized more than nonclassroom. Student relatedness could reasonably be expected to get more emphasis than the nonstudent related competencies.

This kind of systematic analysis of performances, using a variety of dimensions, will yield insights for improving the framework and the specific array of performance statements being considered. A predictable outcome of such performance statement analysis is the recognition that performances need to conform to several criteria. A performance statement serves best when it is *a fairly broad, comprehensive statement of teacher performance applying to a single cell (locale, process, instruction, etc.).*

The overly broad competencies can readily be made more useful by careful revisions. The second item in Exhibit 5.3 needs more focus in terms of all three dimensions. If revised to read "The teacher demonstrates a great deal of stamina and vitality . . . ," then the process is more clearly presented. It could be sharpened still more by specifying "in maintaining the pace of the lesson, keeping students attending, and responding to specific student needs." Such specificity more clearly makes the competency classroom, instructional, and student related.

Another example of the need for revision is found in the following:

> #6 Classwork is interesting and varied. The teacher develops instructional processes that are logical and effective. The teacher uses a variety of methods and materials.

This statement includes elements of planning, organizing, presenting, and evaluation. It is essentially all instruction-related but involves in-classroom and out-of-classroom events. Even so, it represents a coherent pattern of several performances and simply needs to be restructured somewhat. For instance,

> 6a Plans a logical instructional sequence.
> 6b Organizes a variety of materials and methods.
> 6c Presents the learning activities in an interesting fashion.

Such revision gives considerable specificity to a very large pattern of performance. Such revisions lead to still greater refinements to assure more specificity without losing scope.

EXHIBIT 5.3 Analysis of selected teacher competencies by process, locale, instruction- and student-relatedness*

Competencies (Selected)	Process	LOCALE		RELATEDNESS			
		Classroom	Nonclassroom	Instruction	Noninstruction	Student	Nonstudent
Teacher.... ...is dependable and and punctual in meeting commitments	Planning or organizing	X	X		X	X	X
... has a great deal of stamina and vitality ... in maintaining effective teaching techniques	none	X	X	X	X	X	X
... provides for the daily success of each student.	Facilitating or organizing	X		X		X	
... works with parents ... in positive ways	Planning or facilitating		X	X	X		X
... keeps sufficient records for the continuing progress of students	Organizing	X	X	X	X	X	

86

Competency	Category					
... uses open-ended questions to stimulate discussion, probing in ways that keep the questions open-ended	Presenting	X		X		X
... tells and listens to jokes, puns, or amusing incidents in the class-room	Facili-tating	X			X	X
... plans lesson objec-tives and activities that are appropriate to the content and level	Planning	X	X	X		X
... demonstrates the desired skill or competence ...	Present-ing	X		X		X
... gives appropriate attention to student safety	Organizing	X			X	X

*Competencies selected from three different sets utilized in various local school districts.

A rather comprehensive system for categorizing performances was developed by Dodl (1972) and extended by Harris and Burks (1982). While retaining a focus on teacher behavior, the system incorporates a broad array of both in-classroom and out-of-classroom behaviors and extends beyond instruction-related events.

DESCRIBING AND EXPLICATING PERFORMANCES

Descriptions of performance expectations are essential to any evaluation system in a variey of ways. Complex performances need to be explicated in great detail if their specific components and detailed behaviors are to be clearly communicated (Thomas, 1979; Feldvebel, 1980). Explication is also essential before duplications and omissions can be clearly recognized. Above all, careful descriptive explication of teaching performance provides the diagnostic detail necessary to guide the improvement process.

Developing a highly descriptive set of explicated performance statements involves both inductive and deductive processes. Often a literature review, analysis of research, and an inventory of professional judgments yield an extensive list of descriptors. Dodl (1972) utilized this approach in cataloging thousands of teaching competencies. More recently, Pearson (1980) generated over 300 teaching behaviors using such techniques. The task that follows such listings is one of logically clustering or collating them to form more manageable patterns or sets of performance.

Still another approach starts with teaching theory and research as discussed in this chapter. A limited number of clearly recognized categories, patterns, or clusters are selected and these, in turn, are explicated using task analysis techniques. The term "explication" is used to mean describing performances in increasing detail at each of several levels of explicitness. This technique is illustrated in the work of Harris and Hill (1982) in the development of a diagnostic classroom evaluation system. (See Appendix B for details on these performance specifications.)

Regardless of the process by which performance descriptions are developed, their utility is enhanced by careful explication. Practitioners are becoming increasingly aware that performances that only vaguely describe do not communicate with any precision; hence, confusion and misunderstandings arise among those involved. On the other hand, a carefully detailed document, describing major performance areas, but also explicating them in behavioral terms becomes an instrument for communicating to all, a resource for instrumentation, and a guide to growth planning.

Problems Illustrated

Performance specifications that are not carefully drawn to reflect important aspects of the teaching job and explicit events lead to confusion, misinterpretation, and mistrust. For example, Christener, et al. (1979) report a set of teacher evaluation criteria proposed for use in a large school system was studied to see if teachers, administrators, parents and students could agree on their importance. Correlations among elementary and secondary teacher groups were quite high (.78 to .87). However, virtually no other correlations were above .75 and many were too low for comfort. In part, these different views of the importance of various criteria are actual, but they also are derived from the lack of specificity. For instance, a criterion such as "maintains class control in an atmosphere conducive to learning" is simply open to many interpretations without more detailed specification of events or behaviors.

Some efforts at specifying performances provide details in the form of knowledge elements rather than as observable events. "Understand the concept of individualized instruction . . . can define . . . can describe . . . can name . . ." (Clark, 1978:11). Such specifications may be useful for training programs to use in evaluating the efforts of in-service training, but cannot be viewed as very useful in evaluating teaching performance. They do not describe real-life performances.

When performance specifications are not carefully, logically explicated in terms for "breaking down" a performance into specific component behaviors, a confusing set of statements emerges. For example:

III-1 Maintains an effective balance of freedom and responsibility in the classroom.

This is a terribly vague statement that needs much more detail to convey any certain meaning about what the teacher does while maintaining a balance of some kind. However, the breakdown proposed for this competency is even more general (VonFange and Benson, 1978: 8–21):

III-1a [The teacher] recognizes varying abilities of different classes to handle freedom.

III-1b [The teacher] exercises professional judgment.

III-1c [The teacher] organizes, develops, and executes a personal teaching agenda.

These efforts to specify teacher performances simply do not come to grips with the essentials of teaching; namely, how the teacher acts. For instance, what is discipline? What makes it good? And what does a teacher do when "maintaining" it? What is this variety of methods? How do we know when fairness is evident? These performance statements don't describe; they raise questions and sow confusion. One evaluator may interpret "good discipline" as harsh, rigid treatment of any infraction of rules, with certainty of punishment. Another evaluator may interpret good discipline as guiding, advising, encouraging self-control, and avoiding punishment except as a last resort. The same teacher, regardless of his/her practices, is sure to be utterly confused by these two evaluators.

Ideally, performance specifications are explicated so that every type of event identified in the carefully worded elaborating paragraph is made more explicit by a description of behavior and is still further explicated with illustrations of specific teaching events.

Problems of specificity are sometimes found in research on teaching too. In a study of "engaged time," Honzay (1983) identified 24 "discrete teacher behaviors" related to high levels of student engaged time, but only 3 of these "behaviors" explained 84 percent of the variations in effect. If we look at the specification of these three behaviors, they are found to be not so discrete after all. For example, one behavior was: "The teacher checked on students' progress regularly and adjusted accordingly" (Honzay, 1983: ii). Obviously this is not a single behavior but a complex pattern of teaching events. This makes the finding no less important, but cautions against interpretations that are too simplistic.

An Illustrative Explication

A further illustration of this systematic breakdown process called explication is provided below. This is adapted from the work of a study group effort to specify nonclassroom performances as well as those observable classroom events. The same techniques were utilized:

(1), (2) Code and title: #12   Accurate and adequate records maintained.

(3) General statement: Reports are up to date, correct, and submitted on time.

(4) Elaborating paragraph: The teacher submits reports that are accurate. Records are maintained in up-to-date form to facilitate prompt reporting. Deadlines for submitting reports are observed. Minimum requirements for information are exceeded when desirable. Records are maintained that make it possible to prepare special reports as needed.

(5) Specified Behaviors (only one illustration):
    12f   Records are maintained with considerable detail, and are organized so that special reports can be efficiently prepared as needed.

(6) Explicit Indicators:
    12f(1)   Grade books record more than symbols of judgments of quality (As, Bs, etc.). They also include raw scores.
    12f(2)   Records include samples of students papers, tests, and notations about specific assignments.

12f(3)   Records of student performances include written, oral, test, project, and interpersonal evidences.

12f(4)   Records of attendance, behavior, and attitude are objective, both positive and negative, and sufficiently detailed to show patterns rather than isolated crises.

12f(5)   Records of all kinds are clearly self-explanatory in the absence of the teacher originator.

12f(6)   Records are objective, unbiased, and highly ethical in content so that confidentiality is not a serious problem.

(7) Further Illustrations (specific events):

(a) No purely subjective opinions are recorded.

(b) Judgments and recommendations (including grades) are clearly supported by objective evidence.

(c) Gossip and rumor are excluded from records.

(d) Evidence reflects unbiased recording by including every bit of positive evidence along with other kinds.

(e) Records are made secure from those who have no right of access.

(f) Records are open to students, parents, and other professionals who have an interest in the data.

There is no limit to the extent of detail that can be included. Explication is a process of offering details about complex patterns of behavior or performances so they communicate expectations and/or alternatives. The amount of detail should vary, depending on the complexity of the performance being described. Also, explications will be more or less detailed depending on the state of technical knowledge of the profession. More importantly, higher priority performances should be more fully explicated than those of somewhat less importance. Innovative and less well understood performances need to be explicated in great detail to guide efforts of teachers in implementation and improvement efforts.

Exhibit 5.4 illustrates an explication of one of the most widely recognized high priority areas of classroom performance. It shows three levels of explication. Exhibit 5.5 illustrates a still more detailed effort to explicate an area of teacher performance about which there might otherwise be great uncertainty.

Cautions

Too much explication has certain undesirable effects. As performances are explicated teachers raise summative questions about expectations: "Must I do all these specific things to be regarded as adequate or successful?" This is an important question which deserves attention. The specification of performance expectations with considerable explication in terms of detailed descriptions of specific behaviors, indicators, and even illustrations of

EXHIBIT 5.4   Illustration of an explicated pattern of teacher performance*

1a—*Organizes Classroom Activities*
    The teacher organizes classroom activities to produce a smooth flow of events with minimum confusion or waste of time.

    The activities of the classroom are sequenced. Directions are given to facilitate engagement in activities in a clearly understood fashion. Arrangements are made to avoid waste of time with space, materials and assignments since they have been preplanned. Individuals are given opportunities to move ahead without wasting time. Events are coordinated by the teacher (and others) to assure quick and easy transitions from one activity to another. On the other hand, activities have been timed to prevent rushing about or hasty actions.

The teacher—

1a(1) Gives directions for shifting from one activity to another with clarity and simplicity.
    (a) Students are given private directions and assistance, if needed, when others need not be concerned.
    (b) The attention of the student group is secured before giving directions for change.
    (c) Directions are kept brief and only essential details verbalized.
    (d) Individuals who appear confused or reluctant to respond are given prompt, personal attention.

1a(2) Initiates changes in activity for individuals who are ready while others are still busy with prior assignments.
    [(a) through (d) not shown]

1a(3) Arranges all materials for easy distribution as needed during the activity.
    [(a) through (g) not shown]

1a(4) Makes prompt use of supplemental activities or plans modifications to assure full use of all available time.
    [(a) through (f) not shown]

1a(5) Organizes and directs clerical and housekeeping chores to prevent waste of time by teacher and students.
    [(a) through (e) not shown]

*Adapted from Ben M. Harris and Jane Hill (1982). *Developmental Teacher Education Kit* (DeTEK). Austin, Texas: Southwest Educational Development Laboratory.

events is all intended to communicate clearly and enhance understandings among evaluators and evaluatees. These explications are absolutely necessary when diagnostic uses are to be made of the statements. However, guidelines for use of performance specifications must be carefully developed to avoid misuse. Specifications serve to broaden and deepen understand-

EXHIBIT 5.5   Illustration of performance specification—3-level explication with added detail

---

Performance Area #IA: Recognizes and Respects Students
General descriptor: The teacher recognizes and shows respect for each student's individuality, ability, worth, and dignity.

Descriptive paragraph:
   The teacher recognizes that each student is an individual whose learning style and needs must be considered when planning learning experiences. The teacher recognizes the positive relationship between a student's self-concept and his/her ability to achieve. The teacher values and builds upon any abilities which students reveal recognizing the worth of all students regardless of capabilities. The teacher strives to provide emotional support to all students, refraining from imposing or supporting feelings of guilt. The teacher strives to meet needs of students offering dignity and self-respect to all.

Behavior #IA-1:   The teacher gives recognition to each student as a worthy and uniquely different person whose learning style and needs are carefully considered in planning and implementing lessons and units of instruction.

Indicator or Illustrative Events:
IA-1(a): The teacher verbalizes his/her belief in students as worthy individuals.
• Responds to students' ideas in positive, praising terms.
• Avoids using sarcastic remarks toward individuals or the class group.
• Discusses interesting ideas or products of individual students before the class.
• Accepts and makes direct use of students' ideas in developing the content of the lesson.
• (Other?)

IA-1 (b): The teacher openly and objectively refers to differences among individual students, accentuating the positive, avoiding invidious comparisons, and identifying differences as strengths.
• Mentions creative talents of individual student when relevant to classroom events.
• Explains preferences given to certain students in terms of their unique "needs" or strengths.
• Asks students to verbalize their special interests, abilities, and needs.
• Openly refers to ethnic, religious, and cultural differences among students, faculty, and other citizens.

---

ings about performance expectations. They will be utilized differently, however, for summative, formative, and diagnostic purposes. These differentiated uses cannot be ignored. (See Chapter 10 on linking formative and summative systems in this regard.)

COVERAGE AND BALANCE

Performance specifications within any selected category should provide both coverage and balance. Coverage refers to a good match between behaviors described and the total of all important events likely to be worth consideration in the evaluation process. If things do happen in classrooms that are important to teachers and evaluators, then they should be covered in some specific way. Balance refers to explicating at approximately the same level of detail for equally important categories of behavior.

Coverage and balance need attention at each level of detail. Descriptive paragraphs, behaviors, and indicators should each be analyzed to give reasonable assurance that the coverage is similar and balance is maintained throughout.

Verbal Interaction Illustration

In the DeTEK system (Harris and Hill, 1982), one of six performance areas is allocated to "verbally interactive" behaviors. Just three behaviors are designated as shown below. Only the last behavior (3c) is shown as a full illustration including behaviors.

III Verbally Interactive:
3a Communicates clearly and concisely.
3b Encourages and guides student responses and teacher-student interactions.
3c Utilizes a variety of questioning techniques which provoke different levels of thinking on the part of all students.
    3c(1) Uses open-ended questions to stimulate discussion, probing in ways that keep the question open-ended and enhance student thinking.
    3c(2) Adjusts the pace of questioning to allow periods of silence so all students may engage in higher-level thinking.
    3c(3) Uses an array of question types, ranging from simple recognition and recall to analysis, synthesis, and evaluation.

Coverage is obviously limited in this set of specifications, because "wait time," asking and giving opinions and suggestions, and a variety of other types of verbalizing by the teacher are not clearly listed. Similarly, balance is not as good as might be. 3c(3), "uses an array of question types . . ." refers to a complex questioning behavior pattern this is hardly comparable with the skills described in 3c(1) and 3c(2).

Balance and coverage problems are illustrated in Barnes' *Teacher Observation Instrument* (1983). The performance specifications in this instrument include 106 indicators emphasizing verbal interaction in many ways, yet no positively reinforcing verbal events are specified. Such lack of coverage of unusually important teaching behaviors is difficult to accept. From a balance perspective, a performance area "interactions" specifies ten varieties of teacher behavior, largely emphasizing asking, accepting, and explaining. By contrast, this same set of specifications includes a major performance area, "Holds students responsible for behavior," which specifies 33 specific teacher behaviors, largely directive, controlling kinds. Balance is clearly lacking!

Analyzing for Coverage and Balance

Once a preliminary set of performance specifications has been explicated, it can be analyzed using the 15-cell category system shown in Exhibit 4.4 and illustrated in Exhibit 5.1. The forty cells displayed in Exhibit 5.2 provide for even more rigorous analysis. Coverage is suggested by the frequency of behaviors and indicators identified in each cell. By comparing the frequencies for each column, the balance between instructional and noninstructional, in-classroom, and out-of-classroom criteria can be estimated. Row frequencies provide comparisons of balance by performance areas.

SUMMARY

Selecting, specifying, and especially explicating performance criteria cannot be overemphasized. Developmental teacher evaluation demands greater specificity than other forms of evaluation because diagnostic power is provided only with high levels of explication.

Despite much room for argument and debate regarding what teaching practices to focus upon in selecting performance criteria, there seems little doubt that research, theory, and professional wisdom do offer a substantial amount of guidance to practitioners. Much is known about "good" teaching practices, even though much is still to be researched.

Professional wisdom is generated when the highly regarded, effective practitioners are in strong agreement and demonstrate the use of selected practices, even though not widely instituted in other schools or classrooms. One of the clear examples of emerging professional wisdom is found in the wide-spread acceptance of research-based teaching practices in local schools in many places in the U.S. (Stipnieks, 1981).

SELECTED STUDY SOURCES

Biddle, B.J. and Ellena, W.J., editors (1964). *Contemporary Research on Teacher Effectiveness.* NY: Holt, Rinehart and Winston.

An early attempt among many more recent efforts to summarize and draw firm conclusions about teacher effects on learning. Useful for historical perspective since it precedes the late 1970 to early 1980 era giving much attention to direct instruction.

California Teachers' Association (1964). *Six Areas of Teacher Competence.* Burlingame, CA: California Teachers' Association.

>One of the early efforts to systematically define teaching in terms of performance specifications. Six roles provide a broad framework for teaching that reflects a union view of "professionalism."

Dunkin, M. and B.J. Biddle (1974). *The Study of Teaching.* NY: Holt, Rinehart and Winston.

>An extensive review of research on teaching.

Florida Department of Education (1973). *The Florida Catalog of Teacher Competence.* Tallahassee: FL: Department of Education, Division of Elementary Education.

>A landmark effort by Norman Dodl and others to document a vast array of performance specifications in use.

Gage, N.L. (1972). *Teacher Effectiveness and Teacher Education: A Search for a Scientific Basis.* Palo Alto, CA: Pacific Books.

>A brief review emphasizing the very real and solid knowledge base on which teaching can be based despite many unknowns.

Harris, Ben M. et al. (1985). "Competency Specifications for Personnel," in *Personnel Administration in Education,* 2nd edition. Boston: Allyn and Bacon, Inc.

>An analysis of pros and cons in using competency specifications in job descriptions and personnel evaluations.

Harris, Ben M. and Jane Hill (1982). *Developmental Teacher Evaluation Kit.* Austin, TX: Southwest Educational Laboratory.

>A complete instrument system of classroom evaluation of teaching, it includes an example of carefully explicated performance criteria.

Medley, Donald M. (1977). *Teacher Competence and Teacher Effectiveness: A Review of Process-Product Research.* Washington, D.C.: American Association of Colleges for Teacher Education.

>A systematic comparison of research findings of a large number of recent studies emphasizing socio-economic status.

Peterson, P.L. and H.J. Walberg (1979). *Research on Teaching.* Berkeley, CA: McCutcheon Publishing Co.

>An extensive set of reviews attempting to more clearly define the current state of knowledge about teachiing.

Rosenshine, Barak, and N. Furst (1970). "Research on Teacher Performance Criteria," in *Teacher Training: A Symposium,* B.O. Smith, editor. Englewood Cliffs, NJ: Prentice-Hall, Inc.

>Focuses on efforts to synthesize what research clearly indicates about teacher effectiveness in terms of specific criteria.

Ryans, David G. (1960). *Characteristics of Teachers.* Washington, D.C.: American Council on Education.

>An old but unusually important work reporting on a nation-wide study of the elementary and secondary school teacher in the U.S. As the only national

study of such comprehensive proportions, it still serves as a useful frame of reference.

Smith, B.O., editor (1971). *Research in Teacher Education.* Englewood Cliffs, NJ: Prentice-Hall, Inc.

A collection of reviews on teacher education research. Rosenshine and Furst's review of research on teacher performance is especially useful.

6

Instrumentation: Selection, Adaptation, and Design

INTRODUCTION

Instrumentation can be thought of as the systematic development of materials and procedures for data gathering and analysis. Performance criteria provide the frame of reference for instrumentation. Purposes to be served will influence data sources, forms, and analytical techniques. The essence of instrumentation, however, is that objective, reliable, and useful data are produced to serve the developmental efforts of a teacher evaluation program.

Instrumentation considerations nearly always involve the following questions:

1. What purpose is to be served?
2. What data sources are needed and readily available?
3. What criteria, in what form, are most relevant?
4. What procedures are most appropriate?
5. What instrument(s) or data forms are most useful?

It is important to note that the fifth question is properly considered last. It is often considered first and usually results in poor instrumentation.*

---

*"The law of the hammer" suggests that when a child has a new hammer, everything suddenly needs pounding. "*The law of the instrument*" paraphrases that law: "When we know and like an instrument, all situations need to be evaluated with it." Both laws predict serious problems to be prevented if possible.

In this chapter several of these questions will be addressed only indirectly. Purposes have been given attention in prior chapters and will be considered here only to differentiate instrument characteristics for survey, diagnostic, and summative purposes. Specifications are discussed extensively in Chapters 4 and 5 and will be used here only to illustrate instrument selection, adaptation, and design. The primary focus of this chapter, then, will be on data sources and data forms as they are reflected in various data gathering instruments and procedures. Observation procedures are given special attention in Chapter 7.

SELECTION, ADAPTATION, AND DESIGN

The practitioner generally has three options open in instrumenting for developmental teacher evaluation. An existing instrumentation can be *selected*. An existing instrumentation can be *adapted*. Or new instrumentation can be *developed* or *designed*. Instrumentation involves much more than just "getting" an instrument; hence, it is important to consider selection and adaptation as an economical alternative to design of entirely new instrumentation.

Selection Process

Many instruments are available for describing teaching in one way or another. Local districts, research projects, and commercial organizations are sources of instrumentation of many kinds. The selection process, while less involved than adaptation or design processes, is nonetheless not without problems. Promising instrumentation must be identified, reviewed for its appropriateness and then systematically studied *in use!*

A comparative listing of instrumentation alternatives is not available to the best of my knowledge. Hence, a search process is necessary. Simon and Boyer (1970) edited a multi-volume references work called *Mirrors for Behavior*. It has not been up-dated in recent years, however. Borich and Madden (1977) have critically reviewed a variety of instruments in a useful way. Buros' (1978) *Eighth Mental Measurement Yearbook* includes only limited reference to instrumentation of the kind that might be considered by practitioners. Other reference works of some usefulness include Sweetland and Keysers' (1983) listing of tests and Mitchell's (1983) *Tests in Print III*. Beyond these sources the ERIC index and other basic guides to periodical literature are helpful.

The job of selection has just begun with the identification of promising instrumentation. The selection process needs to proceed in several stages:

1. Identification
2. Preliminary review
3. Detailed study
4. Trial use

Preliminary review serves to give assurances that the identified instrumentation includes all necessary material for possible use and, if so, that it is related to the purposes to be served. From a very practical point of view the material available must include actual instrument forms, detailed directions for use, illustrations of data displays, documentation of reliability measures, and information to support validity and utility estimates. If any of these materials are not readily available, then selection efforts need not progress further.

Detailed study of the material is essential to be sure that criteria are well defined, and that the instrumentation is closely related to the purposes to be served. Furthermore, this study is preparatory to actual trial in use and should involve some efforts to apply procedures in preliminary ways.

Trial in use is the most important step in selection of instrumentation. It is rarely possible to adequately assess strengths or limitations until some hands-on experience has been gained. Trials rarely are highly successful in the hands of the untrained user; hence, cautious and balanced estimates of promise need to be made initially. Final selection decisions should be based on full-scale pilot projects.

Adaptations

Instrumentation that looks quite promising in a selection process will often need some adaptations to serve special needs or variations in purposes. Adaptation therefore follows selection and the same rigorous selection process described above should be utilized.

Premature and capricious adaptations are commonly undertaken. Initial study and trial-in-use efforts always produce some uncertainties or frustrations. The tendency to discount the value of the original design and hastily begin adapting is very strong. It is nearly always unfortunate. Even when adaptations are needed, the extent and character of those changes are more clearly evident *after* extensive pilot project trials are completed.

Research instruments are nearly always in need of adaptations. Such instrumentation tends to be strong on quantification and weak on face validity, strong on controlling conditions and weak on flexibility. The practitioner will find that research reports are excellent sources of promising instrumentation possibilities. They, too, should be selected and adapted with great rigor; extensive adaptations are nearly always required.

Designing for Instrumentation

The first rule for practitioners is "Don't create it if you can avoid it." The idea of developing "our own" instrumentation for teacher evaluation is very appealing. It is perfectly understandable, too! The traditions of local autonomy are very strong in U.S. education. Furthermore, the enormous range of differences in the 15,000 school districts and in 100,000 schools is enormous. Even so, selection and adaptation are generally more realistic options. It is not necessary to "re-invent the wheel" in most instances, and the costs of creating an entirely new system, of high quality, are generally prohibitive in staff time and dollars.

Designing new instrumentation almost always involves elaborate efforts of a group with a variety of competencies and experiences (Shearron, 1976). Specialists in curriculum, teaching, learning, training, instrument design, and statistics are needed in the design process. The basic instrument(s) must be developed, tested, and revised using alternate procedures until both instrument(s) and preferred procedures have been developed in fine detail. Instruments and procedural guidelines must be tested for reliability and then training materials developed and tested for feasibility in use.

These designs and testing procedures have to be completed before pilot project trials-in-use can begin. Hence, the design process greatly increases the time required and the cost involved compared with either selection or adaptation alternatives*.

The procedural guidelines that evolve from the testing procedures are necessarily committed to writing and utilized in pilot project trials. These trials also provide the basis for developing training plans and materials to use in training others that will be involved (see Chapter 11 on training for evaluation.)

DATA SOURCES

The sources of information about teaching practices are, for the most part, limited to the teacher, the student, and an administrator or supervisor observer. Where team teaching is in operation, teacher peers may be useful data sources. Peers also may be useful data sources in limited ways even without team arrangements. Other data sources of limited utility include parents, friends, and college instructors, who usually are only indirectly associated with actual teaching behavior. As such, these latter data sources must be used with caution, even suspicion.

Teacher Self-Reports

Teacher "self-evaluation" has been around for a long time in a variety of forms (Hardebeck, 1973; Hartmann, 1978). The rationale for such efforts include: (1) The obvious potential knowledge base of the teacher about his or her own practices. (2) The active involvement of the teacher in generating the data (Johnston and Hodge, 1981). Glatthorn (1984) is one of many writers advocating videotaped self-analysis.. (3) The low cost of gathering-self-reports.

---

*This author has worked with various school districts as a consultant in designing for teacher evaluation. While selection or adaptation processes can often be undertaken in two to three year cycles, design efforts often extend over five to seven years.

EXHIBIT 6.1 Comparison of advantages and limitations of various data sources*

Data Sources	Objectivity	Reliability	Validity	Cost	Involvement	Acceptance	Side Effects	Total Score†
Teacher (Self)	?	+	?	+	+	+	+	+5
Classroom Observer	+	+	+	?	?	?	+	+4
Student	+	+	+	+	+	?	?	+5
Teacher (Peer)	+	+	?	+	?	?	?	+3
Other, Misc.	?	?	?	+	?	?	?	+1

*Advantages and limitations are designated with only two symbols. + = clearly an advantage often gained in utilizing the source. ? = often not an advantage to be gained.

†Total score is the sum of advantages (+), with no effort to give weights to them.

Disadvantages in using the teacher as a data source include bias, subjectivity, and conflict of interest (Trang and Caskey, 1981).

Exhibit 6.1 shows comparisons of estimates of advantages and limitations for teacher self-reports and other sources.

Observation Reports

The use of classroom observations is reviewed extensively in Chapter 7. For observable classroom behaviors this source is perhaps most promising of all. However, some important aspects of teaching are not readily observable. Staff relationships, parent relationships, instructional evaluation and planning are examples of major areas of performance that are not readily observed in classrooms. Other disadvantages for classroom observations includes high cost, limited validity without multiple observations, passive teacher involvement, and acceptance difficulties. Several real advantages in addition to objectivity and reliability are the side effects of promoting morale, building mutual respect, and enhancing the information base of the observer (Stallings, 1977).

Student Reports

The use of data on teaching from students has had only limited acceptance, despite obvious potential. DeVault et al. (1962) reported on the reliability of elementary student data many years ago. Veldman (1970) reported good reliability and limited expressions of bias in using a true-false instrument (Veldman and Peck, n.d.). Farley (1981) reports interesting recent efforts to interview students about teaching.

The obvious advantages for student source data are that students have extensive opportunities to observe teaching and see a variety of teachers over time (Glatthorn, 1984). Their reports can be objective, reliable, and valid; they also are very low in cost. Even teacher involvement can be strengthened as he or she gathers and reviews student responses. Disadvantages stem from the lack of acceptance traditionally accorded such data sources.

Teacher Peers

A "teacher peer" refers to a teacher serving as a data source as a result of pursuing one's normal teaching duties in a peer relationships. This relationship needs to be distinguished from that of a teacher observer, such as a department chairperson, who serves as an observer in addition to teaching. Any professionally trained person can become an observer. The important question is, can the peer relationship be utilized as a data base?

Teachers interact in various ways as peers. They share materials, confer about students, serve on committees, engage in in-service training together, strike, and socialize. These relationships provide an information base that each teacher has concerning any other teacher who is truly a colleague. Contacts with shared students and parents provide still additional information about ones peers.

Teachers do know something about peers with whom they work most closely over the years. Hence, they can be accepted as data sources, but only in limited ways. Teachers know little about their colleauges in terms of classroom practices unless they are actually teaching together in a team relationship. Similarly, they know little about the teacher-pupil and teacher-parent relationships of their colleagues, since these usually are not shared experiences. Furthermore, untrained and unsystematic data gathering characterizes peer relationships.

The one strength in teacher peer data sources is found in the area of staff relationships. Teachers who work together on committees and projects and share in-service training experiences can be objective and reliable in reporting on these aspects of teaching. With appropriate procedures, valid estimates of staff relationships are possible. Unfortunately, involvement, acceptance, and side effects may all be disadvantages.

DATA FORMS

Teacher evaluation data can take a variety of forms essentially distinct from the source. Rosenshine and Furst (1973) distinguish only three types of observational data. They classify data as categorical, sign, or rating. Medley et al. (1984) ignore rating systems as not worthy of use and call attention to multiple coding systems.

As useful as these categories are for thinking about the forms of data, they reflect only modes of recording and omit some worthy variations. Codings, tabulations, rankings, ratings, scores, video, aural, and descriptive-narrative data forms are all in use (Shearron, 1976). Each is sufficiently distinctive to be considered separately. Furthermore, natural artifacts such as tests, worksheets, plans, memos etc. can be utilized as data sources (McGreal, 1984).

Characteristics of Data

Still another way of considering data forms is in terms of their diagnostic characteristics. Instrumentation tends to produce data in forms that range from highly detailed fragments to those that are much less detailed and more global. Closely related to these distinctions is another dimension of data that might be thought of as "rawness." Data in the form of video-recordings is raw as compared to lesson plans or to even more highly artificial forms such as frequency tabulations of events.

Flanders' (1970) interaction analysis utilizes a coding system for recording verbal behaviors of teachers and students. The coded data is very detailed and becomes highly diagnostic when utilized in a matrix analysis format, as shown in Exhibit 6.2. (See illustrations also in Chapter 7.) Interestingly, the Flanders' coded data can be gathered using only a pencil, a sheet of paper, and an observer who has memorized the ten distinct categories. The data, however, is not very raw, in that the specifics of the verbal content are lost in the coding process. Hence, an event coded "4" is a question, but the nature of the question is not preserved as seen in comparing Exhibits 6.2 and 6.3.

EXHIBIT 6.2   Illustration of recorded observation data—narrative descriptive*

> John Carroll was in the midst of explaining. He was at the chalkboard. "When you are adding you have to consider both the numerators and the denominators. Now these numbers don't have the same or a *common* denominator. The easy way is to multiply one denominator by another." Carroll demonstrated, doing two addition of fractions exercises on the board. He explained what he was doing:
>
> Example: 3/4 + 1/3 =
>
> "Now multiply 3 × 1, the numerators. That gives you 3. Then multiply 4 × 3, to get your denominator: 12. You now have a new fraction, 3/12! But you have to reduce that to 1/4th. So, the answer is 1/4th."
>
> A boy raised his hand. Carroll pointed to him. He responded. "I don't understand this." Carroll: "All right, give me an example." The student tells him "5/18th plus 1/6th" Carroll: Goes to board, takes chalk, records the fractions. "OK. Now first just multiply numerators. What are they, Jim?"
> Student: "Uh" (pauses).
> Carroll: "Well it's five times one. Do you see that?"
> Student: "Um-huh."
> Carroll: "OK. Now what do you do next?" (pauses)   *(The lesson continues)*

Ben M. Harris, *Supervisory Behavior in Education,* 3d ed., © 1985, pp. 228–229. Adapted by permission of Prentice-Hall, Inc., Englewood Cliffs, N.J.

EXHIBIT 6.3   Illustrations of four recording forms

Flanders' Codings

10	6	5
5	10	5
5	10	10
5	10	9
5	10	6
5	4	7
5	5	5
9	8	5
2	4	4
6	4	8
8	8	5
2	5	4
6	5	8
4	5	5
8	6	4
10	10	8
5	5	5
4	6	5
8	6	6
2	6	10
5	5	4
10	6	8
5	4	5
5	8	5
5	6	7
4	7	7
8	7	10

Frequency Tabulation of Flanders' Codes

Categories	Tallies	f	%
Teacher talk:			
· Positive reinforcement		3	4
· Lectures		27	33
· Questions and directs		22	27
· Criticizes		5	6
	Total	57	70
Student talk:			
· Direct response		11	14
· Initiates talk		2	2
	Total	13	16
Silence		11	14
		81	100

Exhibit 6.3 (*continued*)

Matrix Analysis

	1	2	3	4	5	6	7	8	9	10	
1											
2				'1	"2						
3											
4				'1	'1			9			
5				5	13	4	'1	'1	'1	"2	
6				"2	'1	"2	"2	'1		3	
7					"2		"2			'1	
8		"2		'1	5	"2				'1	
9		'1				'1					
10				"2	4				'1	"3	
Total	0	3	0	11	27	11	5	11	2	10	80

Descriptive Categorical

a Communicates clearly and concisely
  · Carroll explaining at chalkboard.
  · Has examples on board. Demonstrates process of multiplying
    numerators and denominators. Verbalizes ". . . these don't
    have the same denominators . . ." "Now multiply 3 × 1 . . ."

b Encourages students
  · "Alright, give me an example . . ." as boy asks.
  · "OK. Now what do you do next?" Asks boy who seems
    unsure (answers "um-huh").

c Guides student responses
  · Carroll goes to board to demonstrate for boy. Asks about
    numerators. "What are they, Jim?" No response so Carroll
    gives answer, "Do you see that?"

A tape recording or typescript of a lesson would produce the raw, realistic data representing a series of verbal behaviors. But in this form (a magnetic tape recording), the record has no diagnostic characteristics. Some instrumentation is required to convert the raw evidence. Flanders' coding is only one way of doing this. If a frequency tabulation sign system were employed instead of Flanders' codes, then the same raw data (the tape recording) would be revealed in a different light. Such tabulations have much more limited diagnostic characteristics. If we wish to preserve some of the raw reality of the tape recorded verbal behavior, yet deal with it in a more diagnostic way, the descriptive categorical form of recording is an option (Harris and Hill, 1982). The sequenced verbal events from the tape would be re-ordered to show their relationship to a set of categories, as seen in comparing Exhibits 6.2 and 6.3.

Transcribing data is not the same as re-ordering or translating it. The typescript in Exhibit 6.2 illustrates some of these differences. The typescript could be produced only by a live observer or a video-tape recorder. It could not be derived from an audio-tape recording because non-oral information, such as going to the chalkboard, would have been lost. Given a video-tape recording of events, we can instrument for transcribing them into narrative-descriptive forms, we can code them, tabulate them, etc. However, a transcription of an audio-tape would be significantly different than the record of a video-tape. Similarly, a video or audio-tape will transcribe to descriptive-narrative form quite differently than a live observer's detailed notations. (See Chapter 7 for further discussion of the limitations of mechanical recording devices.)

What emerges, we hope, from this discussion and the illustrating data forms (and sources) is a clear recognition that "data is as instrument does!" The source, the rawness, the diagnostic characteristics, and the mode of recording dramatically influence what is included, what is excluded, and what analyses and interpretations are possible. As a general rule, more than one data source and a variety of instrumentation are superior to singular efforts.

Various Instruments

As suggested by the prior exhibits, data takes different forms as it is gathered, analyzed, and used in various ways. Instruments for initial data gathering place limits on what can be done in later stages of analysis. Hence, it is essential that the data gathering instruments be well-selected or designed, and that they be appropriate for diagnostic and/or survey purposes.

Initial gathering instruments often include tests, inventories, questionnaires, sound recordings, video-recordings, and observer notations. Each of these instrument types will produce data in various forms. Tests may reflect true-false, multiple choice, matching, and other formats. Inventories may use semantic differential scales, forced-choices, multiple choices, rankings, and rating responses, among others. Observer recorded notations may be narrative-sequential, descriptive-categorical, codings, checklists, tabulation, etc.

Each instrument has its special capabilities and limitations. There is no one best instrument. There are uniformly poor ones, however. The brief review of instrument types presented hopefully will encourage the reader to read further in the sources listed at the end of this chapter.

Tests currently are among the most popular instruments for data gathering on teaching practices (Cole, 1979; Popham, 1971; Carey, 1980). Interviews have been widely favored over the years, especially as data sources for selection purposes (Harris et al., 1985). Interest inventories and attitude and personality measures continue to interest researchers more than practitioners, but their ready availability and standardization makes some of them worthwhile. Simulations are still rarely used and generally for selection purposes rather than for developmental or even summative evaluation. All of these must be carefully considered as possibly useful instrumentation.

Tests of Knowledge

Tests tend to be fairly reliable. They are inexpensive to administer and score. They are a way to involve the teacher directly in the evaluation process as a data source.

The use of tests can be justified in teacher evaluation only when their extreme limitations are clearly recognized. Tests can measure knowledge of simple kinds reasonably well. Few tests measure complex concepts of skills very well. They tend to produce reliable scores if well constructed and administered, but they are not valid predictors of teacher performance in many important domains. Tests provide data about what teachers know rather than what they can do.

The abuse and misuse of tests for teachers has a notorious past. Merwin (1978) reports on the most widely used teacher test, the *National Teacher Examination* (NTE). Expressing concern about the lack of demonstrated validity of even such a well developed and tested instrument set, Merwin comments: ". . . the fact remains that after over 35 years of use there is still a lack of empirical evidence to support the predictive validity of these tests" (1978: 515). Weise and Harris (1984) argue further that ". . . testing can only whittle away at the edges of the problem . . ." in assessing competence.

Despite clear and obvious deficiencies, over 30 states had mandated testing of teachers by 1982 (Sandefur, 1984). In 1984, Texas went well beyond most states in mandating a whole series of examinations for pre-service selection, initial certification, advanced certification, and even for promotions to "master teacher" status (House Bill 72, 69th Special Legislative Session, 1984). It is not realistic to expect such extensive uses of such inadequate instrumentation to accomplish much.

Despite their abuse and misuse, diagnostic testing can be useful in developmental teacher evaluation. It is hoped that educators will eventually regain sufficient control of evaluation from politicians to begin rational and effective use of such instruments.

Inventories

Measures of interest, aptitude, attitude, and personality characteristics have many of the same features as tests of knowledge. They are often reasonably reliable, inexpensive, and involve the teacher as a data source. Interest inventories report perceptions but not levels of skill or competence. Attitude measures may identify predispositions toward certain behaviors, but they do not report on practices.

The problem with all inventories is their low level of predictive validity. They do not clearly predict what the teacher actually does or will do. In selecting a teacher from among a group of applicants about whom little is known, any slightly positive predictor may be useful. But for purposes of analyzing the teaching of a member of the faculty, such inventories contribute very little compared with observational data from teacher, student, and observer.

Interviews

Like inventories of various kinds, interviews are not good predictors. They also have the serious disadvantage of being very expensive in staff time. They require a very high level of interview skill to provide reliable information.

The interviewing process may be designed in such a way that better interpretations of other available data are possible. This use of the interview as a feedback, data utilization process is discussed more fully in Chapter 9. However, the use of the interview schedule and procedures as instrumentation for initial data gathering has severe limitations. Interview schedules must be carefully structured and administered by highly trained, self-disciplined interviewers. Their procedures must be standardized (Farley, 1981).

The reliability of interviews under well-structured circumstances can be reasonably high; however, predictive validity is still a serious problem. Interviews, like tests, produce data about behavior that is not directly related to teaching performance. The interviewer can observe use of language, ready recall of information, appearance, and quality of voice with considerable ease, but these evidences are of only limited value in predicting performance, and diagnostic power is generally lacking. Even so, when information is desired regarding parent or staff relationships or specific problem situations, the face-to-face interview may have special utility.

Simulations, Role-Playing and Games

These structured situations in which carefully selected problems are the focus of spontaneous interactions may be the most promising of all data gathering devices beyond direct classroom observations. Games and simulations have been utilized extensively for training purposes. They are reported to have powerful diagnostic characteristics that are not often utilized.

Micro-teaching is one version of a simulation which has been tested extensively with beginning and pre-service teachers. There is evidence that such simulated teaching exercises can promote the development of new teaching techniques (Turney 1969; Tremba 1975).

Modified "lab teaching" techniques, using adults playing student roles, have also been used for training and evaluation (Emmer and Millett, 1968). Both micro-teaching and "lab teaching" seem to have their best diagnostic potential when combined with systematic recording and analyzing of the simulated "teach" sessions, so as to link both evaluation and development (Brown and Kameen, 1975; Eder 1971). From a practical point of view, micro-teaching or lab teaching can be forms of "performance testing" advocated by McNeil and Popham (1973), as distinguished from tests of knowledge.

Video- and Sound Recordings

Electronic means for recording and reproducing simulated or real teaching performances is discussed in considerable detail in Chapter 7 as an alternative mode of observation recording. These mechanisms are utilized increasingly in training and can certainly be applied to research and evaluation (Bailey, 1979; Dranov, 1980).

The equipment is much more reliable now than in prior years. Technological advances have included color, cassette units, light weight portability, and lenses that zoom and focus with ease. But it is the face validity of the recorded evidence that gives recording instruments their greatest advantage.

Questionnaires

These instruments, like interview schedules, provide data of several varieties. Ratings and checklists are perhaps the most common response modes for questionnaires. Their special appeal is in translating opinions and other personal information from individuals into standardized formats. Questionnaires are economical of staff time and are easily analyzed. When properly designed and administered they produce reasonably reliable data.

Teacher self-report questionnaires may be one of the more systematic, yet practical ways of getting truly comprehensive data from teachers on their perceptions of their own classroom teaching practices.

Self-report instruments of nonclassroom practices or perceptions of problems in parent or staff relationships may be the only feasible alternatives in many situations. However, the instability of such responses when utilized in needs assessment "opinionnaires" has limited their usefulness (Harris, 1980).

Student reports of teaching practices can be obtained with simply worded questionnaires. These data can be both reliable and valid when designed to elicit objective reports on observed classroom events (Veldman, 1970). The DeTEK system uses questionnaires that are so simple that even primary age students can respond (Harris and Hill, 1982).

ADAPTIVE INSTRUMENTATION

·A common reality in many local school situations involves a set of general performance categories and a summative, judgmental rating scale already adopted. Board policy in these situations often proclaims: "The primary purpose is to promote improvement". In fact, instrumentation usually calls for (1) observation(s), (2) ratings, (3) reporting to the teacher, (4) reporting to the superintendent, and (5) summative decision making. What is needed is instrumentation for "the primary purpose" of improving teaching practice.

Such instrumentation requires the following:

1. The general categories of performance need to be defined in behaviorally explicit terms, as discussed in Chapters 4 and 5.
2. A survey instrument or instruments with procedural guidelines for its use is needed.
3. Diagnostic instruments and analytical procedures which focus on specific but limited portions of the array of performance category need to be developed.
4. Growth planning procedures with supporting services need to be developed, as discussed in Chapter 9.
5. Linkages need to be established to relate points 1–4 above to the summative decision-making process discussed in Chapter 10.

This section will attempt to illustrate the adaptation and design of the instruments required for steps 2, 3 and 4. These illustrations will not be all inclusive. They draw on discussions of the DeTEK system elsewhere (see Harris, 1985; Harris et al., 1985; Harris and Hill, 1982), but the instruments suggested for this chapter will illustrate still different data forms, recording modes, and procedures.

Starting Point

The summative instrument with which we begin is one of hundreds that are still widely utilized in public schools and in colleges. Exhibit 6.4 is a prototype of such summative, global, judgmental instruments. It illustrates several problems of instrumentation:

1. Knowledge of subject matter (performance category #1) is not observable. One or more tests of knowledge need to be utilized before rational and objective judgments can be reached, "Please circle S N U X" is a direction to make a judgment. Objective evidence must be utilized; otherwise, guessing or personal opinion or both are involved.
2. Student relationships will likely have both in-classroom and out-of-classroom components. As the specific behaviors defining this performance category are not fully explicated, at least two different

EXHIBIT 6.4   Teacher evaluation report

Highlands Public Schools   Highlands, Newstate

Teacher _____   School _____

Grade Assigned _____/ School_____   Subjects _____
                           Year

Directions:
        This instrument must be completed by the administrative supervisor in charge no later than ____(Date)____ of each contract period. A copy shall go to the teacher. The original must be filed with the office of the ____(officer)____.

Remember! The primary purpose of this evaluation is to promote improvement in teaching effectiveness.
        Legend: S = Satisfactory performance   N = Improvements needed
                        U = Unsatisfactory performance X = Not applicable or not observed

Please Circle					Comments/ Notations
S	N	U	X	1. Knowledge of subject matter	
S	N	U	X	2. Student relationships	
S	N	U	X	3. Discipline and control in the classroom	
S	N	U	X	11. Instructional methods	
S	N	U	X	12. Staff and community relationships	
S	N	U	X	Overall Rating_____Recommendation: _____	

Evaluator Signature _____   Date: _____

approaches to instrumentation will be required. In-classroom behaviors can be included in observation instruments. Out-of-classroom behaviors will not be easily observable in a systematic way.
Hence, student questionnaires, teacher self-reports, or interview
may be required.

3. Staff and community relationships will rarely be observable and
will require very careful attention to instrumentation that utilizes
appropriate sources. Peers, parents, and other supervisory personnel will have to be considered as potential sources of data along
with the teacher. Both instrumentation and data gathering can
become quite complicated in such an area of performance.

Practical realities argue against trying to assess each and every aspect
of teaching practice. Exhibit 6.4 calls for "the administrative supervisor in
charge" to be a walking encyclopedia of knowledge about each teacher.
Such fountain heads of knowledge are not readily found. The hard choices
that are offered in instrumenting include (1) ignoring performance categories that are less crucial; (2) attending to less crucial domains of practice—
parent relations, staff relations, etc.—only when persistent symptoms are
detected; or (3) adopting a multi-year schedule attending to different domains in different years on a five to seven year schedule.

The global, summative teacher evaluation report illustrated in Exhibit
6.3 presents still another serious challenge. To instrument for "improvement in teaching effectiveness," both survey data and diagnostic data will
be required.

Survey Instrumentation

Any set of performance categories can be surveyed once they are explicated
in behavioral terms. Checklists, forced-choice inventories, and descriptive
narrative observations are a few types of instrumentation that might be
utilized.

The DeTEK system uses a teacher self-analysis instrument that incorporates both forced-choice and checklist instrumentation (Harris and Hill,
1982). A profile sheet combining the data from both forced-choice and
checklist instruments is illustrated in Exhibit 6.5. The "Comprehensive
Observation of Performance" is also utilized by Harris and Hill (1982) to
produce a survey of observable classroom behaviors. This instrument's use
is detailed in Chapter 7. A sample page is shown in Exhibit 6.6.

The quality assurance program developed by Ron McIntire (1982) for
schools in Houston, Texas utilizes a "list of skills" in a checklist format.
Four major categories are explicated as 29 behaviors. These are used by
observers who simply report on their presence or absence. The format used
is shown on page 116.

EXHIBIT 6.5   Illustration of profile sheet using self-analysis*

DeTEK INSTRUMENT I

TEACHER PERFORMANCE SCREENING INVENTORY

A Self-Analysis Survey Profile

Teacher _John Carroll_   School _Ellsworth Elem._   Date _Jan. 20_

Teaching Assignment: Grade _5th_ Subject(s) _Mathematics and Social Studies_

DIRECTIONS:

After completion of sections A and B

A. TALLY choices from Section A to column A below.

B. Transfer check marks (✓) from Section B to column B below.

C. Check HIGH Performance clusters.
   (4 or 5 choices and 3 or 4 checks)

D. Check LOW performance clusters.
   (0, 1, or 2 choices and 0 or 1 check)

E. SELECT a performance and one or more of its behaviors
   for study.

	A. Performance Choices	B. Behaviors a b c d				Performance Clusters C. High D. Low
1. Businesslike	5					X
2. Friendly	3					
3. Verbally Interactive	2					
4. Stimulating	0					
5. Individual Oriented	4					X
6. Multi-Media Integrative	1					
7. Other						
8. Other						

E. SUMMARY

Selected Performance (1 only): ( )

Selected Behaviors (1, 2 or 3): ___ ___ ___

Comments:

*Reprinted by permission of the authors and Southwest Educational Development Laboratory.

	Yes	No	Not Observed
A. Effectively Uses Instructional Time			
1. follows prepared lesson plans based on—curriculum objectives.	____	____	____
2. focuses students' attention at the beginning of the lesson . . .	____	____	____
(other items not shown)			

Such a checklist, when based on a full lesson, thoughtfully and systematically observed by a trained professional can produce reliable objective data. It provides for a survey of a broad variety of practices. It is not essentially judgmental, even though some subjectivity is present in discriminating between "yes" and "no." A format that would ask observers to check only clearly demonstrated practices might be easier to use and less subject to personal biases.

Q-sort instrumentation is still another approach to producing survey data on a broad array of teaching behaviors. This technique is discussed and illustrated in Chapter 8 where the focus in on diagnostic uses. As survey instrumentation, an explicated array of behaviors are presented to the observer or teacher or both on 3 x 5 cards. These cards are sorted into six or more levels to produce a force normal distribution. The sorter uses his or her memory of actual teaching as observed (or experienced). The sorter is required to classify behaviors as follows:

Levels:	1 Least clearly in evidence	2	3	4	5	6 Most clearly in evidence
Percent of behaviors allowed	2%	10%	38%	38%	10%	2%
Profile value	0	1	2	3	4	5

Such a Q-sort produces forced choices of a relative kind. A profile of choices is shown in Exhibit 6.7. The Q-sort values for behaviors within a category are summed to produce a score for that category.

Diagnostic Instrumentation

Effective diagnostic analysis requires data that offers fine detail regarding what is and is not existent in the teaching behavior. Ideally, diagnostic data would be microscopic in focus and measure frequency, quality, and relationships. In practical terms, we often settle for much less powerful instrumentation.

The microscopic characteristic of the focus on behavior is crucial. Unless data bits are small, their presence, quality, frequency, and relation-

EXHIBIT 6.6 Illustration of discriptive-narrative recording

Performance Area #5 — Individual Oriented
The teacher treats each individual as a unique learner.

No
Evidence

✓_✓5a—Collects, organizes, and analyzes diagnostic data about individual students' current learning needs.

—Girl comes to teacher; shows her a clipping from the newspaper.
T. comes back to the desk to check it with the girl. Girl has other
clippings already pasted.

—T. asks, "Has anyone found all of them yet?" Refers to want
ads. No one responds.

✓__5b—Plans an instructional program which meets the unique needs and learning styles of individual
students.

—T. has all students working on the same activities at all times.

—T. gives directions for assignment. Urges them to "cut, paste and circle".
No variations are suggested. When SS ask for clarification, T.
says, "You can cut a word or an article. What ever!"

✓__5c —Directs instruction in response to the unique needs and learning styles of individual students.

—T. brings a girl up front to show class where she found the "Buick" in ads.

—After several students come to T's desk to ask questions, T. turns
to ask, "Whose having trouble?" Several students raise hands.
T. leaves the front, starts going from desk to desk.

— See 6c—T. asks boy to do more of same.

_____5d—Responds to individuals in ways that assist them in accomplishing their objectives.

—T. moves about the room, assisting individuals in finding the
proper place in the newspaper.

—T. returns to give assistance to a Black girl several times.

—T. moves about, assisting various individuals.

_____*Other Behaviors* (specify):

Performance Summary:

Observed evidence is:	Behaviors							Perf.
	5a	5b	5c	5d	Others			Area
Highly descriptive	HD	HD	HD	(HD)	HD	HD	HD	HD
Moderately descriptive	(MD)	MD	(MD)	MD	MD	MD	MD	MD
Not very descriptive	ND	(ND)	ND	ND	ND	ND	ND	ND

EXHIBIT 6.7   Q-sort profile using DeTEK indicators

Behaviors*	Number of Indicators	Mean Q-Sort Value (0–5)
1. Businesslike		
1a Organizes classroom activities . . .	5	≈4
1b Informs students of objective (etc.) . . .	4	≈1.5
1c Delegates responsibilities . . .	4	≈0.5
1d Paces activities . . .	4	≈1.5
2. Friendly		
2a Speaks . . . in positive . . . ways . . .	5	≈3
2b Expresses interest in individuals . . .	4	≈2
2c Reflects empathy, concern (etc.) . . .	5	≈1
2d Demonstrates interest . . . nonverbally . . .	5	≈2.5
3. Verbally Interactive		
3a Communicates clearly and concisely . . .	3	≈3.5
3b Encourages and guides . . . responses . . .	5	≈4
3c Utilizes a variety of question(s) . . .	3	≈0.5
4. Stimulating		
4a Expresses interest, enthusiasm, curiosity . . .	7	≈1
4b Uses a variety of styles, techniques . . .	5	≈1.5
4c Draws upon interests and current events . . .	5	≈1
4d Responds spontaneously . . .	4	≈4.5
5. Individual-oriented		
5a Collects, organizes, and analyzes . . .	3	≈2

*Source: Ben M. Harris and Jane Hill, "DeTEK Criteria List," in *Developmental Teacher Evaluation Kit*. Austin, TX: Southwest Educational Development Laboratory, 1982. Reprint by permission.

ships to each other cannot be discerned. As a minimum, instrumentation must utilize criteria that are highly explicated and provide for measuring (counting, categorizing, scaling, or describing) these teaching behaviors in a highly discriminating manner.

Colbert (1978) used instrumentation to record the frequency of "instructional/managerial behavior," explicating instructional facilitator as shown below:

Instructional Facilitator	Individual	Small Group	Whole Group
1. Giving instructional directions	I		₩
2. Discussing instructional plans		I	₩ II
3. Discussing instructional progress		III	IIII
4. Discussing topical content	II		IIII
(Continued: others not shown)			

This frequency tabulation format provides diagnostic data by explicating a variety of fairly distinct teacher verbal behaviors, but adds a dimension by separately designating the related student recipient.

Gregory (1969) adapted categories originally developed by Medley and Mitzel (1963) to diagnostically analyze teacher verbal behavior. Thirteen rather explicit forms of teacher and student responses were defined and tallied. However, the format of the instrument for recording is such that every verbal unit is shown in sequence over time. This adds a disgnostic dimension to the data illustrated below:

	Event Sequence										
Informing	(✓) ( ) ( ) ( ) ( ) ( ) ( ) ( ) ( )INF										
Procedural—Non Substantive	( ) ( ) ( ) ( ) ( ) ( ) ( ) ( ) ( )PRNS										
Problem Structuring	( ) (✓) ( ) ( ) ( ) ( ) ( ) ( ) ( )PBST										
Convergent Question	( ) ( ) (✓) ( ) ( ) ( ) (✓) ( ) ( )CVGQ										
Divergent Question	( ) ( ) ( ) ( ) ( ) ( ) ( ) ( ) (✓)DVGQ										
Probing—Same Pupil	( ) ( ) ( ) ( ) (✓) (✓) ( ) ( ) ( )PB-1										
Probing—Other Pupil	( ) ( ) ( ) ( ) ( ) ( ) ( ) ( ) ( )PB-2										
Procedural—Non Substantive Question	( ) ( ) ( ) ( ) ( ) ( ) ( ) ( ) ( )PRNSQ										
(Continued: others not shown)											

This format gains diagnostic power from its graphic display of the event sequence as well as from the explicitness of the criteria.

The DeTEK system utilizes both checklists and descriptive-narrative instrumentation for diagnostic purposes. The device utilized is to narrow the focus from the many behaviors included in the system to only a single behavior. The indicators for each behavior are then utilized as criteria for diagnostic data gathering. This simple conversion from survey to diagnostic instrumentation is helpful since new procedures with additional training is avoided.

Testing for diagnostic purposes, as distinguished from survey purposes, is readily illustrated using a single pair of items. In a survey test of mathematical knowledge, a geometric applications item might look like this:

#34   Calculate the area of the pie-shaped area XYZ:
angle Y = 60°   line XY = 5 inches

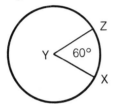

Answer: <u>13.09</u> square inches

If a teacher answers this question correctly, presumably there is no problem to be diagnosed with regard to mathematics knowledge called upon in this item. However, if a teacher leaves the item blank or answers it incorrectly, no diagnostic information is provided.

A diagnostic test item might ask for details of procedures for solving the problem, or each explicit skill and knowledge element could be tested separately. For instance, the following are among those elements essential to solving the problem:

1. The formula for area of a circle is $\pi r^2 = A$
2. $\pi = 3.1416$
3. A circle = 360°
4. 60° is 1/6 of a full circle
5. XY = 5 inches = radius
6. r^2 means radius squared = r x r

Other elements involve multiplication, division, and understandings about angles and areas. In any case, diagnostically useful data will determine the presence or absence of relevant knowledge and skill components.

COMMON PROBLEMS

Each illustration of either survey or diagnostic instrumentation should be recognized as support for several important guidelines on instrumentation and data gathering. (1) Neither survey nor diagnostic instrumentation calls for global judgments or summative decisions. (2) Survey data gives perspective for objectively viewing a complex array of behaviors. (3) Diagnostic data necessarily focuses on only a limited portion of teaching to maximize descriptive detail.

Efforts to utilize simplistic formats and procedures to serve summative, survey, and diagnostic purposes tend to accomplish nothing. Survey instruments may be designed for alternate analyses of data that produce diagnostic information, but these generally are limited in still other ways.

Perhaps, the most common error in designing both survey and diagnostic instruments is the persistent use of judgmental ratings of one kind or another (Medley, et al., 1984).

Judgmental scales are not descriptive of teaching behavior because the standard of values used to scale the observed behavior is unknown and varies in unknown ways with each observer. Hence, a scale like the one shown below is not acceptable, even though a clear criterion is in focus.

	Excellent	Good	Fair	Poor	Comments
a. Clearly defined instructional objectives are uilized . . .	____	____	____	____	

Furthermore, terms like "commendable," "acceptable," and "needs improvement" are essentially judgmental.

A comparative rating scale is rarely an improvement over the judgmental types.

	Superior	Above Average	Average	Below Average
IId Interacts with students in positive ways:				
• smiles	____	____	____	____
• praises	____	____	____	____
• nods agreement	____	____	____	____
• accepts and uses ideas expressed by students	____	____	____	____
• maintains eye contact to show attentiveness	____	____	____	____

The performance criteria in this example are nicely explicated for diagnostic purposes. But the scale confuses; it does not inform. Comparisons with others are implied by the scale, but such comparisons cannot be made readily. Also, such scales are often used with the most casual procedures. Hence, comparisons are vague, subjective, and full of error at best. In many cases the comparison is with the individual rater's stereotype of some ideal. In any case, such scales do little to produce accurate, informative data.

Mixed scales are commonly constructed in the unfortunate belief that a scale with different kinds of terms is more accurate. An unfortunate model offered by the American Association of School Administrators (Gudridge, 1980) included the following:

Degree of competency

	Optimum	Average	Not Shown	Seek More Information
Check one or more for each item	_____	_____	_____	_____

Obviously, any number of points could be logically checked on this scale. It appears not to really be a scale at all. Whatever the rater (observer) checked would require considerable explanation.

The complete avoidance of ratings is advocated by some, at least for initial data gathering (Medley et al., 1984). Certainly, extreme caution must be used when designing any scale to be sure that the behaviors are explicitly described and that the scale calls for objective estimations of those behaviors (Stulac et al., 1981).

A set of scales that can be used by both observers and self-reporting teachers would have special advantages if they could be structured to be reliable and objective. An illustration of such a scale reveals both promise and persisting problems:

Item #1 Did the instructor state the lesson objective clearly?

Did not state the objective	*Hardly.* Only implied the character of the object-ive.	*Somewhat.* Stated the objective but not very clearly.	*Yes.* Stated the object-ive very clearly.
1	2	3	4

(Harris, 1975:184)

This scale defines a category of behavior. The raters are trained to recognize specific practices as related to this category. The scale is further structured to require raters to estimate and record the amount of practice on the scale at one of four levels. Yet there remains a problem even with this carefully structured scale in that observers are required to make small judgments regarding differences in amount of clarity.

The more serious limitation surrounding the use of very carefully structured descriptive rating scales is the difficulty of structuring a large number with care and consistency. In the DeTEK System, scales are utilized by observers as a way of scaling descriptive-narrative recordings at three levels. (For examples, refer back to Exhibit 6.6). The scale used here is a three-point scale. Observers are directed and trained to use an estimating procedure for these ratings.

1. An HD rating = Highly Descriptive. The observed evidence must clearly reflect *all* or nearly all the indicators designated in the criteria list.
2. An ND rating = Not Very Descriptive. The observed evidence does *not* clearly reflect a substantial number of the indicators.
3. An MD rating = Moderately Descriptive. The observed evidence is less than HD and clearly more than ND.

SUMMARY

The selection, adaptation, and design of instruments and procedures for teacher evaluation is a very complex topic. This chapter is less a guide than an introductory statement. The practitioner is well advised to seriously consider adaptations of well-developed instruments instead of designing their own. When instruments are developed, the cautions provided here and elsewhere regarding rating scales and overly simplistic checklists should be the starting point for careful design and testing efforts.

SELECTED STUDY SOURCES

Borich, Gary D. and K.S. Fenton (1977). *The Appraisal of Teaching: Concepts and Process*. Reading, MA: Addison-Wesley Publishing Co.

    Chapter 2 illustrates and discusses a variety of instrumentation (measurement) procedures.

Boyer, E. Gil, Anita Simon, and Gail Karofin, editors (1973). *Measures of Maturation: An Anthology of Early Childhood Observation Instruments*. Philadelphia: Humanizing Learning Programs, Research for Better Schools.

    A review of over seventy different observation instruments.

Carey, Lou M. (1980). "State-Level Teacher Performance Evaluation Policies," *NCSIE Inservice* (February): 9–14. National Council of States on Inservice Education, Syracuse University.

    A survey of state policies on evaluation of teacher performance reveals serious limitations in nearly all current practices when compared with quality standards.

Cole, Robert W. Jr. (1979). "Minimum Competency Tests for Teachers: Confusion Compounded," *Phi Delta Kappan*, 61 (December): 233.

> One of a large array of critical reviews of the competency testing "craze" that is still in vogue in the U.S.

Funkhouser, Charles, editor (1984). "Teacher Competency Testing,' *Teacher Education and Practice*.

> An entire issue devoted to the issue of testing as related to assessing teaching competence.

Glatthorn, Allan A. (1984). *Differentiated Supervision*. Alexandria, VA: Association for Supervision and Curriculum Development.

> Proposals are presented for utilizing a variety of supervisory approaches in promoting teacher growth. Two options (clinical and cooperative) require systematic observation or self-analysis. Emphasis is also given to student data sources and self-analysis using a "reflective journal" and videotape.

Good, Thomas and Jere Brophy (1984). *Looking in Classrooms*, 3rd ed. New York: Harper and Row.

> An elementary view of an array of possible instrumentation techniques.

Government Employee Relations Report, No. 574 (1974). Washington, D.C. Bureau of National Affairs.

> Analyzes and distinguishes between "assessment" for developmental purposes and summative "ratings."

Hardebeck, Richard J. (1973). "A Comparison of Observed and Self-Reported Individualization of Instruction by Vocational, Academic, and Special Education Teachers in Texas". Unpublished doctoral dissertation. Austin, TX: The University of Texas.

> A comparison study of both the problems and possibilities in teacher self-analysis.

Harris, Ben M. (1985). *Supervisory Behavior in Education*, 3rd ed. Englewood Cliffs, NJ: Prentice-Hall, Inc.

> Chapter 7 illustrates a variety of instrumentation alternatives for observation and self-analysis. Rating scale problems are systematically analyzed. Chapter 10 provides illustrations of observation data in use with teachers.

Hartman, C. (1978). "A Longitudinal Look at Self-Appraisal Strategies, *Journal of Teacher Education* 29: 11–12.

> A critical review of various efforts to utilize self-reports of teachers in various forms.

Johnston, John M. and R. Lewis Hodge (1981). "Self-Evaluation through Performance Statements—A Basis for Professional Development," *Journal of Teacher Education* 32: 30–33.

> A somewhat different set of suggestions for employing performance criteria to self-analysis.

Medley, Donald, R.S. Soar, and H. Coker (1984). *Measurement-Based Evaluation of Teacher Performance: An Empirical Approach.* New York: Longman, Inc.

A technically detailed treatment of many aspects of teacher evaluation. Great detail is provided on various instrumentation alternatives. The authors are highly critical of rating devices. They offer details on several instruments using unique recording techniques. Pages 81–110 are especially relevant to instrumentation.

Millman, Jason, editor (1981). *Handbook of Teacher Evaluation.* Beverly Hills, CA: Sage Publications, Inc.

A collection of papers on a wide variety of both technical and practical aspects of teacher evaluation. As a volume sponsored by the National Council on Measurement in Education, it emphasizes measurement problems in largely quantitative terms.

Pearson, H. Delmar (1980). "Development of a Forced-Choice Teacher Behavior Rating Scale." Unpublished dissertation. Austin, TX: The University of Texas at Austin.

A study gives evidence to support forced-choice scales as highly discriminating for survey purposes.

Shearron, Gilbert F. (1976). "Developing and Improving Instruments for Measuring Competence of Pre-Service Teacher Education Students." A paper presented at a conference on Competency Based Teacher Education in Special Education Assessment. New York: August 11, 1976. Research in Education ED 129 803.

Stallings, Jane H. (1977). *Learning to Look.* Belmont, CA: Wadsworth Publishing Company, Inc.

A detailed handbook of guidelines for using the SRI observation instrument and procedures.

Stulac, Josef F., et al. (1981). *Assessment of Performance in Teaching: Field Study Instrument.* Columbia, SC: South Carolina Educator Improvement Tast Force.

The details of instrumentation developed for field testing in South Carolina are presented. Emphasis is placed on "statements of evidence" associated with assigned scores.

7

Classroom Observation Technique

INTRODUCTION

Observing and recording classroom events, is, perhaps the oldest of all personnel evaluation procedures in the field of education. It remains uniquely important in teacher evaluation of any kind and is certainly crucial to developmental teacher evaluation, since it aims to know, analyze, reinforce, and guide the improvement of teaching and learning.

Classroom observation techniques for gathering data, as related to teaching and learning, have a special place in teacher evaluation because they demand focus on (1) reality, (2) the classroom, and (3) the complexities of teacher/student/lesson/material interactions. A further, importantly unique, feature of classroom observation for data gathering is that there is always more than one data source available. Students, teachers, outside observer, and technical devices (microphone, camera, etc.) are all potential data sources. It is not possible for one to be utilized without at least one other source also actively observing. This fact provides enormous advantages that have generally been neglected in both theory and practice.

Using more than one data source frees practitioners from reliance on a single type of instrumentation or a single viewpoint. The evils of relying on only one data source are clearly evident in teacher selection (Harris, et al., 1979) and in student achievement testing. While similar mistakes are common in current efforts of "teacher testing" (Weise and Harris, 1984), and in past efforts to rely exclusively on principal judgment to evaluate teachers (Eckard and McElhinney, 1977), they need not persist. And, to the extent that use is made of the various information sources nearly always available, teacher evaluation can be enormously and economically improved.

Multiple data sources disperse power and influence in the evaluator/ evaluatee relationship. Principals generally are expected to evaluate as though they and they alone command all relevant data. In fact, they rarely have sufficient data, often are less knowledgeable than the teacher evaluatee, and may utilize crude observation techniques (Medley, Coker and Soer, 1984). Even so, when there are two or more data sources utilized in ways that offer alternative perspectives on teaching, then no one person— teacher, principal, supervisor, evaluator, or student—can claim a privileged position as "the authority"; nor can the perspectives of others be ethically ignored. Such a dispersion of knowledge-based power can promote collaboration and promote more rigorous analysis. It can also discourage the use of biases and overgeneralizations on the part of all parties.

Another important advantage of recognizing two or more potentially useful observers in the classroom is the opportunity offered for specialized analyses. Chapter 8 elaborates on the use of multiple data sources for congruence analysis purposes, taking advantage of this potential.

This chapter will elaborate on the rationale for making observations in classrooms an essential part of all teacher evaluation efforts. The characteristics of systematic professional observations will be identified. Basic skills and techniques for utilizing various observation instruments will be discussed. Distinctions between comprehensive and diagnostic observation and recording techniques will be developed with special attention to electronic/photographic recording and possible computer applications. Finally, attention will be called to myths and misconceptions that abound regarding classroom observing.

BASIC TECHNIQUES

Classroom observation techniques involve a set of procedures for attending to events in progress in such ways as (1) to see and hear what is transpiring, (2) to focus on a selected number of events, and (3) to record them for future use. Such procedures can be rather casual, as in the case of a visitor to the school or class who makes notes for future reference. Systematic classroom observations, however, call for rigorous, standardized procedures utilized by trained observers. Observations generally need to be more systematic than those of the casual observer and should always be as rigorous as possible.

Systematic observations vary in the way they structure the focus of the observer, the mode of recording utilized, and the nature of the intervention itself. Foci for observations vary from the extremely comprehensive and unstructured, as in ecological or ethnographic techniques, to those with extremely narrow, microscopic attention to specific details. Recording modes range from the photographic, electronic, and narrative/descriptive to checklists, rating scales, tabulations, and coding systems. Interventions also vary widely. One-way viewing screens or hidden cameras provide for observing with virtually no interference with classroom events in progress. At the other extreme, participant observations presume that the observer will be actively engaged in these events. Most observation procedures in current use avoid both extremes, calling for unobtrusive entry into the classroom, and minimizing observational influences on classroom events (Samph, 1976).

The strengths and limitations of these various foci, recording modes, and interventions will be discussed later. They will necessarily all have some techniques in common and must also conform to essential standards of evaluation.

Evaluation Standards

Four standards for assuring that evaluation efforts are of high quality have been proposed by Stufflebeam (1979). They have relevance in thinking about classroom observations. These standards are:

1. *Accuracy*   Technically accurate information is provided.
2. *Utility*   Practical information is provided.
3. *Propriety*   Information is obtained legally, ethically, and with proper regard for all concerned.
4. *Feasibility*   Procedures are realistic in terms of time, energy, and values derived (Carey, 1980:9).

These standards, when applied to classroom observations, suggest specific procedures. For instance, since classroom events are numerous, rapidly changing, and complex, accuracy is very difficult to attain and sampling procedures generally must be employed. This complexity also limits the use of electronic and photographic recordings. The utility standard often requires that the observer carefully select certain sets of events for attention, while ignoring others. Gathering a vast array of information beyond current levels of need is wasteful and complicates the analysis and interpretation processes. The feasibility standard influences the length of the observation period, the frequency of observations, and the need for more than one data source. Propriety calls for prearranged observations, with clearly defined purposes, and proper review procedures. This standard also limits the use of hidden cameras or microphones.

Factors Characterizing Observations

A specific observation can be characterized by a variety of factors relating to techniques employed. A list of factors that incidentally or purposefully influence the nature of the observation is presented in Exhibit 7.1. All of these are important to consider in selecting procedures and planning for observations.

EXHIBIT 7.1   Characteristics of professional, systematic classroom observation

Precursor Factors

Training—Both teacher and observer have training regarding instruments, criteria, procedures, and techniques employed.

Criteria explication—Criteria are utilized to directly guide the observation procedures; they are explicit and public.

Instrumentation type—Instrumentation, including procedures for observing, sampling, and recording, is predetermined and selected with purpose.

Purpose—The purpose(s) for which the observation data is gathered is clearly determined and limited.

Focus—Consciously made decisions to focus on certain categories of events are accompanied by exclusions.

Observer/observed relationship—The roles and relationships of observer and teacher to each other and to the students are differentiated.

Prearrangements—Time, length of visit, activities planned, and any special arrangements are designated in advance.

In-process Factors

Sampling events—Systematic sampling procedures are employed to assure representativeness of recorded evidence.

Time utilization—Available time for observing/recording is carefully allocated to assure a full record of a full lesson.

Categorization—Clearly defined categories are systematically utilized to guide observing and recording.

Involvement—Observer involvement in classroom activities is avoided completely or minimized drastically.

Observability—Observable events are the exclusive focus for recording (with opinions, summaries, and speculations eliminated).

Scanning bias control—Environmental scanning is consciously utilized periodically to prevent unconscious omission of relevant events. Biases are consciously controlled by compensatory attention to an array of other events.

Recording technique—Recording techniques are utilized faithfully throughout time periods.

Post Hoc Factors

Forgetting—Recorded notations of observed evidence, regardless of form, made as complete as possible with as little time lapse as possible.

Transcribing—Recorded events are transcribed to assure accuracy, completeness, and legibility.

Analysis—Analytical procedures of one or more kinds are undertaken based on the purpose(s) to be served and the unique character of the data (instrumentation).

Interpretation—Meanings are ascribed to analyses based on trends, patterns, comparisons, omission, or other features that emerge!

Training is an essential factor in any observing effort. Untrained observers cannot see adequately, fail to control biases, do not sample events, and produce inadequate records. The accuracy standard demands training of all who are providing observation data. The DeTEK system illustrates this emphasis on training for all in providing a "Trainer's Manual" with different sessions depicted for various personnel groups. The amount and kinds of training required will vary widely among observers and be different for various situations, foci, purposes, and instruments. For instance, if student observers are employed, the instrumentation must be highly simplified, but even with such safeguards, students must be given at least a few minutes of training to be sure they know how to respond and are cautioned against biases. Teachers to be observed need training to assure they are knowledgeable about expectations. Teachers also can profit from having detailed information on procedures. Furthermore, they need to be trained to assist in interpretations and valuing processes.

Training for principals and supervisors working closely with classroom teachers must include several hours of study of instruments, procedures, purposes, and cautions. Training should also include basic skills in looking, relating events to criteria, and scanning the environment. Recording will require additional training. Usually twenty to thirty hours for a specific system or instrument will be needed. Once basic techniques are mastered, each additional instrument or procedure may be trained for in less demanding ways. An outline of basic observation training procedures is presented in Appendix D.

Criteria explication has been discussed and illustrated in Chapter 5. The extent to which criteria are highly detailed to reflect observed events, the less uncertainty for the observer. Such explicit criteria are referred to as "low inference." They assist the observer in being objective, reduce errors of omission, and reduce bias. Unfortunately, the more explicit the criteria, the more numerous they become; hence, new problems are introduced for the observer. With many criteria, the observer must be more alert, make classification decisions quickly, and record more quickly. These demands can cause errors too.

Instrumentation influences observation procedures and each instrument has its own special advantages and limitations. Instrumentation is carefully discussed in Chapter 6 and is only briefly considered here. Instruments of various types demand alternative forms of recording, amounts of time, sampling procedures, and, of course, training. Regardless of type of instrument, the constants in observation involve matching actual events with criteria and recording the "matches" in a clear and useful way.

Observation purpose influences instrument selection, timing of observation, and the recording forms. If an observation is intended as a "get acquainted" activity by a supervisor, then it will be broadly focused or comprehensive, be timed at a mutually appropriate time, and reflect recording techniques that are most helpful to the observer. If purposes are diagnostic and developmental, then a focused instrument will be needed, the time should match the appropriate classroom activity, and the recording should be readily interpretable by both observer and teacher.

The focus of observation in a classroom refers to the range of events regarded as important. It would be nice if all observations could be comprehensive and include all that might conceivably be relevant. But teaching is so complex that such comprehensiveness is never attainable. In fact, choices are always being made to include and to exclude events. It is the explicit, purposeful, and systematic ways that observational foci are selected that makes the evidence accurate and useful. If we decide to focus on all verbal interactions, then the nonverbal events may be consciously and systematically excluded. But if both verbal and nonverbal events are to be in focus, then some limits must be placed on each, since it is unlikely that all can be accurately embraced.*

Relationships between the observer and the teacher being observed are important factors to consider in observation planning. When an observation is anticipated for the first time, anxiety levels may be unduly high and need attention. If an observation is explicitly requested by the teacher for a special purpose, then those expectations must be carefully considered in advance (Cogan, 1973). Even when an observation is part of a routine system of monitoring, teachers have an ethical right to be informed about the time, purpose, and procedures to be utilized (Glatthorn, 1984). Moreover, pre-observation planning between observer and teacher is essential for very utilitarian reasons. Observations are potentially extremely useful, but expensive too. Both the observer and the teacher are contributors to the process. The observer needs to know enough about lesson plans, activities, subject content, student characteristics, and classroom arrangements to plan and time the observation well. The teacher as a simultaneous informal observer will want to know the observation focus and purpose to sharpen his or her attention to events and to advise the observer on procedures. Effective observations are nearly always cooperative and reciprocal in nature (Rayder and Taylor, 1979).

Other elements in assuring good working relationships between observer and teacher involve reviewing procedures and expectations for all involved. Teachers need to know whether students will be interrupted, what equipment will be used, whether movement about the room is required, how the observer will exit, what follow-up will be provided, and where the recorded information will go. Many of these details can become

---

*It is often presumed that videotaping is a suitable method for recording comprehensively in an ecological mode without limiting the focus to be utilized (Medley et al., 1984). Such a presumption simply ignores the extreme limitations inherent in electro-mechanical devices. The decisions of the camera operator, the type of lens, the amount of light, the loudness of the voices, and the overlapping of events will conspire to produce a variety of special problems (Kaplan 1980).   •

standardized procedures that are well understood. When this condition prevails, much time and worry is saved.

Constants in Observations

All classroom observations have a few basic techniques that must be applied to produce useful information. Criteria must be systematically used, all relevant observable events must be considered, accurate recordings must be made, and extraneous or biasing events must be controlled. These are never perfectly accomplished but are essential to systematic observation.

Criteria Utilized　The systematic use of criteria in the observation process presumes that the observer clearly understands how the criteria relate to the real events of the classroom. Beyond this, understanding is the requirement that the observer systematically employ all criteria, neglecting none and favoring none over others. If five types of questions are to be tabulated, then all five categories must be used consistently with a full understanding of what each question category stands for in terms of actual teacher talk. On the other hand, if ten categories of behavior are specified, then all ten must be systematically utilized. Only variations in the events themselves should produce variation in the record.

All Events Considered　Since all events cannot be fully observed and recorded, special procedures may be needed to assure that no variety of event is ignored. Sampling procedures, formal or informal, may be useful in assuring complete representation of all events among those recorded. Sampling procedures often involve time sampling and a constantly roving eye.

Event sampling usually involves systematically allocating time frames to specific portions of the teaching space during observations (Hiatt and Keesling, 1979). If many different activities are underway in a single classroom at the same time, time sampling will facilitate observing. The observer might decide to allocate three minutes to each of five groups, for instance. In a 45-minute period, each group would be observed three times for a total of nine minutes. No group would be ignored either accidentally or by biasing events.

Scanning the environment with a constantly roving eye is often essential to assure that all relevant events are equally well represented in the observation record. The observer uses the "roving eye" technique consciously and deliberately. Care is taken to avoid attention to only one or a few events. Instead the observer remains alert to the numerous locations where relevant events might be observable. Hence, the roving eye constantly attends to first one person or space and then to another, always returning quickly to attend to "where the action is," but not allowing any person or place to monopolize the observer's attention. Attending only to the teacher, or an active student, or a particular group is certain to produce incomplete recordings.

Bias control requires that the observer be aware of his/her tendencies to overvalue or undervalue various events. We all have biases; the need is for their control. Those who are very fond of bright, colorful, decorated, visually stimulating classroom displays must avoid excessive attention to these events while ignoring others. Those who are impressed by knowledge of subject-matter, or orderliness, or logical sequence must not allow these interests to overshadow attention to other types of events. To a degree, the careful and systematic use of explicit criteria will minimize biases. Additional efforts should include consciously giving attention to those events likely to be neglected otherwise. The observer must "know thyself" as well as the criteria.

Adequate Records   The variety of precursor, in-process and post hoc factors being discussed here will determine the adequacy of the record that is finally produced by the observer/analyst. Training in using criteria, in using instruments properly, and pre-arrangements suitable to the purpose and the focus selected are all essential to an adequate record. In-process factors are all, of course, related to producing an adequate record, but time utilization, recording technique and emphasis on observability may need special attention. Forgetting and transcribing are post hoc factors of special concern.

Time utilization is crucial in assuring a complete observation record because there is always too much to do, too many alternatives, and events keep "marching on." The more narrowly focused the observation, the more clearly defined will be the use of time. Even so, the observer always must gather some context information such as date, time, number of students, teachers, room, subject, etc. It may be desirable to describe the general sequence of events. It may be important to make a sketch of the classroom. Identifying students by name may be useful (see Appendix C-2).

Decisions on what to include and how to record each category of information is important. Since very bit of recording takes time, simple forms for checking off context information are helpful. Unimportant information needs to be eliminated. However, nothing is so frustrating or wasteful of time as to need some information and not have it in the record.

Use of time should be planned in advance as much as possible, but spur of the moment decisions are also required. What do you do when the focus is on verbal interaction and no such events are transpiring? When events that have already been thoroughly recorded are repeated over and over should the repetitions be enumerated? When unanticipated events, unrelated to purpose, dominate a portion of a lesson, should they be included or omitted? There are no easy answers to these questions of time utilization. The observer must be flexible without losing focus or corrupting the observation purpose.

Recording techniques vary widely, ranging from narrative descriptions to checking, tabulating, coding, and rating. Training in (1) using the specific techniques, (2) applying them to the particular format of the instrument, and (3) relating each event to a criterion is essential to quality recording. Beyond such training, the observer/recorder must review his/her procedures carefully before every observation, check to see that all material is in hand, arrive in the classroom in plenty of time to get settled, and remain for an entire class period or at least through a full sequence of a lesson. Above all, the recorder must be disciplined to attend to the dual tasks of observing and recording, allowing for no interruptions or moments of relaxation.

Observing in classrooms can be "fun" derived from what the observer learns. It cannot be fun in the sense of relaxing, interacting, or socializing.

Emphasis on observability is important to producing an adequate observation record. The observer must record only what is clearly observable and must be alert not to miss such events. Conversely, the observer must avoid recording opinions, speculations, summaries, or inferences. When a teacher is heard to remark, "Tomorrow we'll try to have more discussion on that topic . . .," the observer can record what the teacher said (descriptive-narrative recording), or record it as code 5—"Lectures using Flanders' categories," or check the item—"Teacher informs students of future plans." What the observer must *not* do is record "The teacher uses a variety of discussion leading techniques," based only on this bit of evidence. What discussion leading techniques the teacher uses will be observable tomorrow. Today we can only speculate.

Forgetting is a very human phenomenon. The human mind tends to retain certain memories and not others for a variety of reasons. In general, however, we cannot expect to remember details of observed events. There are generally so many events and such a variety ocurring in rapid succession that, if not recorded immediately, they may not be recalled. The observer is therefore obligated to record rapidly and as completely as possible any relevant event. The time lapse between an event and its recording should be minimized. Descriptive recordings are especially challenging in this respect because new events occur while past events are being described. To minimize this problem brief notations are utilized that are later transcribed as more complete descriptions.*

Codings and frequency tabulations put the observer under time pressures too. Events may occur very rapidly, even overlapping each other in time. The coder or tabulator must keep up because few events can be accurately recalled in proper sequence.

The fear of forgetting too much is one of the strong motives for using a tape recorder or a video-tape camera-recorder. Obviously, the "memory" of these electronic devices can be very useful. Unfortunately, they rarely hear or see as much as the live observer can.

---

*Many years ago stenographic recordings of classroom talk were made by Stevens (1912) in efforts to study teacher questioning. The courts still utilize such recording techniques. Useful as stenographic recording was and is, it also illustrates the principle of limitation. No procedure or instrument is without severe limitations. In this instance, the nonverbal events are almost completely ignored.

Transcribing one's observation record involves post-observation efforts to assure the accuracy, completeness, and legibility of the record. Accuracy can be enhanced by careful review of recordings to correct omissions or errors. The teacher may be able to clarify the factual character of certain events. Completeness is enhanced when details can be added to the record from memory.

Legibility is an important factor in developmental use of observation records because the teacher needs to be able to fully understand the recorded evidence. Legibility is enhanced by rewriting, elaborating, adding explanatory comments, and typing.

COMPREHENSIVE OBSERVATIONS

When the purpose is to survey and develop an overall view of the teaching practices, then the focus must be rather broad and an effort to be comprehensive is in order. Comprehensive observing is extremely challenging. Teaching is so terribly complex that no truly comprehensive view is possible. Hence, the instruments and procedures for approximating comprehensive observations must resort to sampling procedures of appropriate kinds.

Comprehensive observation implies that a very broad array of performance criteria will be employed. Furthermore, a series of observations will normally be required to assure samples of various times of the day, subjects, class groups, and types of lessons. While a single comprehensive observation may be useful, that utility will be necessarily limited (Hiatt and Keesling, 1979).

The requirements of comprehensive observation are potentially served by checklists, descriptive-categorical instruments, and rating scales. The strengths and limitations of these have been discussed in Chapter 6. Descriptive-categorical instruments offer the greatest promise for being truly comprehensive, retaining objectivity, and providing reasonable levels of reliability and validity. Their strength is that they facilitate the use of a great variety of criteria without loss of descriptive detail. They also have "face validity."

Descriptive Categorical Recording

Observing with a large array of performance categories or criteria involves selectively describing events in narrative form as they occur. The observer is required to write almost constantly during a class period. The essential skills involved are (1) associating events with criteria, (2) locating the appropriate criterion or category on the instrument, (3) describing the events in brief narrative form (using shorthand notations as needed), and (4) continuing to focus and refocus one's attention on events as they occur.

A descriptive observation record of this categorical type is illustrated

EXHIBIT 7.2   Illustration of categorical descriptive recording

Rough Original Observer Notations	Rewritten Record
The teacher . . .	
6a. *Uses a variety of audio-visual and manipulative aids as integral parts of lessons and assignments.*	
• Paper in lesson—marking pens— clip—paste	• Newspapers are used for much of the lessons' activities. Searching, marking, clipping, and pasting are involved as well as reading.
• Record play—plugged in	• Record player in front of room. A record is on the turntable. The cord is plugged in. No actual use.
• Chart—tree	• A chart rack is used to display a tree. Work assignments are shown.

in Exhibit 7.2. The crude descriptive notations of the observer are carefully rewritten following the observing period. Hence, a more legible and complete set of descriptions of events emerge.

Harris et al. (1975) note the sequence of standardized procedures found to be most reliable in producing descriptive observation records (DORs) of this categorical type include the following:

1. *Enter the classroom and sketch the facilities* (5 minutes). Select an observation post in the rear or at the side of the room. Remain as unobtrusive as possible. Do nothing, initially, but sit, observe, and record. The first few moments are well utilized in preparing a sketch of the physical facilities and displays in the room. This is useful to orient the observer, may be useful for discussion purposes later, and permits the observer to set a "tone" from the very beginning that this is a business visit, not a social call. Both students and teachers are encouraged by the busy observer to go on about their work in a normal way. This pre-lesson sketching and recording of date, time, grade, teacher's name, etc. can occupy the observer constructively even while students are assembling and class is yet to begin. See Appendix C-2 for an illustration of a classroom sketch.

2. *Observe and record classroom events sequentially* (20 to 35 minutes). Using a guide that lists an array of categories of criteria to be utilized, the observer describes any event that relates to each category. Approximately one minute time samples are utilized. Each

category is reviewed. Presently occurring and immediate past events are considered and, *if* relevant, they are quickly described. The observer moves the focus every minute to another category of criteria, repeating the three step process—read category descriptors, review events, record as appropriate. When no event relates to a criterion under focus, the observer checks (√) that item after one minute has transpired as both a signal to "move on" and as a record of "no evidence."

Using an observation guide with 20 to 30 categories of criteria, 100 or more specific criteria are under scrutiny, since a single category may reflect a cluster of 3 or more specific criteria. (See discussion and illustrations of performance specifications in Chapter 5).

3. *Observe and record classroom events spontaneously* (15 to 20 minutes). Continue with the three step process utilized sequentially, but now make every effort to relate each event to a category and to record a descriptive notation of the event under that category. The observer is now charged with matching events to categories without concern for sequence. Since events may occur very rapidly, the observer must be simultaneously looking, remembering, associating with categories, and recording. This is a demanding set of skills, but the human observer learns to do it quite well with training and hard work (and no recording device can do it better).

The observer, when unable to keep abreast of all events, utilizes sampling and abbreviation techniques. Repetitive events are noted with ditto marks or the word "repeat." Special attention is given to new events in the sense that a comprehensive observation report should not err in overlooking a kind of event even if it may err in not cataloging all repetitions.

The observer uses a roving focus even while writing to describe prior events. It is crucial that the observer not allow events of special interest, intensity, or frequency to detract from his or her attention to the full array of events transpiring in the classroom. The roving focus technique involves a conscious and systematic process of periodically moving away from any given locus of activity to scan the entire classroom and focus on any potentially relevant event that is found.

4. *Move about the classroom* (10 to 20 minutes). The observer moves to one or more locations in the classroom to focus on objects and events at closer range. Such movements must be unobtrusive, of course. However, most classes are accustomed to the presence and movement of a second or third adult from time to time. The observer quickly looks over students' shoulders, moves closer to an activity center, looks at displays, exhibits, and in other ways uses these few minutes to add descriptions of relevant objects or events, and to clarify the recorded evidence with greater detail.

5. *Review "blank" categories* (1 to 3 minutes). Glancing through the pages of the DOR, the observer takes note of any category in which no events have been described. An effort to recall events is made, and the classroom is scanned in a final effort to observe related events. If this fails, the observer checks the item (√) to record this "absence of observable evidence."

6. *Leave the classroom and rewrite* (20 to 30 minutes). At this point an observer has been in the classroom for nearly an hour. Less than 40 minutes is rarely adequate for a comprehensive observation period; more than an hour is not usually necessary.

On leaving, the observer continues to be unobtrusive, leaving silently, nodding and smiling if the teacher's attention is available. Since the teacher has been informed of follow-up procedures and understands that the observer's work is not done, there is no need to communicate with the teacher at this time.

The observer leaves and goes to a quiet place (away from office interruptions and telephones) to undertake the rewrite! Observation notations recorded in the classroom may be very complete and legible, but this is not usually the case. The rewrite consists of the following:

- *Read* every descriptor of each category and review the specific performance criteria clustered in that category.
- *Review* descriptive notation in the category.
- *Revise* the descriptions to make them more legible and descriptively detailed.
- *Add* descriptions of events from memory that were not included.
- *Check blank* categories carefully in a last attempt to recall any event related to that category of criteria. If no evidence can be recorded, the observer should insert the words "No observable evidence" in that blank space.

If any scaling or other analysis of the observation record is to be completed, it can be done profitably at this time while the reality that the DOR tries to reflect is fresh in mind. On the other hand, the teacher can often profit from being involved in the scaling or other analytical techniques. The teacher's input may be also needed before such analysis is undertaken for the sake of accuracy and validity. Appendices C-2 and C-4 illustrate completed portions of descriptive observation records.

Record Objectivity and Adequacy

The use of the descriptive observation recording techniques and procedures detailed above assume disciplined objectivity on the part of the observer. The procedures described are intended to promote objectivity as well as reliability (Medley et al. 1984). However, there is no substitute for

self-discipline and the hard work that rigorous application of these techniques requires.

Four problems commonly associated with learning to be an objective
observer-recorder have been recognized (Harris and Bessent 1969:149).

#1   The Use of Value Judgments   All events must be described as objectively
as possible with no values, opinions, or feelings included. A criterion implies a set of values about the teaching behaviors sought. Furthermore, the
omission of criteria may imply judgments about relative worth of such
behaviors. However, once criteria are publicly determined, the observer is
responsible only for observing and recording with optimum levels of objectivity and reliability.

It is easy to err in being slightly subjective. For instance, a notation
"The teacher failed to adjust the blinds properly," includes two judgmentally loaded terms—"failed" and "properly." Both imply observer opinion
or judgment and neither add to the descriptive information offered. The
observer can record with equal clarity the same objective events as "The
blinds were not adjusted to prevent sun from shining on desk tops." This is
negative evidence but implies no judgment. A more careful observer might
record, "The blinds were slanting down, sun shining through them was
striking eight desks near the windows."

A positive example reflects the same problem. "Teacher had the room
beautifully decorated." This is an opinion and not very informative. Instead
the observer might record: "Two bulletin boards used color photos, spray-
painted letters, and colored yarn. Student work was mounted on colored
construction paper. Green plants growing on window sill have aluminum
foil around their pots." No opinions, no judgments, and more information!

It normally requires more words to objectively describe an event.
Hence, brevity may be a virtue when observation notations are used during
a busy class period. But the post-observation rewrite period should be used
for writing fuller descriptions.

#2   Descriptions Are Too Vague and Too Abbreviated to Clearly Reflect Events   For
instance, the descriptive notation, "Teacher smiles" is surely objective, but
not terribly informative. The tendency of the inexperienced observer is to
record: "Teacher smiles a lot." But this leaves the interpretation of this kind of
event wide open to speculation. Does the teacher go around smiling all the
time? Are smiles wide and "toothy" expressions of real pleasure? What related events produce smiles, and which do not? Are smiles accompanied by
any other events of positive or supportive kinds?

To illustrate further, if the category calls for evidence that "the objectives for the lesson are clearly communicated to students," then explicit,
vividly descriptive evidence needs to be recorded to reflect what happened.
In one classroom the observer might write:

Teacher had objectives written on chalkboard.

Teacher asked students to read the board. Asked for questions. Commented on several terms.

Teacher gave illustrations of how lesson objectives would relate to vocations.

Teacher talked with Bill about objectives after others began the assignment.

In another classroom a contrasting set of events is equally carefully described:

Teacher gave assignment as "Reading pages. . . ." No explanation or reason mentioned.

Student complains assignment is "tough." Teacher does not respond.

Bill sits after others begin. Teacher talks to him, "Better get started." Bill looks worried, shuffles papers. Teacher does not clarify.

#3 Lack of Relatedness of Events to Criteria All recorded descriptions of events under a particular category should relate in some way to one or more specific criteria subsumed under that category. Often events are clearly related to more than a single criterion or category and should be recorded in more than one location on the instrument or guide. However, rather remote or unlikely relationships between events on criteria should be discouraged.

If a criterion calls for "Teacher involves students in evaluating their own progress," then a description such as "Students record their own test scores on an individual progress chart" seems clearly related. However, a notation "Tests show many students earn A's" seems inappropriate. What the latter observer may be doing is recording anything related to evaluation of student progress under a criterion that is much more narrowly defined.

#4 Negative Evidence Neglected or Described Judgmentally Since all recorded observations need to be as objective as possible, many observers fail to recognize negative evidence. Negative evidence is a description of an event that is clearly negatively related to a criterion or category. Two types are commonly observed: (1) events that are clearly contrary to a criterion, and (2) events that are not in evidence when a rational person would clearly expect them. Examples of the first type might include the following:

Teacher scolded class for poor tests results. (This is negative evidence in relation to a positive reinforcement criterion or a self-evaluation criterion.)

Teacher questions were almost all "closed," demanding only recognition and recall responses. (This is negative evidence with respect to a criterion asking for use of both open and closed questions, as well as for a criterion calling for questions of a variety of kinds.)

Negative evidence of the second type involves inference making by the observer regarding what would be expected to occur. As such, the observer must be cautious not to inject value judgments or opinions about what the teacher should have done. Nonetheless, some omissions are clearly omissions that can be described:

Bill completes his report. Teacher calls on next student without comment. (Depending on the circumstances it seems appropriate to include "without comment.")

Students start working. Several hold up hands indicating need for attention. Three students just sitting. Teacher stands at rear of room, does not respond. (Such "evidence" of lack of attention to individual needs and inefficient use of time are, perhaps, permissible if cautiously and objectively described.)

Cautions in recording negative evidence include avoidance of judgments. The observer is not objective if Bill's neglect above is described as "Teacher ignores Bill." The evidence does not support such a judgment and observers should not record judgments. Similarly, an observer would not be justified in recording, "Teacher stands at back of room, ignores students, wastes time."

Levels of Inference

Evidence may be "low inference" or "high inference," but there is no absolute objectivity. Inferences are drawn by an observer about every event as to whether it is related to a criterion or not, which criteria it related to, whether it has already been adequately represented, and so forth. Since inferences must be drawn and objectivity sacrificed to some extent, the observer should be alert to drawing inferences that are not essential to a full and useful record.

Comprehensive observing runs risks in sacrificing objectivity that are not acceptable when more limited observational foci are utilized. If the observer has only ten categories of verbal behavior to code, each one can be defined in mutually exclusive ways (Flanders, 1970). When a hundred or more criteria are employed, ranging over widely different kinds of events (in contrast with purely verbal behavior), criteria must be clustered together for logistical reasons because frequency tallies cannot suffice and events may relate to multiple criteria. These difficulties have led researchers to avoid comprehensive observing and focus instead on fragments of teaching (Barnes, 1983; Martin et al., 1980; Stallings, 1977; Stow, 1979). Practitioners have no such luxurious freedom of choice; they must strive to understand teaching in its broader dimensions.

Consider the problem of inference control reflected in Exhibit 7.3. The evidence observed was recorded as follows:

> Record player in front of room, a record is on the turn table. The cord is plugged in.

The observer has been extremely objective in providing only verifiable, factual information. However, deciding to record these facts about an unused piece of equipment under the category (6a—Uses a variety of audiovisual aids . . ." is to draw an inference. The existence of the record player is very low inference evidence but relating it to teacher use makes it high inference and less objective.

Fortunately, in this illustration, the observer was sensitive to such a problem and detailed additional evidence about a recording in place and the electric cord connected to give some credence to the relationship between the factual evidence and the selected criterion. It would have helped the observer if the teacher had actually utilized the record player during the observation period. But that did not happen and the observer is forced to choose between ignoring the evidence as too inferential or recording it with cautious objectivity.

To carry our illustration further, suppose the observer noted while moving about that the title of the recording appeared closely related to the topic under discussion in the classroom. This added information, while calling for inference making by the observer, strengthens the total pattern of evidence about using the record player. Conversely, if this observer found the title completely unrelated to lesson content, or if a student on leaving commented, "We never get to listen to our records in this class," then the accumulated evidence can be weighed more heavily.

Inferences might be crudely classified at several levels and illustrated with evidence as shown in Exhibit 7.3.

Since comprehensive observing is so important and demanding, it behooves observers to emphasize recording the low inference evidences most rigorously, giving some attention to evidence that calls for medium levels of inference, but avoiding high inference recording. When interpreting an observation record, the low inference evidence needs to be given greatest weight.

Reliability estimates for observers who are properly trained and disciplined are reasonably high (Semmel, 1978). Interobserver reliability coefficients of 0.80 are obtainable even with such complex procedures as those required for comprehensive observing. Chapter 12 suggests simple methods of checking reliability levels for observers. This is important because teachers have a right to expect both objectivity and reliability from those intervening in the classroom.

EXHIBIT 7.3   Illustrations of evidence recorded at various inference levels

Level of Inference	Types of Evidence	Illustrations
High	Values, opinions, speculations, crude estimates generally related to clusters of criteria.	• Not multi-media oriented • Seems bored • Students are happy • Excellent • Satisfactory
Medium	Careful estimates more specifically related to a criterion or a cluster	• Uses both open and closed questions • Makes little use of record player, flannel board, or charts • Does not respond in positive, friendly ways • Students respond enthusiastically • Smiles frequently
Low	Observable events described and clearly related to explicit criteria	• Has record player ready, flannel board bare, chart of assignments only • Does not smile, laugh, joke, or compliment • Students laugh, smile, respond with hands waving • "Is it orange or red?"

Teacher Self-Reporting

The teacher as observer of self has been all too often ignored, or considered only when electronic devices are employed. In fact, the teacher is always aware of his or her own teaching performance and can offer evidence of a most comprehensive kind. The teacher and the student group are the ones who directly experience a full array of classroom events. Their observations have special potential for comprehensive validity.

The problems of reliability and objectivity in teacher self-reports have been well documented (Hardebeck, 1973; Hartmann, 1978; Hook and Rosenshine, 1979; and Thomas, 1971). Studies indicate that teacher self-reports are not clearly related to observer reports. This is hardly surprising. However, Mills (1980) Irving (1983), and Newfield (1980, 1981) all suggest that self-reports of well-trained teachers are useful. Hardebeck's unreplicated study indicates that teachers accurately report the practices they know and utilize, but understandably have problems estimating their use of those they do not know well.

Teacher self-reporting must be recognized as one of the promising approaches to comprehensive observation of teaching. It is an inexpensive source of data. It is as valid as that derived from most other sources, and it has special value in promoting teacher acceptance of the evaluation process.

Because the teacher is very emotionally and personally involved in the evaluation process (Trang and Caskey, 1981), special safeguards are required in securing self-reports that are both objective and reliable. A forced-choice inventory technique was discussed previously as a way of helping the teacher report discriminatingly about his or her teaching. The Q-Sort technique is also useful for this purpose. The problem of securing objective data from the teacher on his or her own teaching is quite different than that faced in using an outside observer. This latter observer must attempt to see enough to be able to generalize (Hiatt and Keesling, 1979). The teacher has seen too much to remember or differentiate. Glatthorn (1984) suggests the use of a "reflective journal" by the teacher as a way of assuring better recall of practices.

The classroom observer must be cautious not to assume that differences in perception are errors on the part of either the teacher or the outside observer. In fact, they may be, but who is in error? There is almost certain to be substantial amounts of error in all measures (Capie, 1978). Hence, in Chapter 8 we talk of discrepancies and differences in perceptions because objective reality is rarely fully verifiable.

FOCUSED OBSERVATION

When a limited array of events is selected to be observed, the alternatives for both data gathering and recording procedures are greatly increased. Unlike comprehensive observations, focused observations can utilize checklists, coding, and frequency tabulations, as well as descriptive techniques. Mechanical/electronic/photographic devices that are of so little use in comprehensive efforts become unusually valuable when a clear and limited focus has been selected. Even self-report and student report procedures gain in reliability and utility when a few specific teaching practices are in focus.

Regardless of focus, instrumentation, and data source, many of the essential characteristics of systematic observations still apply. Observational criteria must still be explicit. Observers must be trained. Objectivity and reliability still require self-discipline and standardized use of procedures. Sampling methods may still be required because only the narrowest focus assures recording all events.

Selecting a Focus

Decisions on observing a limited array of events are dictated by purposes to be served. Diagnostic foci are frequently utilized, based on some preliminary survey of a wider array of practices (Colbert, 1978). In the DeTEK system, any of 22 behaviors can be selected on the basis of a comprehensive observation and a teacher self-report. Clinical supervision systems tend to rely on the teacher to identify a focus for observation with or without formal procedures (Goldhammer et al., 1980). Tillman (1982) proposes a "troubleshooting" model utilizing student problems as the starting point for focusing upon "teacher performance deficiencies."

A special observation focus is often derived from a personal interest, an institutional concern, or a popular notion. Time-on-task analysis represents a recent focus of considerable popularity (Denton, 1982). Problems or pressures in a school or community may promote the use of a focus on "discipline," "academic learning," or verbal interaction opportunities for minority students (Paley, 1979).

A danger in selecting an observational focus in an ad hoc fashion is that teaching as a complex process may be viewed as a set of discrete actions (Doyle, 1981). Furthermore, a limited array of events may be given a distorted level of importance. A focus should relate to a larger frame of reference and be only as narrow as required to produce useful information. For instance, a focus on pupil time-on-task should properly embrace teacher behaviors related to enhancing or restricting time-on-task (Davidson and Bell, 1975).

Descriptive Recording

A narrowed focus makes it possible to utilize the descriptive categorical recording techniques already discussed with even greater efficacy. In the DeTEK system, for instance, a single behavior may become the focus instead of the 22 behaviors utilized for the comprehensive observations (see Appendix C-2). Hence, the observer, using identical procedures, can now focus attention on only a few performance criteria called "indicators." The use of these criteria gives focus in being fewer in number, but they are also more explicitly defined. Thus a more detailed and reliable descriptive report is produced. Such specificity also promotes face validity.

Sequential, descriptive recording is especially useful when a limited focus has been determined. Hunter (1983) advocates the use of such observations referring to the record and the descriptive recording as "script taping." Unlike descriptive categorical recording, the observer holds the limited set of criteria in mind and uses a blank sheet for recording descriptions of events. Every relevant event is described in sequence as it occurs. The observer ignores all unrelated events, concentrating on both the sequence and description of events that relate specifically to the focus. This is a useful and practical technique when fewer than a dozen explicit criteria or categories of events are selected.

This particular technique of sequential descriptive recording has been widely utilized to focus on the elements of a didactic lesson. It can also be utilized when attending to types of questions or when a few discussion-leading behaviors are in focus.

Coding and Frequency Tabulations

Systems of focused observations often utilize coding or frequency tabulation techniques. Flander's (1970) famous interaction analysis categories illustrate the special utility of coding events to produce a very accurate and complete record of a limited array of events.

Frequency tabulation recording techniques are much like those employed in coding. A limited array of criteria must be selected, they must be defined in ways that make each one mutually exclusive. When codes are recorded in sequence, frequency tabulation requires a special format to retain a record of sequence. Such recording requires special training. Its effectiveness is illustrated in the extensive use of the several OScAR instruments by Medley and Mitzel (1963) and the dyadic-interaction categories by Brophy and Good (1974).

The enormous advantages of well-designed coding or frequency tabulation records are to be found in the analytical techniques that can be applied to them. The Flander's matrix analysis technique has proved to be unusually valuable for developmental purposes (Harris, 1985). Profiles and graphs illustrated in Chapter 8 are readily prepared from such detailed observation data. Colbert's (1973) instrumentation utilized tabulations relating teaching acts to time, type of lesson, and type of grouping utilized.

Scaling Techniques

A limited number of categories or criteria of teacher performance can be recorded by an observer using scaled estimates of events. As always with focused observations, systematic procedures must be applied to carefully define criteria for utilizing each point on the scale.

The classroom observation scales utilized by Emmer (1978) include 12 broad categories of events. Each category was carefully defined and observers were trained to estimate the extent to which each category of event was in evidence during 15-minute time samples. For example, Emmer's second category refers to "Teacher-Initiated Problem Solving." A 5-point scale is used every 15 minutes by the observer to report little or no such behavior (designated as "1") to "most of the teacher's behavior is teacher-initiated problem solving" (designated as "5").

Such scaling techniques are convenient for purposes of research, but lack a great deal when used for developmental evaluation purposes. Unless highly focused on very explicit criteria of performance, they lack face validity and utility.

Broadly defined scales can be used in focused observation instruments, using coding or frequency tabulation techniques. For instance, a broad category such as "Personalized Planning" (McDaniel, 1979) may be thought of as more than "one type of behavior" (Emmer, 1978). A category, "Teacher Presenting" can be coded or tabulated as an array of specific teacher acts:

1. Teacher lectures.
2. Teacher reads to the class.
3. Teacher answers pupil questions (substantively).
4. Teacher points to or shows picture, chart, or map.
5. Teacher demonstrates or illustrates writing on the board.
6. Teacher demonstrates or illustrates by manipulating objects.
7. Teacher shows film, filmstrip, transparency.
8. Other presentation acts (specify).

If coded in a fashion that preserves the sequence of these events and with rules governing timing, a rich and accurate description of events can be produced. It is still possible to scale such tabulations or codings, but the detail of descriptive information is better retained by coding. When scaling is utilized for broad categories of diverse events, the loss in vividness often exceeds the gain in simplification.

Student Reports

Use of student reports on instructors is fairly common in colleges and universities and is gaining attention in elementary and secondary schools. Comprehensive reports on teaching from students are not likely to be either reliable or valid for various reasons. The student is limited by reason of forgetting, halo effect, and personal involvement (Korth, 1979). However, it is possible to derive focused, objective reports of specific teaching events. DeVault et al. (1962) validated student reports on elementary teacher practices in implementing the "new math" many years ago.

Describing teaching practices (or absence of practices) should be the essence of efforts to use students as observers. Since they are not trained as observers and have limited experience in differentiating practices, the instrumentation must be highly simplified. The language used to describe performance criteria must be simplified. The responses of students should be highly structured, and objective reporting of events should be emphasized over opinions and feelings.

The DeTEK system (Harris and Hill, 1982) has been successful in securing student report data from students at all levels above kindergarten and first grade. Once students can read simple descriptions of teaching practices, they can identify those that do and do not characterize the teacher in the classroom. Opinions, judgments, and speculations need to be avoided, of course, as with any observation effort. It is also essential to carefully restrict criteria to those that relate to readily observable events from the students' point of view.

Electronic/Photographic Recording

The refinement and invention of electronic/photographic recording devices has been revolutionary in recent decades. Whereas the "box" or "flash" camera offered only very limited assistance in observing and recording teaching at the turn of the century, motion picture film seemed to offer more promise in the 1930s. In fact, it was not until the 1950s that light weight, quiet equipment, using high speed film became available in both 16mm and 8mm sizes. This made it possible for pioneers like Frances Fuller (1967, 1969) to combine live observations with photographic recording. Other developments quickly emerged to add variety to the technology available. Presently, observers can use film, audio-tape, video-tape, closed circuit telecasting, and computers as tools for observing and recording.

The audio-tape recording is most widely used. Despite its limitations, recording only teacher and student talk (and noise), the recorders are inexpensive, transportable, and easy to operate. Obviously, an audio-tape recording must be restricted to focused observing since much nonverbal behavior is eliminated. But the live observer can work in tandem with the audio-recorder, recording nonverbal events as well as the audio events.

A special advantage of the audio-tape recorder is its simplicity of operation. Once set-up to record events, it requires little attention; hence, the observer can do other things simultaneously. A serendipitous benefit is the opportunity for the teacher to record his or her own teaching, with no other observer involved.

Audio-taping, like all recording techniques, presents serious limitations. A single microphone is rarely adequate to "pick-up" both teacher talk and student talk, unless both are close together and the microphone is there, too. Most inexpensive recorders have a very sensitive microphone built into the case and its tends to pick up all kinds of sounds, including papers, shuffling feet, and hall noises. Really clear and complete audio-tape recording generally calls for two or more microphones (one on the teacher) and high quality equipment.

Video-tape recording of teaching in the classroom offers advantages over audio-tape, including providing for both audio and video recordings. Furthermore, the video-tape offers a colored image and immediate play-back capability. These advantages are so great as to discourage the use of photographic film, except for special purposes. If nothing else, the reusability and erasability features of video-tape would be difficult to contest in offering teachers self-analysis opportunities (Kaplan 1980).

Recent technical developments offer still further convenience and usability features to classroom observers. Video-cameras are now very light weight and portable. Microphones are built into the camera. Zoom lenses are available to provide both wide-angle and telephoto images. Video-tape players are now widely available as cassette players, making play-back very simple.

As with any recording technique, there are numerous problems and limitations associated with the use of video-taping. Video cameras are very light sensitive and cannot function well when shooting into a window area. Detail is lost when moving from a poorly lit area to a bright area (Kaplan, 1980). Microphone problems discussed in the previous section on audio-taping all prevail with video, too. Additional problems may emerge if the camera operator is not professionally trained to focus on relevant events (Rissel, 1978).

Limitations of technology as applied to classroom observation must be carefully assessed and realistically accepted if they are to make maximum contributions. In our enthusiasm for the new and unique features of technology, we overestimate its capability and foolishly (if not dangerously) misuse electronic devices. First, we must recognize that they are not observation instruments, only recording devices; they see and hear and record within limits only what an intelligent observer has arranged. Secondly, these devices are confronted by some of the same problems the live observer faces; namely, too much to see, hear, and record. The camera has no recall; if an event is not in focus when it occurs it is simply not recorded.

The electronic/mechanical/photographic devices are useful tools in the hands of skillful observers. They can assist but not (to date) replace human observation, and they do not analyze or interpret, value, or make decisions.

The superiority of the human observer needs a few words of attention. Humans have two ears and can simultaneously tune into a variety of messages. The human observers have two eyes with peripheral vision and enormous speed in moving from one focus to another. The human mind of a trained observer can guide, direct, and record enormous numbers of events. To date, the human observer is not only indispensible but superior to electronic media on most counts.

COMPUTER APPLICATIONS

Computerization of some aspects of observing and analyzing teaching is a likely development in the very near future. For years, computer programs have been available to analyze data. This is perhaps best illustrated by the programs that take coded data from Flanders' interaction analysis and generate a completed matrix. This saves enormous amounts of time for users, who can concentrate on interpreting such matrices. Computer-based storage and retrieval systems for observation records can be developed with little new technology.

A more futuristic application of computer technology to observation and analysis of teaching is to be found in interactive uses of both the computer and video-cassettes or video-discs (Floyd, 1982). Industrial and military uses of such advanced technology is emerging for training purposes (Donahue, 1983). It is quite feasible with existing hardware for a teacher and an observer to use the micro-computer to assist them in reviewing specific video-taped events and analyzing a variety of such events. More sophisticated uses of such interactive electronic systems are subject to imagination, development, and cost.

MYTHS AND MISCONCEPTIONS

Classroom observation has been so clearly associated with summative evaluation over the years that those practices have contaminated observation in both thought and practice. Furthermore, confusion surrounds classroom observation practices due to the influence of research emphasizing the quantification of data. A few basic concepts about classroom observation, if clarified, can avoid much confusion. A host of myths and misconceptions still need careful attention because they are deeply rooted in fear, tradition, and ignorance, and will not disappear easily.

Concepts that need to be clearly recognized to avoid confusion about classroom observations include the following:

- Observing is data gathering not judging or even evaluating.
- Observing must involve recording because memories are not capable of adequate recall.
- Observing is a systematic, objective procedure guided by explicit performance criteria.
- Observing, when done properly, is not casual, social, or surreptitious.

With the clear acceptance of these concepts certain misunderstandings and some inappropriate practices are identified. Since observations are not judging sessions, judgmental instruments are not properly used. Since recording is essential, training also is essential for observers. Teachers must be reassured that the record will be available for review. Systematic, objective procedures with explicit criteria inform the teacher of expectations and offer protection against mistreatment. Since observing is businesslike and straightforward, anxieties building on uncertainty are reduced.

Myths or serious misconceptions about classroom observations have been widely circulated by both word of mouth and the print media. Harris (1985) has listed and discussed many of these most commonly held beliefs:

1. Teachers just won't accept being observed.
2. Testing students makes observations unnecessary.
3. Observations disrupt the lesson.
4. Observers only see a "special performance."
5. Writing in the classroom is disruptive.
6. Unannounced observations are best.

7. Systematic recording gets in the way of really seeing what is going on.
8. Watching pupils and how they study and learn should be the primary focus.
9. Using tape- or video-recordings makes it unnecessary for observers to record.
10. Recordings permit the teacher to be his/her own observer; no "outsider" is needed.
11. Observation data are neither reliable nor valid.
12. Casual "drop-in" visits or strolling down the hall are just as good as systematic observations.

Most of these items have been given some attention in this and previous chapters. All of these are either complete myths without any factual basis, or they reflect serious misconceptions. Items 1, 2, 3, 4, 5, 7, 11 and 12 are not supported in any substantial way. Items 6, 9, and 10 must be viewed with considerable suspicion, even though there may be some truth in them. Unannounced visits may have a special utility in some summative evaluations, but for general use they offer only disadvantages. We have discussed at length in this chapter the contributions of electronic/photographic recording, but their limitations are all too real. The teacher as one's own observer-analyst is full of controversy and special conditions must prevail, in any case. The chapters on feedback and growth planning give more attention to this issue.

SUMMARY

Classroom observations are useful to nearly any meaningful form of evaluation of curriculum and instruction. For developmental teacher evaluation, observers are indispensible. Observations produce data—they are not to be equated with evaluations, but are ways of implementing the data gathering step in an evaluation process.

While observations are usually viewed as an outsider "visiting" the classroom, other observers are always present: namely, teacher and students. The use of at least three observation data sources offers unusual opportunities for better data and better collaboration, too.

Comprehensive observations are most demanding and, unfortunately, not often systematically employed. Despite the difficulties, descriptive-categorical recording and teacher self-reporting techniques are available and practical. Comprehensive efforts to view all aspects of the teaching learning process promote insights for both observers and teachers that are not likely to be produced otherwise.

Focused observations, while much more common and less demanding, still require rigorous procedures. They offer a great variety of forms of instrumentation and analytical techniques. With careful selection and specification of performance criteria, focused observations permit detailed diagnostic analysis of teaching that is essential in guiding the improvement process.

SELECTED STUDY SOURCES

Beegle, Charles W. and Richard M. Brandt, editors (1973). *Observational Methods in the Classroom.* Washington, D.C.: Association for Supervision and Curriculum Development.

A forward looking monograph emphasizing the potential for observation in supervisory practice. Still worthy of review.

Bennett, Neville and David McNamara, editors (1979). *Focus on Teaching: Readings in the Observation and Conceptualization of Teaching.* London: Longman Group Limited.

A diverse array of brief papers on systematic procedures, observational research problems, and related topics. Includes work from many known sources. Excellent source for many ideas.

Blease, Derek (1983). "Observer Effects on Teachers and Pupils in Classroom Research" *Educational Review* 35 (November):213–17.

Intensive observing for five weeks in a dozen classes. Evidence gathered that constant (and excessive or intensive) observing has effects on both teacher and students. Even so, only 1 of the 12 teachers seemed to be dramatically affected. Students reported to be trying to cover up for teacher inadequacies.

Borich, Gary D. and Kathleen S. Fenton, editors (1977). *The Appraisal of Teaching: Concepts and Process.* Reading, MA: Addison-Wesley Publishing Co.

A collection of papers on a variety of studies by well known authorities. Chapters 7 and 9 focus on technical concerns.

Descamps, Jorge A. and Norma G. Hernandez (1981). "Constructing Classroom Observation Instruments," in *Improving Classroom Practice Through Supervision,* Robert H. Anderson, editor. Dallas, TX: Texas Association for Supervision and Curriculum Development, pp.18–26.

Discussion of problems of instrumentation. Illustrates several promising forms.

Good, Thomas and Jere Brophy (1984). *Looking in Classrooms,* 3rd ed. New York: Harper and Row.

A very introductory treatment of the topic with emphasis on teachers analyzing teachers. Many specific suggestions for focusing upon specific aspects of teaching are presented. Details of simple observation forms illustrated.

Harris, Ben M. (1985). *Supervisory Behavior in Education.* 3rd ed. Englewood Cliffs, NJ: Prentice-Hall, Inc.

Chapter 7 presents many of the basic ideas included in this chapter, giving more detail on instrumentation. Chapter 10 reports in case study fashion on a variety of applications of observational practices with teachers.

Harris, Ben M. and Jane Hill (1982). "The DeTEK Handbook," in *Developmental Teacher Evaluation Kit*. Austin, TX: Southwest Educational Development Laboratory.

The *Handbook* for this kit describes observational techniques in detail. Attention is given to both comprehensive and focused observations. Other instrumentation, teacher self-report, and student reports are illustrated.

Gump, Paul V. (1980). "Observation of Persons and Contexts," A paper presented at the American Educational Research Association Meeting, Boston, MA. (April). ED 193 362.

Options used to observe and record analyzed. "Diary specimens," time sampling, event sampling, and critical incidents are discussed. Limitations are also analyzed.

Hough, John B. and James K. Duncan (1970). *Teaching: Description and Analysis.* Reading, MA: Addison-Wesley Publishing Co.

Chapter 5—Analyzing Instruction—presents the OSIA system for classroom observation and matrix analysis techniques. Both verbal and nonverbal behavior of students and teachers are analyzed.

Kowalski, Joan (1978). *Evaluating Teacher Performance*. Arlington, VA: Educational Research Service, Inc.

Reports on a survey of many teacher evaluation practices in U.S. schools. Emphasizes various common practices.

Medley, Donald, Homer Coker, and Robert S. Soar (1984). *Measurement-Based Evaluation of Teacher Performance*. New York: Longman.

A systematic treatment of nearly all aspects of measurement of teacher behavior. Chapter 9 is especially useful for its emphasis on operationalizing teacher evaluation.

Stallings, Jan A. (1977). *Learning To Look: A Handbook of Classroom Observation and Teaching Models*. Belmont, CA: Wadsworth Publishing Company.

A detailed account of observation training for use of the SRI instrument is provided. The general problems of observation or their applications to teaching models is quite limited.

Stodolsky, Susan S. (1984). "Teacher Evaluation: The Limits of Looking," *Educational Researcher,* 13 (November): 11–18.

A report of a small study of 5th grade teachers who are teaching both mathematics and social studies to the same students. The researcher makes much of differences in format, pacing, and cognitive levels between subjects.

Stubbs, Michael and Sara Delamont, editors (1976). *Explorations in Classroom Observation*. London: John Wiley and Sons.

Aptly titled, it explores teaching from a variety of view points, focusing largely on pupil teacher interactions. Techniques illustrated largely depend on brief critical incidents recorded in descriptive sequential form.

8

Analytical and Diagnostic Techniques

Data gathering for evaluation is normally followed by analytical techniques of one or more kinds, "rendering" the raw data and making them more suitable or manageable for interpretation, valuing, and decision-making. In practice there may be little clear separation between the steps of data gathering, analyzing, and interpreting. This is, in fact, part of the problem faced by practitioners because analysis techniques must be tailored to purposes (see Chapter 3 for a review of purposes). Analysis techniques are also constrained by the character of the raw data.

Various forms of analysis are available in teacher evaluation. Some are very simple and easily utilized without specialized techniques. Other analytical tools are very complex, requiring specialized procedures, computer processing, and expert interpretations.

In an effort to be practical, this chapter will concentrate on illustrating a few analytical techniques that avoid both the very simple and the overly complex techniques of analysis. Basic analytical techniques are reviewed here to provide a frame of reference for concentrating upon their use in diagnostic analysis of teacher performance. Various diagnostic analyses are illustrated, drawing on the work of Flanders (1970), Mager and Pipes (1970), Brookover (1980), Borich and Fenton (1977), Tillman (1982), and Harris (1985). However, the real emphasis of the chapter is on the use of a conceptual model of teaching as the basis for diagnosis. Practical applications of this model for diagnostic analysis are illustrated using instruments and procedures provided in the DeTEK system (Harris and Hill, 1982).

Analysis and diagnosis applied to teaching behavior calls for clarity about the purposes and uses to which the evaluative results apply. The author continues to assume that teaching behavior is very complex, multidimensional, not fully observable, and not easily represented statistically, graphically, or in narrative forms. Hence, we approach analysis and diagnosis with limited purpose and much humility.

When the purpose is essentially developmental, both survey and diagnostic frames of reference are useful. The former calls for analytical techniques that aggregate raw data in ways that offer patterns, profiles, or other ways of communicating about great complexity in meaningful and useful ways. A new or different gestalt is derived.

In sharp contrast to the survey approach is diagnostic analysis. This calls for sifting and sorting of data, not for aggregating them. Instead, diagnosis calls for selecting out of a mass of data only those elements that have special meaning for specific kinds of actions—training, reinforcement, corrective feedback, etc. In using such techniques, the larger picture, the gestalt, is systematically sacrificed or ignored. The microscope replaces the wide-angle lens.

Exhibit 8.1 shows relationships among various types of evaluation, placing a special focus on diagnostic analysis as a form of developmental evaluation. Initially, educational evaluation is seen as instructional or noninstructional. Assuming an instructional focus, program evaluation vs. teacher evaluation can be differentiated. This is a somewhat artificial distinction, since teachers or personnel are inevitably related to other elements of program and vice versa.

A crucial distinction within teacher evaluation shown in Exhibit 8.1 includes the formative/developmental vs. summative/administrative evaluation. These distinctions have been discussed in previous chapters. The special distinction shown in this exhibit is between diagnostic analysis and survey uses of formative data.

BASIC ANALYTICAL MODES

Analytical techniques most commonly used for evaluation of teaching are rating, ranking, tabulating, coding, testing, computing, and plotting. These basic techniques are utilized in various forms, separately and in combinations, to produce displays of various kinds. Other techniques not so widely utilized include Q-sorting, branching, and a host of statistical computations involving specific techniques for manipulating raw data.

All analytical techniques presume the ready availability of data that are in appropriate form for use in a specific analytical process. For instance, ratings are applied to numerical values along a continuum of opinions, perceptions, or other raw data. If the data are not clear, then ratings are not applicable. Similarly, the tabulation technique presumes that the data represent discrete categories of behavior, such as nods, frowns, smiles, questions, etc. If the phenomena are not readily categorizable, then some other analytical technique is in order. Testing presumes that specific

Exhibit 8.1   Types of evaluation and analytical forms

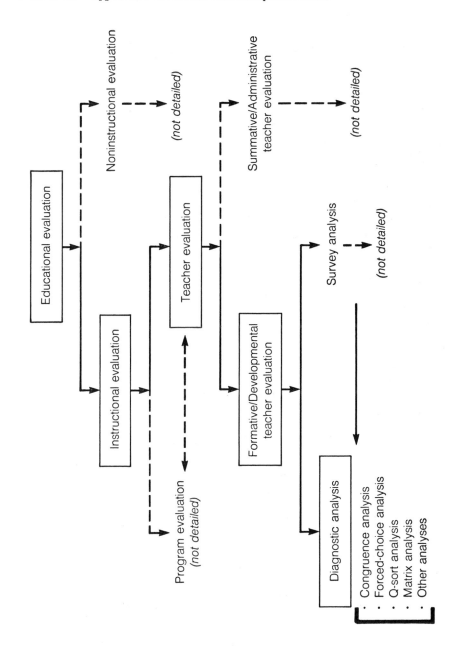

knowledges are likely to be possessed as raw data in the mind of the teacher. It is useless to test for knowledges that are irrelevant or not likely to be existent.

Evaluation specialists often distinguish between descriptions and measurement of teaching behavior (Borich and Jemelka 1981). This is very difficult because they are often intertwined. However, to the extent that we can separate description and measurement, clarity and utility are enhanced. The problem is complicated even more because measurement in a purely quantitative sense may be less useful than combinations of both qualitative and quantitative methods. Eisner (1977:346) gives perspective on this point in asserting, ". . . the improvement of education will result not so much from attempting to discover scientific methods . . . but rather by enabling teachers and others . . . to improve their ability *to see* and *think* about what they do." (italics added)

Flander's (1970) use of coding to analyze live or recorded verbal interactions between teacher and student illustrates an approach to raw data handling which is both qualitative and quantitative, but highly enlightening when displayed in a matrix analysis format (Anderson and Hansford, 1974).

Frequency Tabulations

When raw data is in appropriate forms simple tabulations of these data provide displays that can be quite easily interpreted. Frequency tabulations provide profiles or tabular displays such as the one below that facilitate simple comparisons.

Teacher questions coded by type may be analyzed to produce a profile as shown here:

Question Type	Frequency of Use	Total	Percent
Recognition	⊬⊬ ⊬⊬ 111	13	31.7
Recall	⊬⊬ ⊬⊬ ⊬⊬ 111	18	43.9
Comprehension	1111	4	9.8
Demonstration	1	1	2.5
Opinion	111	3	7.3
Analysis	1	1	2.5
Attitude or Value	1	1	2.5
Synthesis or Application		0	-0-
Total—All Questions		41	100.2

Further analysis using simple computations are reflected in row and column totals and percentages. Without further analysis some interpretations can be drawn about this sample of observed teacher questioning.

A 2 x 2 analysis using the same raw data on questioning could provide still additional interpretations.

Question Types	Questions Directed To:		
	Anglo Students	Minority Students	Total
Lower Level			
(Recognition recall)	11 =26.8%	20 =48.8%	31 =75.6%
Higher Level			
(All except recognition and recall)	7 =17.1%	3 =7.3%	10 =24.4%
Totals: Questions	18 = 43.9%	23 = 56.1%	41 = 100%

This tabulation forming a 2 X 2 table of frequencies has a different form and a different purpose than did the previous illustration. Interpretations of such displays are also a bit tricky, and further computations as well as related information are important for interpreting purposes.

Two by three analyses are also sometimes utilized for comparing frequencies in six categories. These tend to become somewhat unwieldy for interpretation.

Scattergram Analysis

Two independent types of data can be analyzed and displayed using the scattergram as a type of graphic analysis. The relationship of teacher questions to students by grade average are shown to illustrate such analyses.

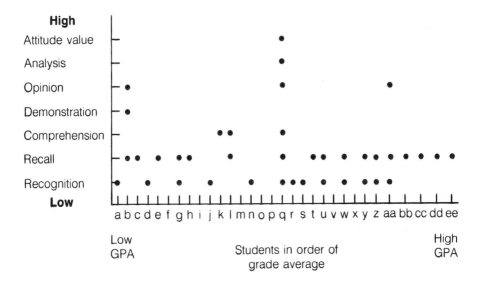

This display offers opportunities for somewhat different interpretations of teacher questioning. Little tendency to challenge the more able students with higher level questions is shown.

Bar and Line Graphs

These simple graphic displays are widely utilized in other fields to make comparisons, usually over time. Such displays have been utilized in teacher evaluation to a limited extent (Borich and Fenton, 1977). A line graph showing the same teacher's use of individualization techniques over three different observations is shown here:

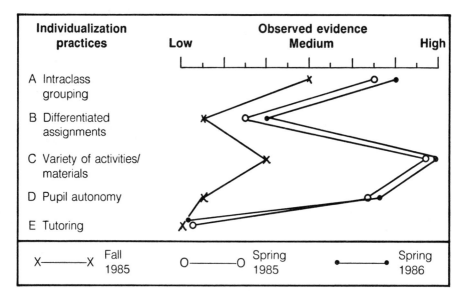

This set of lines can be interpreted to reflect meanings of a variety of kinds. Growth is evident in all but one area of practice. Most growth occurred between Fall and Spring, 1985. Little or no growth in "tutoring" leaves it the weakest area of practice, while striking growth in C, "variety of activities materials," makes it the teacher's strongest area of practice.

Bar graphs involve much the same analytical techniques as line graphs but permit more comparisons. Estimates on specific indicators in the DeTEK system over time are shown below.

Forced-Choice Analysis

Although widely studied, forced-choice techniques, including Q-sort analysis, have been utilized only in limited situations for teacher evaluation. Pearson (1980) recently studied one very simple form of forced choice analysis and found it useful in describing teacher behavior. DeTEK (Harris)

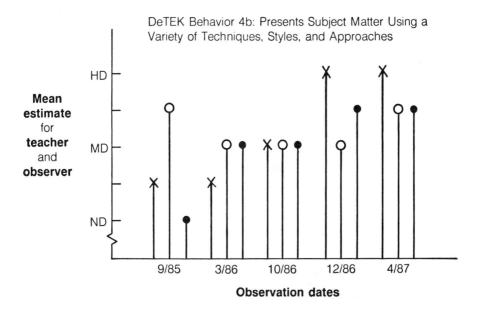

DeTEK Behavior 4b: Presents Subject Matter Using a
Variety of Techniques, Styles, and Approaches

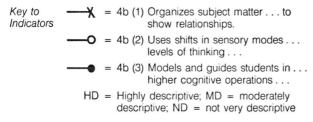

Key to   ━━✗   = 4b (1) Organizes subject matter . . . to
Indicators   show relationships.

             ━━O   = 4b (2) Uses shifts in sensory modes . . .
                            levels of thinking . . .

             ━━●   = 4b (3) Models and guides students in . . .
                            higher cognitive operations . . .

        HD = Highly descriptive; MD = moderately
              descriptive; ND = not very descriptive

utilizes a simplified forced choice inventory for teacher self-analysis (see Appendix C-1).

Forced choices as utilized by Pearson involves both discriminating choice making and weighting those choices. Exhibit 8.2 provides an illustration of the analysis involved.

In all, eighty teacher behaviors are displayed in clusters of four. The teacher is described (or describes self) by choosing only two of each of the four behaviors as most descriptive of actual performance. The specific behavior choices are then re-analyzed showing the pattern of choices within eight performance categories.* As illustrated in Exhibit 8.2 weighted values are assigned to chosen criteria to reflect their importance in this situation or assignment. Such analytical techniques can reveal patterns of practice by major categories based on either self-reports or observer reports. This

---

*Only 1 of 20 clusters and only 3 of 8 performance patterns are shown in this illustration.

Exhibit 8.2 Self-analysis inventory*

Teacher _John Bills_   Date _October 11, 198-_

PART I- Forced Choices

(✓) 1. Speaks quietly and slowly   / / / / / / /X/ / / /
                                            Low   High

( ) 2. Challenges students with difficult
        material   / / / / / / / / / / /

( ) 3. Uses lots of different teaching
        methods   / / / / / / / / / / /.

(✓) 4. Talks with a pupil after school
        about an idea the pupil has had   / / / / /X/ / / / / /

PART II - Profile Summary

Directions: Transfer check marks for "chosen" behaviors to the
corresponding numbered parentheses.
         Compute sum of scaled values for "chosen", checked
items only. Record sums in score boxes.

Performance Categories	Behaviors			Score
1. Clarity	✓# 1(**8**) # 7( ) ✓#16(**6**) ✓#23(**5**)	#29( ) #33( ) ✓#41(**9**) #50( )	✓#48(**10**) #74( )	**38**
2. Variability	# 3( ) ✓#12(**6**) #18( ) ✓#26(**5**)	✓#38(**8**) #46( ) ✓#51(**9**) #57(**9**)	✓#65(**7**) #72( )	**44**
3. Enthusiasm	#14( ) ✓#22(**2**) #34( ) #47( )	✓#59(**4**) ✓#64(**3**) #68( ) #69( )	✓#70(**8**) #77( )	**17**
4. Relationship to Students	# 9( ) #20(**9**) #21( ) #32( )	#35( ) #44( ) ✓#60(**5**) #66( )	#75( ) #78( )	**14**

*Based on *Pearson's Teacher Behavior Profile, (1980).*

analysis is not, however, highly diagnostic. Instead, it tends to provide
more information of the survey type.

An adaptation of this forced-choice technique to congruence analysis
is illustrated in the next section of this chapter. It suggests possible diagnostic outcomes. Furthermore, Q-sort analysis, also a forced-choice technique,
can be highly diagnostic.

Profile Analysis

A profile analysis technique was developed in the DeKalb (1975) assessment project in Georgia to utilize a wide variety of instruments and data
sources. Tests, observations, interviews, and self-reports were among the

EXHIBIT 8.3 Profile analysis

Teacher **Virginia Abrahams**   Date **Nov. 20, 198-**

School **Southmost Jr. High**   Assignment **Homemaking**

Competency   **03- The teacher plans and prescribes**
objectives appropriate to each student's/group's iden-
tified needs.

Performance Criteria	Data Source by Items					Summary	
	Observations			Inter-	Ques-	Score/	
	Supv.	Teach.	Adm.	view	tionnaire	Possible	%
#1- Selects objectives...	3 [X] 4 [X]	3 [X] 4 [X]	3 [X] 4 [ ]		15a [X] 17 [ ]	**6 / 8**	**75**
#2- Reviews learner style....				6 [X]	12 [X] 15d [ ]	**2 / 3**	**67**
#3- Matches.......	8 [ ]	8 [X]	8 [X] 11 [X]			**3 / 4**	**75**
TOTAL: Competency	---					**31 / 42**	**74** %

various types of instruments utilized. The challenge was to combine these data to produce a single informative profile. Exhibit 8.3 is an illustration of this type of profile. For each of the twenty "competencies," a separate profile is utilized. Specific performance criteria are scored for two or more sources. The profile reports both the specific item and the performance estimate based on an established criterion of success. An item is marked with an "X" if the item is at or above the criterion level. Items are left unmarked if below the success level.

Such a profile shows that overall level of success in demonstrating a major competency. Additionally, specific performance criteria are shown to be high or low as scored on various data sources. The most diagnostically useful information is retained by reporting specific items yet to be "passed." Those items marked with an "X" indicate pass, while those left blank are yet to be demonstrated, using a criterion-reference made of scoring.

Other Analytical Techniques

The use of matrix analysis and rating scales are illustrated in a variety of other works and need no further attention here. Less well known techniques for analysis, both quantitative and qualitative, that have been utilized, include branching diagram analysis (Haris, 1984), path analysis (Borich and Fenton, 1977), and Q-sort analysis. Space does not permit depicting each of these in detail. However, a brief description of some lesser known analytical techniques should alert the reader to possibilities for new and better practices. Q-sort techniques for diagnostic purposes are illustrated in the following section of this chapter.

Mager and Pipes (1970) detailed a simple but useful analytical sequence. Starting with the assumption of a "performance discrepancy," they chart a sequence of steps.

1. Is there a discrepancy? If yes . . .
2. Is the discrepancy important? If yes . . .
3. Is the discrepancy a skill deficiency? If yes . . . see #4. If no . . . see #7.
4. Is the skill one that was previously present? If yes . . .
   a. Arrange feedback to reinforce its use.
   b. If no . . . arrange training opportunities.
   . . .
7. If discrepancy is not a skill, then consider situational factors.

A series of logically sequenced questions continues to guide the diagnostic use of the information available.

Tillman (1982) employs a similar logical-analytical technique for "trouble-shooting" classroom problems. A logically sequenced series of questions is utilized to diagnose the character of a problem about which there is information.

Assessment center techniques for analysis of performance have utilized a wide variety of kinds of data—interviews, questionnaires, tests, simulations, etc. The unique analytical techniques involve a panel of "judges" utilizing common data sources and standardized procedures for summarizing and valuing. The assessment center project of the National Association of Secondary School Principals (Hersey 1982, Schmitt et al., 1982) is related to principal selection but purports to have diagnostic capabilities, too. It is probably too early in the testing stages of this project to know how useful the assessment center approach might be. Apparently, it has been effective for selection purposes (Campbell and Bray, 1965; Byham and Pentecost, 1970; McConnell, 1971), but such summative purposes are likely to pose additional constraints on these techniques for routine use in teacher evaluation (Merritt, 1973).

A DIAGNOSTIC MODEL OF TEACHING

Because of its enormous complexity, teaching behavior can be viewed more clearly using one or more simplified models that make the complexity manageable for analytical purposes. Such models are widely used in nearly all fields of professional endeavor. The physical models of the struc-tures of atoms and molecules that are utilized by chemists are crude and simple but useful. The architect's model of a proposed new building is neat and simple, helping to convey some limited understanding about the real structure as it might emerge. All maps are models of terrain in that they are extremely simplified but useful tools for geographers, pilots, and truckers, too.

A model of teaching to serve both survey and diagnostic analysis purposes is illustrated and discussed below. It is only one way of viewing teaching. Its merits are in its usefulness in thinking about teaching in comprehensive yet diagnostic ways and its value in explaining conflicting views.

In earlier chapters the research on teacher effectiveness and the utility of detailed specifications of behaviors for evaluating teaching have been discussed. Our state of knowledge about teaching has been presented as substantial, even though all too limited. Given our current understanding, the following assumptions about teaching can be proffered:

1. Teaching involves an enormous array of behaviors (thinking, act-ing, and feeling).
2. Teaching occurs in a variety of places over extended periods of time.
3. Teaching is *not* all behavior of the teacher, but only that which is related to instructional goals and, hence, student learning.
4. The most crucial manifestations of teaching are those of the class-room when students are involved.
5. Teaching behaviors are known well enough to be crudely classified as effective, not effective, and uncertain.

With these assumptions in mind, we can define and classify teaching behaviors in a variety of useful ways. Some of these include:

- All known teaching behaviors . . .
  a. in common use and known to be effective
  b. not in common use but known to be effective
  c. effectiveness uncertain—still to be fully established
  d. known not to be effective
- All other behaviors (nonteaching) . . .

A Map of Known Teaching Behaviors

Exhibit 8.4 presents a view of these various kinds of behavior as a map. The irregularly outlined area represents all known teaching behaviors, with nonteaching behaviors falling outside this area. Within the irregularly de-fined area is a square representing both known and uncertain areas of

Exhibit 8.4   A map of teaching

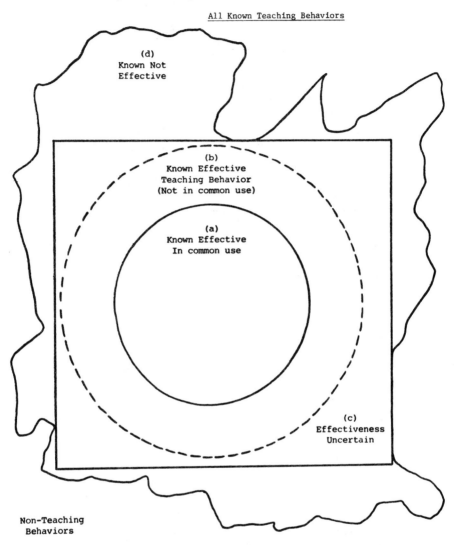

effective teaching behavior. Area "a" embraces behaviors in common use and known to be effective in promoting student learning. Area "b" embraces known effective behaviors not in common use. Area "c" embraces behaviors of uncertain effectiveness that may or may not be in common use. Area "d" lies outside the square area and embraces known teaching practices that are not effective. These may range from harmful to neutral in their effects on student learning.

This map is an overly simple representation of the state of the science and art of teaching (Gage, 1978). It defines areas of practice, but does not specify the behaviors themselves. It addresses the "field" of teaching practice, not the individual teacher. No special attention is directed by this model (map) to the distinctions between generic and specialized behaviors.

Mapping Specific Behaviors

Exhibit 8.4 defines and classifies four arrays of behaviors that presumably can be explicated as specific practices. Without attempting such an explication (see Chapter 5 for illustrations), the map can be made more useful by designating a hypothetical array of such behaviors, as shown in Exhibit 8.5. Small circles in various forms represent designated behaviors of each of the four types defined in the legend.

In reading Exhibit 8.5, it should be recognized that the designated behaviors are illustrative of a much larger array. Area "a" probably could embrace at least forty behaviors of the broadly specified kinds in common use. If explicated at more detailed levels, two hundred behaviors might be included in Area "a". A substantially larger number could be embraced in Areas "b" and "c", if we can judge by the enumerations in Dodl's "catalog of teaching competencies" (1972) or those by Harris and Burks (1982). To my knowledge, there is no systematic study or enumeration of the behaviors included in area "d." Surely these are also numerous.

A Map of Six Performance Areas

Exhibit 8.6 uses our map of teaching practices to focus on categories of behaviors. It would be less than helpful if our model (map) of teaching practices gave the impression that hundreds, even thousands, of known behaviors are exhibited by teachers as isolated events. Obviously, there are patterns of behavior exhibited in the work of all except the most disorganized. In this exhibit, the full array of known and promising behaviors is divided into six performance areas based on the DeTEK system of specifying teaching behaviors. Other categories could be superimposed on our map, so long as they are behavioral and related to teaching.

Plotting Individual Teaching Styles

The utility of the map as a model of teaching practices for survey purposes with individual teachers is explored in Exhibit 8.7. If our map reflects a full array of behaviors that are known and have some potential value in helping students learn, then by surveying the demonstrated behaviors of any individual teacher, a pattern of practices or the "teaching style" of the individual teacher can be plotted.

Exhibit 8.7 illustrates the plotted teaching style for hypothetical teachers "x" and "y." The styles are characterized by differentiated patterns of use of the array of specified behaviors in each of the six performance areas. The styles are further characterized by the extent of coverage of behaviors in area "a" as distinguished from "b" or "c." In these two illustrations, the plotted "styles" do not extend into area "d," reflecting the

EXHIBIT 8.5   A map of teaching with behaviors designated

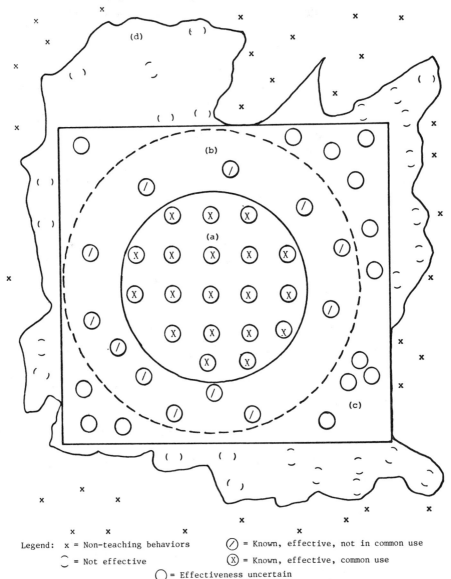

Legend: x = Non-teaching behaviors   ⊘ = Known, effective, not in common use

⌒ = Not effective   Ⓧ = Known, effective, common use

◯ = Effectiveness uncertain

use of noneffective behaviors. Such plots, as well as many others, are possible.*

---

*The utility of plotting teaching patterns or styles in a map like this can be "tested" by the reader using Exhibit 8.6 and a piece of tracing paper or transparency film. With a designated set of behaviors and a specific teacher in mind, plot his or her demonstrated behaviors, outlining the areas to be included. Then plot a contrasting teacher (yourself perhaps). Note similarities and differences.

EXHIBIT 8.6   A map of teaching: six performance areas*

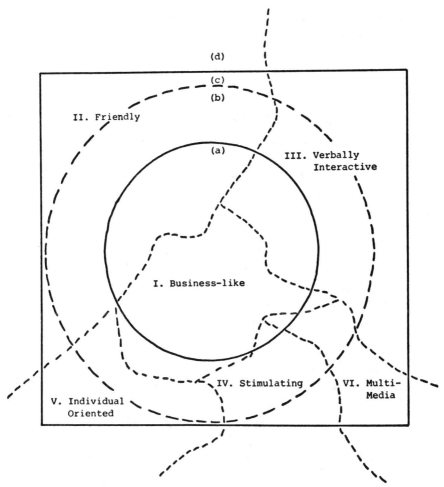

*This representation of a map of teaching was first presented in a televised lecture by Ben M. Harris, entitled, "Improving Teaching Thru Diagnostic Assessment", Region IV Education Service Center, Instructional Television Network, Project InterAct, Houston, Texas, November 1, 1983.

As crude as these plotted styles may be, they still are more realistic and useful than many in current use. Certainly, such ways of thinking about and analyzing teaching behavior are distinctly more promising than continued classification of teachers as "excellent," "poor," "average," or "very talented," or "conscientious."

The maps presented so far in this chapter have been models of teaching, not actual descriptions and analyses of real teaching. Hence, we are proposing ways of thinking about teaching, its patterns and differing styles.

EXHIBIT 8.7   Illustrations of plotted teaching "styles" for two teachers

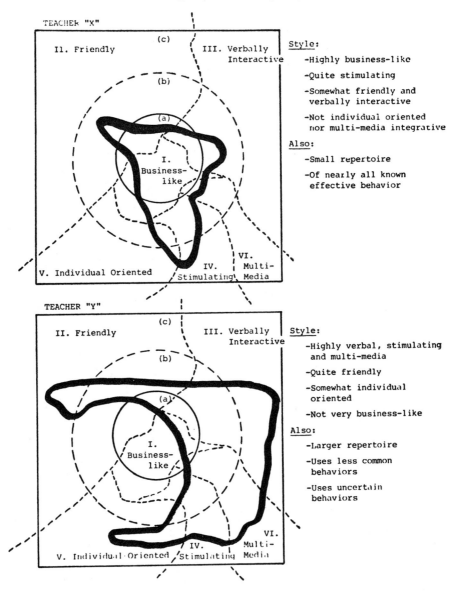

The maps might serve as analytical techniques as well as models, but much more precise procedures would be required. Again, an analogy may be useful. A simple physical-political world globe is an excellent model for use in thinking about the land and sea areas of the earth and recognizing important relationships, distances, directions, elevations, etc. Nonetheless, much more precise maps and tools are needed by navigators.

Comparing Contrasting Perceptions of Teaching

One of the perplexing concerns about teaching practices is that of differing perceptions. Teachers, students, principals, supervisors, and fellow teachers all have somewhat divergent ways of perceiving the same teacher. This is hardly surprising, since teaching is very complex and no source of data is truly adequate. What is promising is the fact that there is substantial agreement among trained observers on many teaching behaviors (see Chapter 7).

What is truly exciting, from a developmental evaluation perspective, is the ease with which simple survey techniques produce strong agreements on behaviors not clearly in evidence.

A map of teaching behaviors is useful in thinking about the differences in perceptions of teaching and their use in selecting foci for diagnostic analyses of teaching. Figure 8.8 illustrates a map of teaching behaviors with only two perceptions plotted for a single teacher. In this instance, the

EXHIBIT 8.8   A map of teaching behavior: two contrasting perceptions

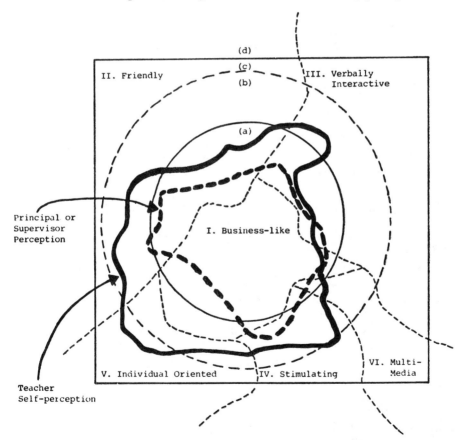

self-perception of the teacher is plotted with a solid line, while the perception of a principal, supervisor, or other knowledgeable observer is plotted as a broken line.

Even at first glance, both similarities and differences are apparent. Both maps embrace much common area, especially regarding businesslike behaviors. Individual-oriented behaviors are not included in the map of perceptions of the observer, as they are in the teacher's self-perceptions. There is close agreement in perceptions of multi-media behaviors. There are differences in the total area plotted, indicating that teacher self-perceptions embrace more behaviors in five of the six categories of practice.

If we concentrate on differences in perceptions graphically represented in Exhibit 8.8, they are numerous and might cause great concern. Obviously, both views cannot be completely valid. The differences in many instances are so discrepant that serious challenges might emerge, promoting confrontations, conflicts, and even frustrations.

However, if we concentrate on agreements rather than disagreements, they are numerous, interesting, and useful. Based on Exhibit 8.8 there is agreement that the teacher is perceived as:

1. More highly businesslike than anything else
2. Not eliciting multi-media behaviors.
3. Exhibiting friendly behaviors of limited kinds.
4. Eliciting friendly behaviors of both common and not-so-common varieties.
5. Exhibiting rather limited, verbally interactive, behaviors, largely of commonly used kinds.

Such agreements in perceptions, both positive and negative, are the basis for selecting one or more foci for diagnostic analysis procedures.

Selecting Foci for Diagnostic Analysis

All illustrations of the use of a map of teaching behaviors presented to this point represent survey efforts. We have yet to use these models in diagnostic ways. Diagnostic analysis of teaching practices requires a specific focus to deal with a few sharply defined performance criteria in sufficient detail to clearly differentiate those to be reinforced and those needing to be improved.

Exhibit 8.8 suggests ways of selecting foci. One or more areas of disagreement could be selected. However, at least five areas of agreement are also available. Using a crude map of two contrasting perceptions offers at least three alternative kinds of foci for diagnostic analysis.

1. Areas of agreement on demonstrated analysis.
2. Areas of disagreement on demonstrated practice.
3. Areas of agreement on practices not demonstrated.

When a third or fourth perception is utilized, further comparisons can be made and still other kinds of foci for diagnosis often emerge. For instance, if students or peer-teacher observers are utilized, their plotted perceptions also show both similarities and differences.*

When three or more perceptions of informed observers are compared, the foci that are available to consider for diagnostic analysis include:

1. All agree—behaviors are clearly demonstrated.
2. All agree—behaviors are *not* demonstrated.
3. Two of three agree—behaviors are demonstrated.
4. Two of three agree—behaviors are *not* demonstrated.

There are generally too many foci for all to be utilized. Some selections need to be made. (1) Focusing one or more areas where all agree positively can lead to confirmation of accomplishments. (2) Focusing one or more areas where all agree negatively can lead to confirmation and clarification of needs. (3) Identifying areas of disagreement reveals the uncertainties that need more attention in survey format.

Exhibit 8.9 illustrates the map of teaching practices shown in Exhibit 8.8, with a third set of perceptions added. For the sake of clarification, the areas of "(2) All agree—behaviors not demonstrated" are unshaded and lie outside all the plotted areas. The inner-shaded area clearly reflects "(1) All agree—behaviors clearly demonstrated." The cross-hatched areas are "(4) Two of three agree—behaviors *not* demonstrated". The remaining unshaded areas represent "(3) Two of three agree—behaviors demonstrated."

Selecting one or a limited number of areas for focused diagnostic analysis involves a variety of considerations. Areas within the circle of common practices might deserve special attention if all agree such an area is "not demonstrated." Areas outside the circle of "known to be effective" might warrant less attention (see Exhibit 8.5).

Areas within any category that is largely not demonstrated might deserve special attention. For instance, in Exhibit 8.9 performance categories III (Verbally Interactive), V (Stimulating), and VI (Multi-media) are all relatively neglected and, hence, might warrant selection for diagnostic analysis.

Three behaviors are designated in Exhibit 8.9 to represent selected behaviors for diagnostic analysis. Selections in these instances—X, Y, and Z—reflect three different areas of the map and three different categories of performance (I, III, and VI). They also reflect areas of behavior of three different kinds.

---

*Try analyzing the teaching presented in Exhibit 8.8, hypothesizing a third perception. Using tracing paper or a sheet of film, draw a similar but somewhat different map representing a third perception. Now find agreements.

EXHIBIT 8.9   Foci for diagnostic analysis from three contrasting perceptions

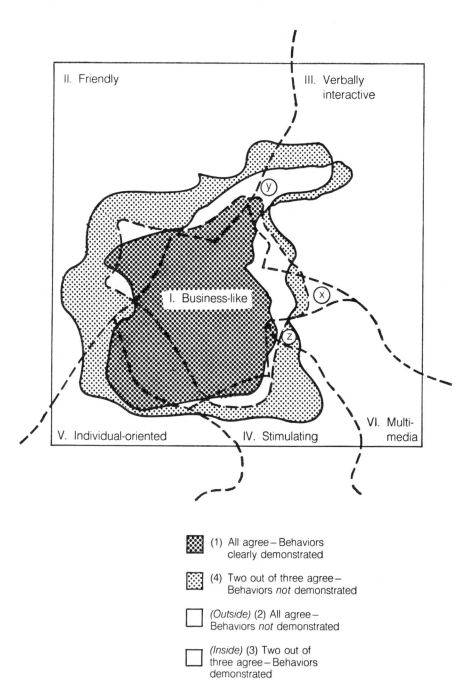

II. Friendly

III. Verbally interactive

I. Business-like

V. Individual-oriented

IV. Stimulating

VI. Multi-media

▨ (1) All agree – Behaviors clearly demonstrated

▧ (4) Two out of three agree – Behaviors *not* demonstrated

☐ *(Outside)* (2) All agree – Behaviors *not* demonstrated

☐ *(Inside)* (3) Two out of three agree – Behaviors demonstrated

DIAGNOSTIC ANALYSIS BY CONGRUENCE

A diagnostic analysis technique especially useful in working with teaching practices is congruence analysis. The preceding illustrations of contrasting perceptions of teaching using the mapping model represents a kind of congruence analysis for survey purposes. Diagnostic analysis builds on this same model of teaching, but demands more precise procedures.

Congruence with Three Sources

The illustration of three perceptions of teaching behaviors in Exhibit 8.9 can be a useful point of departure for demonstrating diagnostic congruence analysis techniques. If X, Y, and Z represent three major behaviors that are made explicit, the analysis can draw upon carefully focused observation data from three sources. Exhibit 8.10 presents the required information for diagnostic congruence analysis.

In this illustration the selected behaviors are (or had previously been) explicated according to procedures presented in Chapter 4. The twelve explicit criteria or indicators of performance are each utilized in careful classroom observations. Three observers are utilized independently. Their estimates of observed evidence are reported at three levels:

Yes = The teacher demonstrates the criterion behavior clearly, unequivocally, in high quality, and in appropriate ways.
No = The teacher demonstrates little or no behavior consonant with the criterion that is clear, high quality, and appropriate.
? = Evidence is observed that falls between the other two levels. Uncertainty is suggested.

Congruence analysis utilizes the three sets of estimates of performance to generate at least four types of diagnoses as follows:

A = *Accomplishments.* Diagnosis based on complete positive or high levels of congruence of estimates from the three sources.
N = *Need for Improvement.* Diagnosis based on complete or nearly complete congruence of negative or low levels of estimates from all sources.
U = *Uncertainty.* Diagnosis based on considerable incongruence of estimates from the three sources. (*Note:* Yes, ?, No represents maximum incongruence. ?, Yes, ? is still a high level of incongruence since ? often implies uncertainty within data sources. No, No, Yes is incongruence, suggesting real disagreements.)

EXHIBIT 8.10   Diagnostic congruence analysis: an illustration with 3 behaviors, 3 sources, and 12 criteria

Selected Explicated Performance Criteria		Self-Report (Teacher)	Observer Report (Principal)	Observer Report (Supervisor)	A = Accomplishment N = Need U = Uncertainty R = Refine or Upgrade
		Observe Evidence from Three Sources			*Diagnoses*
X Behavior 1d–Paces activities to assure task accomplishment.					
(1) Moves about the room surveying individual student activities.	(1)	Yes	Yes	Yes	A
(2) Reminds student group of time allocations.	(2)	Yes	?	No	U
(3) Adjusts time allocations to fit needs of individuals.	(3)	No	No	No	N #1 Priority
(4) Provides direct assistance to individuals and small groups in completing assigned tasks.	(4)	Yes	?	?	R
Y Behavior 3b—Encourages and guides student responses and interactions.					
(5) Gives information and makes suggestions to stimulate and guide student activity.	(5)	Yes	Yes	?	R
(6) Asks students for information and for suggestions beyond recitation and routine.	(6)	Yes	No	No	U
(7) Waits extended periods of time, (3-5 seconds) following questions, to allow for a student response.	(7)	?	No	No	N #4 Priority
(8) Listens thoughtfully to student questions and ideas, nodding, keeping eye contact, and avoiding interruptions.	(8)	Yes	No	No	N
Z Behavior 6b—Involves students actively in multi-sensory experiences.					
(9) Directs students in role playing in connection with assignments.	(9)	No	No	No	N #2 Priority
(10) Arranges laboratory-type experiments for students.	(10)	?	?	?	R or U?

	Observe Evidence from Three Sources			Diagnoses
Selected Explicated Performance Criteria	Self-Report (Teacher)	Observer Report (Principal)	Observer Report (Supervisor)	A = Accomplishment N = Need U = Uncertainty R = Refine or Upgrade
(11) Assigns and outlines action-research projects for students as regular assignments. (11)	No	No	No	N #3 Priority
(12) Utilizes games that simulate real situations. (12)	?	No	?	U

R = Refine or Upgrade. This diagnosis is based on incongruence that involves only positive estimates along with question marks (?). To the extent that question marks may represent some uncertainty but also a more limited level of positive evidence, they often support the "refine and upgrade" diagnosis.

When all estimates are congruent with question marks (?, ?, ?), then an R diagnosis might still be justifiable.

The various diagnoses generated in Exhibit 8.10 are straightforward and logically derived from the data displays. The diagnostic ground rules suggested above in defining the four types of diagnosis make practical sense, given some faith in the data sources and the purposes of diagnostic analysis. The three sets of data must have some validity. Completely subjective, biased, or speculative data sources would hardly be trustworthy for this or any other purpose. Also, diagnostic analysis has as its prime objective the clear differentiation of behaviors that, on the one hand, can be reinforced, recognized, and rewarded because they are technical accomplishments or competencies. On the other hand, diagnostic analysis aims to clearly differentiate specific behaviors which are not part of the teacher's repertoire of competencies and, hence, are candidates for improvement through training, coaching, modeling, etc.

By-products of this relatively simple diagnostic congruence analysis technique are diagnoses of "up-grading" or "refinement" of practice. This need to differentiate between lack of capability requiring basic training and those capabilities needing supportive services and self-initiated efforts was hypothesized long ago by Mager and Pipes (1972). It has been largely neglected in in-service training, evaluation, and clinical supervision practice as well as in the literature.

Modified approaches to diagnostic congruence analysis are worthy of consideration. The same techniques can be utilized in the absence of systematic classroom observation focused upon specific selected behaviors. A carefully developed checklist of explicated criteria can be utilized by three or more knowledgeable individuals. This procedure runs risks of generating data with too little validity to be useful. In the DeSCAS system for diagnostic analysis of supervisory competencies, simple ratings of explicated criteria by a variety of subordinates, peers, superordinates, and self have been used to produce seemingly discriminating diagnoses (Harris, 1982).

Another approach utilizes the frequency of responses of students as one of the three data sources. This is illustrated in the DeTEK system discussed below.

Forced-Choice Congruence

The map of teaching behaviors can produce a clear focus for diagnostic analysis, which then can be used with forced-choice instrumentation and congruence analysis techniques.

Forced-choice inventories, when utilized with both self-descriptions and the descriptions of knowledgeable others, permits congruence analysis of diagnostic value. A limited number of very explicit criteria are utilized, with each criterion paired with every other one. Once choices are completed, a profile of frequencies of preferred choices emerges (see Appendix C-1).

This analytical format is shown in Exhibit 8.11. Only the one focus X has been selected, and it has been explicated to produce six specific criteria of performance. These are instrumented in pairs, with each criterion paired with every other one. For example:

> *The teacher . . . .*
> (   )—Moves about the room surveying individual student activities. (1)
> or
> (   )—Provides direct assistance to individuals in completing their assignments. (4a)
> –
> (   )—Reminds the entire group of students about time allocations. (2)
> or
> (   )—Moves about the room surveying individual student activities. (1)

A complete inventory of this kind will have fifteen pairs for six criterion statements. The frequency tabulations shown on the illustrative profile (Exhibit 8.11) are for only two knowledgeable respondents. Three or more could be utilized. The diagnoses that emerge are necessarily somewhat more limited. "Needs for improvement" diagnoses seem plausible for those criteria being chosen very infrequently by both respondents. High levels of frequency of choice can hardly be regarded as "accomplishments," since the focus was selected in an area of the teaching behavior map that suggested lack of demonstrated performance.

Q-Sort Congruence

Q-sort technique offers still another alternative for use in diagnostic analysis. Q-sorting of an array of explicated criterion statements has advantages

EXHIBIT 8.11 Diagnostic profile illustrating diagnostic analysis by forced-choice data

Focus X: Behavior: 1d-Paces student activities . . . .

	Frequency of Choices			
Explicated Criteria of Performance (Selected)	Self	Supervisor or other	Diagnoses	Priority
(1) Moves about the room surveying individual student activities.	1	0	Need	#1
(2) Reminds the entire group of students about time allocations.	5	4	—	
(2a) Reminds individuals of time allocations when needed.	2	5	Uncertainty	
(3) Adjusts time allocations to fit needs of individuals.	0	2	Need	#2
(4) Provides small group work to assist students with their assignments.	5	4	—	
(4a) Provides direct assistance to individuals in helping complete assignments.	2	0	Need	#3
Total tallies =	(15)	(15)		

in permitting the analysis of a larger number of selected criteria and thus more selected foci. Disadvantages are found in the time required, the special materials (cards, etc.) to be prepared, and the special procedures that need to be followed. (See Chapter 6 for instrumentation details.)

Keeping in mind that the Q-sort technique requires the forced ordering of criteria to form a normal distribution, several steps are required after a full array of explicated criterion statements are placed on small (3 X 5) cards. Using a self-analysis format, the procedures include the following:

1. Distribute cards, place each card in one of six categories, ranging from
   a—Not something I do, and I can't do it.
   b—Not something I do, but I probably could do it in limited ways.
   c—Something I do, but only in limited ways.
   d—Something I do fairly well, but maybe not well enough.

e—Something I do reasonably well, but not often.
f—Something I do quite often and quite well.
2. Redistribute each stack of cards, category by category (a through f), to form a normal distribution.
   5% or 1/20 in categories a and f
   15% or 1/7 in categories b and e
   30% or 1/3 in categories c and d
3. Eliminate all cards in categories c and d. (Put them aside; they are not to be used further at this time.)
4. Redistribute all cards from categories e and f, using five levels of "competence" as follows:

C-1	C-2	C-3	C-4	C-5
5%	20%	50%	20%	5%
Least clearly competent				Most clearly highly competent

Again, use a forced distribution, putting approximately half of the cards in the middle category and only one in twenty (but at least one) in each of the extreme categories. All other cards go into C-2 and C-4.
5. Redistribute all cards in categories a and b in the same manner as above. Your scale now is:

N-1	N-2	N-3	N-4	N-5
Most clearly a need				Least clearly a need

6. Transfer criterion statements to a profile (See Exhibit 8.12) for C-4 and C-5 and N-1 and N-2 *only.*
7. Have informed observers—principal, supervisor, and team leader—repeat the procedure.

An illustration of the diagnoses that derive from a Q-sort completed by three observers is shown in Exhibit 8.12. A set of forty criteria, all related to (1) clarity of presentation and (2) giving directions, produced this diagnostic profile.

Q-sorting is combined with congruence analysis techniques to produce a few very clear diagnoses of both accomplishment and needs for improvement. Uncertainties continue to emerge, reflecting incongruence in perceptions of the three observers. The forced ordering of a full array of

EXHIBIT 8.12   Congruence analysis illustration using Q-sort data from 3-sources

| Explicated Criteria Statements | Weighted Values* | | | | |
	Self-Analysis	Principal Analysis	Other Supervisor	Sum of Weights	Diagnosis
#6. Teaches things step by step	(++)	(+)	(0)	+3	Refine
#13. Gives specific details	(+)	(−)	(+)	+1	Uncertain
#1. Explains things simply	(+)	(++)	(++)	+5	Accomplish-ment
#17. Explains, then stops so students can think about it.	(−)	(−)	(−−)	−4	Need
#21. Shows examples of how to do the work.	(−−)	(−)	(−−)	−5	Need
#24. Asks questions to find out if students really understand.	(−)	(−)	(0)	−2	Uncertain
#4. Stays with topic until students understand.	(−)	(0)	(0)	−1	Uncertain

*Assign values as follows: ++=+2   +=+1   Insert zeros (0) for all blanks.
                            −−=−2   −=−1

explicated criteria, followed by a re-ordering of only the top and bottom portions of the distribution, increases the discrimination among criteria if observers are really knowledgeable. The use of weighted values (++, +, 0, −, −−) in making final diagnostic decisions adds still more to the precision of the analysis.

SUMMARY

The systematic analysis of teacher evaluation data is essential to the translation of raw information into meaningful interpretations. Even the simple, unsophisticated modes of analysis illustrated in this chapter can be revealing. However, the complexity of teaching behavior calls for much more sophisticated analysis than is currently in general use. This is especially important with regard to diagnostic analysis.

In focusing on diagnostic analysis, a framework for viewing teaching, mapping the known and unknown realities, provides ways of thinking about teaching that are manageable. The various uses of forced-choice instrumentation and congruence analysis techniques appear to be quite promising. Above all, such diagnoses can be made without imposing global values and without resort to complicated statistical analysis.

SELECTED STUDY SOURCES

Borich, Gary D. and K. S. Fenton (1977). *The Appraisal of Teaching: Concepts and Process.* Reading, MA: Addison-Wesley Publishing Co.

Chapter 3 discusses a variety of applications of appraisal processes. Diagnostic, formative, and summative differences are analyzed.

Brookover, Wilbur B. (1980). "A Model for Research and Goal Achievement," in *Measuring and Attaining Goals of Education,* Alexandria, VA: Association for Supervision and Curriculum Development.

A series of flow charts are presented to graphically illustrate hypothesized relationships between school variables and educational outcomes. Teaching-learning process variables are shown as only one link in a chain of events. Figure 10 is most useful in relating teaching behavior to learning outcomes.

Flanders, Ned (1970). *Analyzing Teaching Behavior.* Reading, MA: Addison-Wesley Publishing Co.

A systematic review of both procedures and related research on which interaction analysis is based as applied by Flanders. Of unusual significance is matrix analysis technique.

Harris, Ben M. Harris (1985). *Supervisory Behavior in Education,* 3rd ed. Englewood Cliffs, NJ: Prentice-Hall, Inc.

Chapters on classroom observation and evaluation of instruction discuss qualitative vs. quantitative analysis, illustrate analytical techniques applied to observation data, and compare a variety of multi-factor evaluation techniques.

Harris, Ben M. (1979). "Orientation on Branching Diagram Analysis". *Studies in Educational Evaluation* 5 (1979): 157–161. Permagon Press, Ltd.

A description of an analytical system based on systems theory that has practical significance in many evaluation efforts.

Kulka, Richard A. (1979). "Interaction as Person-Environment Fit," in *New Directions for Methodology of Behavioral/Science,* Lynn R. Kahle, editor. Volume 2. San Francisco: Jossey-Bass, Inc.

Presents suggestions for using congruence estimates in studying personal/environmental fit. Cautions about potential hazards in using congruence scores.

Georgia Department of Education (1983). *Guidelines for the Implementation of Performance-Based Certification by Georgia Department of Education.* Regional Assessment Centers, and Local School Systems, Division of Staff Development. Atlanta, GA. mimeographed.

A detailed explanation of the new teacher certification/assessment process being utilized in Georgia Schools. Analytical techniques and instrumentation are both discussed in this document.

Shoemaker, David M. (1977). "The Contribution of Multiple Matrix Sampling to Evaluating Teacher Effectiveness," in *The Appraisal of Teaching: Concepts and Process* by Gary D. Borich and Kathleen S. Fenton, Reading, MA: Addison-Wesley Publishing Co. pp. 292–300.

A brief description of a multiple matrix sampling applied to student achievement testing. Translation of this technique for use in teacher assessment promises useful outcomes.

Tillman, Murray (1982). *Trouble-Shooting Classroom Problems.* Glenview, IL: Scott, Foresman and Co.

A vertical practical guide to systematically diagnosing problems observed in real classroom situations. The reader is guided to logically move from identifying a problem to fixing it.

9

Feedback, Action
Decisions, and Growth

INTRODUCTION

Well-analyzed information about teaching can affect classroom practice and learning only as it promotes desirable change. This chapter is concerned with the promoting of change in teaching practices by making use of evaluation data. The processes of evaluation discussed in Chapter 3 distinguish analysis, interpretation, valuing, and decisions from actions. The previous chapter emphasized analysis and introduced interpretation, but gave no attention to decision making and actions for improving teaching. This chapter will focus upon relating these final steps in the evaluation process to data gathering and analysis.

A transition from evaluation to staff development is involved in the latter steps of the evaluation process. There is no clear point of transition, however, because the entire process of evaluation influences attitudes, provides insights, and may even affect behavior. This is especially true when the evaluation process is highly collaborative, as illustrated in the DeTEK system (Harris and Hill, 1982), or in clinical (Garman, 1982) and collegial systems (Alfonso and Goldsberry, 1982). Both formally and informally, a truly developmental evaluation system is likely to affect both evaluator and evaluatee thinking, feelings, and behavior (Valverde, 1982). As Marcel Proust observed, "The voyage of discovery consists not in seeking new landscapes, but in having new eyes."

The feedback interview or conference is widely accepted as a primary vehicle for putting evaluation data to work. This may reflect too much reliance on face-to-face verbal interaction. In fact, a broad variety of activities has utility in the process of interpreting, valuing, and deciding on actions toward growth. Reading, re-analyzing, discussing, explaining, viewing, planning, prioritizing, and scheduling are a few terms suggesting possible follow-up events. Using this broadened perspective, this chapter will discuss a variety of procedures for what is traditionally thought of as feedback. The concept of collaboration and the practices that give special meaning to this term are discussed and illustrated. Finally, this chapter analyzes growth planning as a practical form of decision making and as a guide to action.

FEEDBACK

This term, so widely utilized in the various human professions, is unfortunate in many ways. It was borrowed from the field of electronics, where it refers to an amplification process that produces annoying, screeching noise (Jenerette, 1981). In many minds, feedback tends to emphasize telling and selling by an authority figure with passive listening by the teacher (Maier, 1976). Recent efforts at so-called "peer supervision" have sometimes utilized feedback in such crude and unstructured forms that negative effects clearly dominate (Pac-Urar and Vacca, 1984). Since we are not likely to replace the term with any that is acceptable, a clear and technically defensible set of practices needs to be defined. At least the warnings of Gerhard can be taken into consideration:

> Any amount of random tinkering with or expansion of unsystematic activity can only produce greater confusion and randomness . . . (1981:10).

Using Information

Feedback should be systematic, purposeful effort to utilize information from one or more sources to make decisions and project plans for constructive action. Two or more persons are generally involved. Information sources are often multiple, but even more importantly, information extends beyond evaluation data to include professional wisdom, known practices, traditions, constraints, perceptions, attitudes, and values.

In the context of developmental teacher evaluation in a formal school setting, decisions and plans for improvement will be constrained by job descriptions, goals, and resources of the institution. But overriding considerations are both personal and professional. A unique individual with feelings, concerns, insights, and motives is the object of the evaluation process, and we should not ignore the human side of education.

Alternative Strategies

Feedback that is not highly directive tends to follow a number of patterns including telling, asking, and probing.

Pattern #1—Tell the teacher all the nice or positive things you can think of, suggest at least one problem area, then ask for reactions, and hope something productive emerges. This pattern has no clear strategy beyond the first two steps. The flow of events is unpredictable, objectives are unclear and thus not often accomplished. The evaluator assumes the role of judge, conferring positive valuings on a host of practices. The teacher may accept a submissive listener's role, enjoy the compliments, agree with the problem innuendo, and fall into line by agreeing to do what the evaluator suggests. Such a passive/authoritarian relationship is hardly conducive to development. Furthermore, many teachers reject such roles and insist on being a party to the interpretation, valuing, and decision-making steps. When this is so, this pattern simply won't work.

Pattern #2—Ask how the teacher "feels" about the teaching, hope that a problem will be verbalized, and then hope a quick agreement can be reached. This pattern has a sharply conceived strategy: appear permissive, let the teacher talk, pounce upon any acknowledged problem to get quick and easy decisions for action. Unfortunately, this pattern promotes ignoring the data; as such it is unsystematic, assumes the teacher has diagnostic powers and insights, but limits their use.

Teachers have been known to make a game of this situation. Knowing the evaluator, the teacher may volunteer a problem that is closely related to the evaluator's biases. Other teachers choose a problem that is not focused on teaching—suggesting a student or a text or a curricular problem instead. Other teachers tell about the quality of the lesson, mention no problems, and force the evaluator to abandon his or her strategy.

Pattern #3—Probe the thinking of the teacher with a series of pointed questions that encourage critical review of self. This pattern is a bit more straight forward, more honest, than either of the two previously depicted. The strategy often is one of encouraging the teacher to relate his or her perceptions of the available evaluation data. Unless extended to include consideration of values, priorities, and decisions it may be only an exercise. Another problem associated with this pattern emerges if the teacher accepts the probing and comparing as an exercise in self-defense. Every perception may be either supported by the data or challenged because of "insufficient" or "unreliable" data.

Other patterns and combinations of these are often utilized. It is not possible to speak with any assurance about good, better, and best feedback practices. Blumberg (1980) and Patterson (1969) demonstrated the primitive nature of many supervisory conferences long ago. Real progress in understanding the dynamics of conferencing is being made through the efforts of clinical supervisors (Garman, 1982; Snyder, 1981). Recent emphasis on "collegial evaluation" (Roper et al., 1976) and "colleagueship" (Alphonso and Goldsberry, 1982) offer promise for extending practice beyond the assumptions of both clinical and peer supervision. The use of video-taping in feedback techniques offer still additional possibilities for practices that make the teacher a co-analyst (Kaplan, 1980).

Anxiety Levels

Much of the literature on classroom observation and feedback is preoccupied with concern for teacher anxiety (Withall and Wood, 1979). As discussed in Chapter 7, much of this concern about the presence of an observer in the classroom has been unwarranted, being either not serious or stemming from malpractice rather than from professional, sytematic observation. This concern for anxiety may also be unwarranted as related to feedback conferences.

Moody and Blackbourn (1980) report on a rather extensive study of both elementary and secondary teachers' perceptions of post-observational conferences by their principals. They found teachers to be generally positive toward conference situations and less positive toward principal practices. Most interesting was the finding that experienced teachers and older teachers were distinctly more positive about post-observation conferences than their younger peers.

In a more recent study, Blackbourn (1983) reports very high correlations between the collaborative behavior of the principal in evaluating instructors and their attitudes toward post-observational conferences. Pac-Urar and Vacca (1984) report failure for a peer observation-feedback project due to lack of training and faulty design, yet found teachers still ready for assistance from a variety of colleagues. The Glickman and Pajak (1984) study of teacher responses to supervisory conferences, stressing information vs. suggestions vs. directives, shows a clear pattern of acceptance of information and suggestions, with combinations of both information and suggestions being most well received by teachers. An extensive array of studies leads us to conclude that teacher acceptance of feedback on their teaching varies widely in response to style, content, the background of the individual and the situational context; yet these wide variations reflect more acceptance than resistance.

Experiences with the highly structured DeTEK approach to using both teacher self-report and observation data to guide diagnostic decision making continue to produce very positive teacher responses. Somewhat typical of such responses is the following:

> You know, this is the first time in 13 years of teaching that an administrator actually observed me and (then) attempted to help me.*

Such individual expressions of acceptance were further supported by a confidential survey in which 90 percent of participating teachers reported very positively (Harris, 1981).

---

*Reported by conference tape recording between a high school teacher and the assistant principal, 1983.

Hunter's Six Types

The six types of supervisory conferences suggested by Hunter (1980) are becoming widely recognized. A distinction is made between "conferences designed to improve instruction . . ." and those that are "evaluative." Five conference types suggested for the instructional improvement category are really differing purposes to be served:

A. To identify, label, and explain effective behaviors.
B. To stimulate a repertoire of additional behaviors.
C. To identify teaching behavior with which the teacher is *not* satisfied.
D. To identify teaching behaviors that are less effective, but not recognized by the teacher; and to develop alternatives.
E. To promote continuing growth.

Any one or any combination of these purposes might be worthy for a single feedback session. However, they can hardly be fully accomplished except over a long period of time. Hunter's type B and E are really overall, long-range goals. All feedback activities are likely to be concerned with these outcomes if the evaluation system is developmental. On the other hand, Hunter's types suggest to this writer a strategy, sequencing the efforts of the evaluator and evaluatee as follows:

- First, A—Identify, label, explain effective behaviors (evaluator).
- Second, C—Identify teaching behavior with which the teacher is *not* satisfied (evaluatee).
- Third, D—Identify teaching behaviors that are less effective, but not recognized by the teacher (evaluator).
- Fourth—Develop alternatives.
- Fifth, B and E—Promote growth in alternative behaviors directed toward a broader repertoire.

Except for the danger of such a strategy being needlessly authoritarian, the logic of the sequence of purposes has much to commend it. As a sequence of purposes, it gives focus and direction to the feedback activities.

A COLLABORATIVE MODEL

A feedback model serving developmental purposes will be necessarily collaborative in nature. If it is also data-based, it must give considerable attention to interpreting the data that is to be utilized for ". . . the validity of inferences go beyond the data . . ." (Cronback, 1980:7). However, interpersonal dynamics must still be considered, especially in the valuing process.

Finally, decision making leading to commitments for action will involve exploring alternatives, prioritizing, and consensus building.

Four Phases

Phase I of such a feedback process will focus on the data as analyzed and the meanings that can properly be attached to these data.

Phase II will engage conferees in assigning values to the interpretations derived.

Phase III will involve decision making regarding alternative courses of action.

Phase IV will involve planning for implementation of selected actions.

An Illustrative Scenario

To illustrate this four phase model for feedback, consider a conference in which the DeTEK system is being employed. Three sets of data have been generated and analyzed as shown in Exhibit 9.1. (See also Appendix C-6.)

Events

3:20 The teacher (**T**) enters the conference room, says "Hi," smiles a bit nervously. The evaluator (**E**) smiles broadly, "Hi. How are you?" (**T**) "Just fine, I guess." (**E**) "Sit here so we can look at the Diagnostic Analysis Worksheet together."

3:21 (**E**) "You've seen this worksheet before. I've just recorded all the data so we can begin to think about diagnoses."

(**T**) "Um huh. I see." (**T**) looks at worksheet as (E) moves it over toward (**T**) on the table so they both can see. (Pause)

3:22 (**E**) "We need to review these data from the three sources and see what diagnoses make sense."

(**T**) "I see. How do we do that?"

(**E**) "Well, you recall the three sources: me, the observer; you describing yourself; and your students reporting on your practices as they see them."

(**T**) "Yes, I put my instruments on your desk yesterday."

(**E**) "Right. I've analyzed what you gave me, and summarized it here in columns (2) and (5)."

Analysis Preliminaries
- Teacher shows some anxiety.
- Tries to be reassuring.
- Anxiety is evident. Phase I—Interpreting
- Structuring. (**E**) sets tone for working "together". Also places the data in focus.
- Emphasis is on procedures.
- Terminology. (**E**) refers to diagnoses rather than interpreting or analyzing.
- Time is provided for the teacher to become familiar with the data.
- Collaboration is stressed in positioning the worksheet.
- Interpretation is defined as the task at hand.
- Diagnosis is identified as outcome sought.
- Review of procedures for data gathering gives perspective to tasks at hand.

- Shared responsibility is acknowledged by teacher.
- Responsibility of evaluator for this aspect of data analysis recognized.

EXHIBIT 9.1 DeTEK instrument V: data analysis worksheet

Teacher _Albert Simpson_ Grade _10th_ Subject _Biology_ Date _Jan 10,19-_

School _Highlands Secondary_ Collaborator(s): ___ Prin.( ) Supv.(X) Other( )

PERFORMANCE # _1-Business_ BEHAVIOR # _1d - Paces activities to assure task accomplishment like... Plishment, arranging ... assistance ... to make progress..._

(1) Indicators (Write abbreviated description of indicators)	(2) Self-Report II	(3) Observation Report III	(4) Agree or Disagree	(5) Supplemental Student Report IV	(6) Accomplishments (Circle)	(7) NEEDS Yes-Uncertain
(1) Moves about...	ND	ND	Agree	5*	✱	Yes-Need #2
(2) Reminds group...	HD	HD	Agree	33	⊛	–
(2a) Reminds individuals...	MD	HD	Disagree	25	✱	Uncertain (need to refine?) #3
(3) Adjusts time... to fit...individuals...	ND	MD	Disagree	15	✱	Yes-Need #1
(4) Provides small group...	HD	HD	Agree	42	⊛	–
(4a) Provides direct assistance to individuals...	MD	ND	Disagree	19	✱	Uncertain #4

✱ Number of Student Reports = _48_

(8)
If "uncertain" is designated in col. 7, set date for an observation here.

Day _Thursday_
Date _Jan.23,19-_
Time _9:35_

3:23 (T) "OK. I see—I think. ND means I didn't think I was good at moving about . . . You agreed with me and the students too!"

• Teacher is demonstrating ability to interpret the data.

(E) "That's quite correct. One minor change in your interpretation though! ND only means that you estimated that practice as not very descriptive of your work in the classroom and my observations produced the same estimate."

• Reinforcement with some corrective feedback.

(T) "Now what do we do with that?

• Task orientation.

(E) "Well, why not look at the whole set of data first, then think together about whether we think the evidence strong enough for clear diagnoses."

• Task clarification.
• Collaboration in using data.

3:24 (T) "OK. Now that second indicator shows all of us agreeing that my practices are strong there. Right?"

• Initiative is shown as teacher moves on suggested next step.

(E) Nods and smiles. Waits. (Pause).

• Initiative is encouraged so teacher is as fully involved as possible in verbalizing the interpretation.

3:24 (T) "This is a curious set of . . ." T points to a set of estimates numbered (2a)]

(E) "Performance estimates"

• Terminology is clarified.

(T) "Yes. I estimated my practices as only moderate, but you observed me doing more." (Pauses. Frowns.)

• Intrepretation involves considering inconsistent and unclear data.
• Collaboration reinforced by allowing wait-time for teacher to use.

3:25 (E) Waits. Then says "What about the student estimate of your practice. 'Reminds individuals of time allocated . . .'?"

• Guiding attention to other data source as a question allows teacher an opportunity to extend the interpretation.

(T) They are divided on this practice. Only about one-half checked this one." (Frowns. Pauses.)

• Verbalizing the meaning of data.

3:26 (E) "Your interpretation is quite accurate. This illustrates inconsistency among data sources. You and your students seem to be estimating the practice very much alike. It is the observer whose estimate is different. This is very common.

• Reinforcement.
• Verbalizing an interpretation of data.
• Accepting incongruence in estimates.

Interpretation of data continues in this general way until all data are given at least some attention and their meanings considered. Then, a shift to valuing is initiated.

Events	*Analysis Phase II—Valuing*
3:30 **(E)** "Let's see if we can convert these data sets into diagnoses. We have guidelines to follow, but we will also have to consider how strongly we feel about these results."	• Structuring as well as shifting and refocusing on the next phase. • Guidelines identified.
(T) "You've lost me. How do we get to 'diagnoses'?"	• Clarification is being sought.
(E) "Good question! First, our diagnoses. We want to determine the following if we can:	• Acceptance of the right to question, even challenge.
(1) Accomplishments—When all estimates agree on HD—Highly descriptive.	• Identification of terms and specific guidelines to be used.
(2) Needs for Improvement—When all estimates agree on ND—Not very descriptive. (3) Uncertainty—when no consistent, congruent pattern of estimates is reported."	*Note:* These are standards built into the system and are presented as such. They are clearly not negotiable.
3:23 **(T)** "So this first one is a need for improvement. Right?"	• Acceptance of the guidelines is evidenced.
(E) "It is if we think the data are valid. They are certainly highly congruent."	
(T) "OK! Here's an accomplishment then. Or is it? The students were not unanimous—only 33 out of 48 responded."	• Reinforcement. • Judgments about validity of the data recognized as legitimate. • Attention to data is shown. Even when data is unclear, its meaning and importance is still considered.
(E) "How can we handle that?" **(T)** "What rule do we follow?" **(E)** "Well, it's a judgment call. Do we feel pretty confident about this practice? Does your evidence and mine as observer clearly reflect *accomplished* use of this practice in your classroom?"	• Structuring. Both conferees are systematic in approaching the problem. • Using rules. • Judgment is called for, but judgments emphasize careful review of the evidence.

3:34   At this point the conferees turn to the raw data, especially the observation record describing this category of events. The teacher is encouraged to review the narrative descriptions of events and talk about them. Probing questions are raised:

• Is the evidence of the practice rather abundant?
• Is the evidence all positive, without contrary practices observed?
• Do you utilize this practice quite regularly?
• Do you have related practices you also employ?
• Do you feel quite good about your skill in utilizing such practices?
    If all of these are answered yes, then an accomplishment is clearly diagnosed.
    Once a set of diagnoses have been agreed upon (see Exhibit 9.1, columns 6 and 7), then the conference continues with decision making in focus:

Events	*Analysis*
	Phase III—Decision Making
3:40 (E) "OK. These diagnoses seem reasonable. Can we agree on how important the needs and uncertainties are? Do you *need* to attend to some of these practices with more urgency than others?"	• Collaboration is emphasized by calling for prioritization.
	• (T's) perceptions of needs are legitimized.
(T) "I'm not about to work on all of these at one time!?	• Reality and perspective emphasized.
(E) "That seems realistic to me."	• Acceptance of limitations as well as feelings expressed.
(T) "Can't I just start with number one—'Moves about the room surveying individual student . . . ? I can improve that, I am sure!"	• Initiative. A desire for quick remediation.
3:41 (E) "That's your first priority for improvement. Is that what you are proposing for our consideration?"	• Reflecting and also structuring toward prioritization and seeking consensus.
(T) "Yes." (Matter of factly)	
(E) "What shall we decide about these other *needs,* and what about these uncertainties?"	• Structuring for a set of decisions that can guide follow-up plans.

3:42   The conferees discuss possible courses of action for each of the four practices—(1), (2a), (3), and (4a). Decisions are sought in terms of prioritizing each as to importance. Decisions also are made regarding follow-up on uncertainty (see column (8) in Exhibit 9.1).

Events	*Analysis*
3:50 (T) "OK. We've agreed on a diagnosis for each practice and given top priority to '(3) Adjusts time . . .'. I feel good now about dealing with (1) and (2a) by myself. When you come to observe me providing direct assistance (3), I think you'll see lots of improvement in those others, too."	• Ownership and initiative expressed as (T) makes commitments to self regarding efforts at improving practices.
3:51 (E) "I like that! Shall we turn now to a *growth plan* for practice (3) or set another date for that."	• Structuring. (E) identifies task yet to be accomplished.
3:52 (T) "We need some time for that, right? Let's do it Monday."	• Initiative.
3:52. (E) "I'll be away Monday, what about Tuesday instead? That gives us both time to do some more thinking."	*Phase IV—Planning* • Scheduling • Collaborating.
(T) "Great! What time? 3:20?"	
(E) Looks good to me! Now let's do come together with some concrete ideas on growth and development activities."	• Structuring. (E) clarifies what need to be undertaken.

(E) "Here is a reprint of a journal article you might want to review. It deals with pacing practices."

(T) "OK. Hope I can find the time."

(E) "Here is a sample copy of a growth plan. It illustrates the form and substance of a plan. We will want to develop something like that on Tuesday. Not a carbon copy, of course."

(T) "Oh". Looks at plan with curiosity. "It's like a lesson plan!"

(E) "Yes. A growth plan. We develop it together. Be thinking about the activities for your plan that could help you learn more about pacing and adjusting time."

(T) "OK. I will."

(E) "Why not make some notes on possible activities? Bring them with you on Tuesday."

• Continuity. Interim events are suggested to keep interest alive.

• Reservations.

• Clarifying and goal setting by making clear what the end product of their planning will look like.

• Terminology reinforced.
• Collaboration emphasized.
• Continuity encouraged through interim activity.

• Commitment.
• Structure given to interim responsibility.

The session is concluded. Phase IV continues later.

Common Problems

Resistance or evasiveness is sometimes encountered in feedback conferences. This is to be expected when the model discussed above is not understood by the teacher. It is difficult to be a good collaborator when you don't understand the process. However, high levels of anxiety may also result from nonfunctional interactions on the part of either conferee. Evaluators sometime ramble and talk around the task when they are anxious about the situation. Resistance is also manifest simply because the teacher has other things on his or her mind—another agenda.

An evasive teacher case reported by Harris (1985: 248, 51) was dealt with by an assistant principal in a patient and time consuming way; then the pressure of time was used to justify a mild form of confrontation:

> **T:** . . . You know, I'm probably as businesslike as I'll ever be and I don't have time to be more individual with kids. I'll be that way no matter what.
>
> **S:** I didn't know what to say. She was so determined in her tone of voice. . . . I just sat there looking at her . . . We both sat there, staring at the profile sheets. She broke the silence . . .
>
> **T:** I'd really like to look at this verbally interactive area . . .

Silence can be an effective tool; it allows time for thought, with opportunity for the evaluatee to take the initiative. Confrontation, by contrast, is hazardous, since it is clearly not collaborative in nature. However, when resistance is such that no real collaborative engagement exists, confrontation may be worth trying.

When the agenda of the teacher is diversionary, yet urgent, the evaluator may want to postpone the feedback conference until later:

> **T:** I really am worried about Jane and Sue. I'm not getting to first base with them.
>
> **E:** I don't have any specific data on your work with Jane and Sue. Have you been doing a special study of them?
>
> **T:** No—not a study . . . but they were the ones I had to separate when you were there observing.
>
> **E:** I see. Well, why don't we look at our data on your practices involving classroom management and positive reinforcement? Perhaps, we'll diagnose some needs for improvement that will have usefulness in dealing with that kind of problem.
>
> **T:** But those two are special. I've tried everything! I'm at my wit's end. I really don't know what to do next! (Tears seem to be welling up in the teachers eyes.)

The evaluator (E) really needs to make a decision here. Is this teacher so upset that counseling and catharsis is more important than developmental evaluation? Can this teacher collaborate in diagnosing his or her needs in this state of mind?

The danger in this situation comes from not clearly making a decision. For instance:

> **E:** I see you are really very upset. Do you want to tell me about the way you feel?

The evaluator has arbitrarily shifted the strategy and changed the plan of action. The evaluator is now a counselor. Data on teaching practices is no longer being utilized, and diagnosis is being replaced by nondirective techniques emphasizing feelings and catharsis. The focus is shifted from teaching practices to student behavior.

Tacking on Course

Such a situation can be approached collaboratively, and the stage set for dealing with *both* agendas, if necessary:

> **E:** (Alternate response) Are you asking to postpone our feedback conference so we can talk about your concern for these two students?
>
> **T:** Gee. I don't know! I'm really upset. Can you talk with me about this now. I'm really not ready for diagnostic analysis.
>
> **E:** Surely. We can reschedule our feedback conference. Now, tell me about Jane and Sue.

It is equally probable, that the interactions would take still another turn:

T: (Alternate response) Gee, I don't know! I'm really upset, but let's go ahead with this diagnostic analysis. I know I'm probably doing some things that add to the problem.

E: Very well. As we complete our work, review the data, see what accomplishments and needs we can diagnose, then we can still consider priorities. And your concerns about Jane and Sue need not be ignored.

The focus on developmental evaluation, using data, collaboration, and growth planning are presented in either of these two scenarios, for "the evaluator is an educator; his success is to be judged by what . . . is learned" (Cronbach, 1980:11).

Oververbalization

A most common problem in the feedback conference is the tendency of the evaluator to talk the data to death. If properly analyzed and displayed the data should "speak for itself" to a large extent (see Chapter 8). Furthermore, the teacher should be encouraged to verbalize the meanings he or she attaches to the data. Hence, the evaluator should be parsimonious in talking about the data. Instead, the evaluator should emphasize the process for using the data to address the task at hand. The four phases are used to expedite moving from interpreting, to valuing, decision making, and planning for growth.

COLLABORATION

The term "collaboration" is one of a great variety that are utilized in business, government, and education to imply various forms of nonauthoritarian relationships among people. Cooperation, participation, involvement, teamwork, and democracy are but a few such terms. The term "democratic processes" currently is out of favor while "collegiality," a very old concept, seems to be gaining new favor (Alfonso and Goldsberry, 1982).

Regardless of terminology, there appears to be wide-spread and persistent support within the field of education for employing nonauthoritarian methods for some evaluation purposes. The highly authoritarian supervisory conferences reported by Blumberg (1980) are probably less widely employed than claimed, but are surely not supportable. The common emphasis on extremely unstructured, laissez faire relationships between secondary supervisors and teachers has been documented by Carthel (1973) and has been further documented for elementary schools in a variety of case reports (Harris, 1975). There continues to be great interest in self-assessment (Bailey, 1979; Johnston and Hodge, 1981) despite considerable skepticism (Hartman, 1978) and some evidence of limited utility (Hardebeck, 1973; Hook and Rosenshine, 1979; Glickman and Pajak, 1983). Self-assessment may or may not reflect collaborative processes.

Some form of collaboration between teacher evaluatee and evaluator(s) seems essential to effective developmental evaluation. The problems are (1) defining the character of the collaborative processes in realistic ways, (2) resisting temptations toward old habits of authoritarian kinds, and (3) developing the newly required skills. Clive (1984) stresses the place of self-appraisal in a multiple, data-based evaluation process. He emphasizes, however, the importance of teacher training in exercising such responsibilities. Cronbach and associates emphasize collaboration as negotiation. "What is needed is information that supports negotiation rather than information calculated to point out the 'correct' decision" (Cronbach, 1980:4). This is highly consistent with the notions of "participative decision making" (ERIC, 1977). Glatthorn's (1984) concerns for differentiated supervision, like Glickman's (1980) emphasis on developmental supervision, reflect efforts to reconcile conflicting evidence on authoritarian vs nondirective relationships in evaluation or other aspects of supervisory practice. It seems unlikely that the best answers will be found using simple one- or two-dimensional models that generally are in present use.

The Character of Collaboration

In a task-oriented evaluation endeavor that calls for utilization of data sources for diagnostic purposes, collaboration tends to extend well beyond the traditional pre- or post-conference. Every step in the total evaluation process is potentially subject to collaboration (see Chapter 2, Exhibit 2.1). Although differentially applicable to various steps in the evaluation process, collaboration has process characteristics of its own. Some of these are:

1. Mutual respect for each other within the limits of known responsibilities and expertise.
2. Tolerance for differing values and interpretations.
3. Acceptance of developmental purposes.
4. Adherence to the laws, regulations, and ground rules that give the system its unique character.
5. Willingness to commit reasonable amounts of time and effort.
6. Acknowledgement of differentiated responsibilities on rational bases.
7. Readiness to influence each other without seeking to control or dominate.
8. Activeness in seeking to communicate.
9. Humility in approaching complexities with simple methods.

This is a demanding set of process characteristics. Few of us can expect to operationalize evaluation efforts at this ideal level. Furthermore, these characteristics are mutually required and must be trained for, modeled, and developed over time. But it is also important to recognize that the sytem of evaluation can be designed to promote or constrain such collaborative efforts. For instance, the DeTEK system utilizes a ten-step sequence that clearly delegates responsibilities of different kinds to evaluators and teachers (Harris and Hill, 1982). The design of this system utilizes two separate stages of data gathering and analysis (I. Pre-Diagnostic Survey and II. Focused Diagnostic Analysis), which gives time for both collaborators to learn to communicate and forestalls hasty decision making (see Exhibit 3.4). Furthermore, the system utilizes ground rules requiring shared decisions and offering specific alternatives for resolving disagreements.

Resisting Old Habits

Since collaboration, depicted as nine mutually exhibited process characteristics, is very demanding, the temptation to use old habits or easier alternatives is very great. When data are shared from two or more sources and are not highly congruent, an understandable tendency is to reject one set and cut off communications about the other data. When the teacher resists accepting an interpretation, it is easy to assume the mantle of authority! For evaluator, it might come out like this: "Well, you just can't argue with that. I saw rather clear and persistent evidence. . . ." For the teacher the authoritarian stance may sound like this: "Well, you just have to be there facing these problems and you'll get a different view!"

Knowing oneself is important in resisting old habit patterns and consciously avoiding those words or action that are inconsistent with collaboration. Avoiding "I," while stressing "we" is helpful. Focusing on the data as a basis for forming opinions is important. Listening hard and asking for clarification, even when you think you understand, makes a big difference; so does asking for suggestions and information while giving suggestions and information parsimoniously. Avoiding negative terms, but avoiding flattery, too, allows others to think. A common habit that undercuts collaboration is "building rapport" via elaborate praise of the teacher. Giving praise, especially when it precedes collaborative interpretation, emphasizes opinions and imposes values.

Developing New Skills

Training in using collaborative techniques in conferencing is desirable, if not essential, for both evaluator and teacher. It is especially crucial for the evaluator because he or she can model these techniques as they are actually applied. Chapter 11 makes suggestions regarding training for all parties to assure quality in evaluation. Much can be learned in process if evaluator and teacher take time to review their behavior. Video-taping or audio-taping conferences provides opportunities for both collaborators to review their actions.

Essential attitudes in developing truly collaborative techniques include respect for the data and the mutuality of the endeavor. Both collaborators need to be developing and sharpening their skills because the process will not succeed except by mutual efforts. The knowledge and skill of both evaluator and teacher are essential. Similarly, the focus on data that both collaborators respect gives them a common base for thinking, comparing, interpreting, valuing, and deciding. Traditionally, opinions and feelings tend to prevail in decision making in our schools, so respect for data needs to be given emphasis in all we do when implementing an evaluation system. This emphasis on data must be balanced, of course, against the reality that the data are always very limited.

A Broader Base of Involvement

Collaborative efforts in developmental teacher evaluations are not restricted to the feedback conference; in fact, strong arguments can be made for collaboration in every step of the evaluation process from criteria selection, to instrumentation, data gathering, and analysis. The extent of teacher involvement in various evaluation steps will be determined by policy, system design, technical skill required, time availability, and interest.

Collaboration can and often does extend beyond the two individuals usually involved—teacher and evaluator. The Georgia teacher assessment system, for instance, involves assessment center teams as well as principals and teachers in a fairly elaborate system (Georgia Department of Education, 1983). Many schools are gradually including students as data providers (Penn-Harris-Madison School Corporation, 1981), while Houston Texas schools once attempted to include parents as a data source (Houston ISD, 1977).

The DeTEK system (Harris and Hill, 1982) may be unique in its design for fostering collaboration in every aspect of the evaluation process. This system has a specific set of performance criteria explicated, and instrumentation is provided. However, all other steps in the evaluation process are highly collaborative. Data gathering involves both observer and teacher in differentiated but compatible ways. Analysis of the data from two or three sources is undertaken in conference with the teacher actively involved. Diagnostic analysis leads to interpretations regarding needs, priorities, and decisions are all made in a context of collaboration. The final steps in the DeTEK system are carefully structured to assure collaborative implementation of growth plan activities (see Appendix C-7).

A carefully structured system of procedures can promote collaboration. By incorporating certain procedures and ground rules, collaboration becomes an expectation for all. Neither the whim nor preferences of teacher nor evaluator are allowed to prevail in such a system.

GROWTH PLANNING

The last two steps in the evaluation process call for decisions and follow-up planning for action. Decisions and actions in a developmental systems are most appropriately those that focus on reinforcing strengths and initiating improvement efforts. Some sort of growth planning is an essential link in the evaluation process between decision making and action.

It is a curious fact that many systems directed toward improving teacher practices do not clearly specify the process of improvement, even though it is inferred. Perhaps, the long established tradition of separating evaluation and staff development has had this effect. There has also been some influence from the traditional notion that professional growth is a purely personal affair (Harris, 1980), or at least not one of high priority in school operations.

For whatever reasons, growth planning tends to be neglected and separated from the evaluation process. Anderson and Snyder (1981), for example, describe "supervisory conference" and "post-conference analysis" in considerable detail, but do not suggest an improvement process. Instead, there appears to be considerable faith in the conference itself to produce growth. The Penn-Harris-Madison system calls for "interim conferencing" as the opportunity to ". . . discuss the progress of the teacher towards goal achievement . . ." and does provide a "goal setting conference form" for this purpose (1981:13).

The Carrollton-Farmers Branch (1980:33–35) system provides the principal with a checklist of "recommendations for improvement of teaching performance." Twenty-one general suggestions are provided to guide such planning. But growth planning is such a crucial link between evaluation steps that specific directions for teaching improvement should not be slighted. Such a crucial step needs both rigor and imaginativeness.

The Planning Process

If the needs have been identified, accepted by collaborators, and given priorities for action, then the process of growth planning is like that for many other plans of action:

1. Break the desired outcome into its component parts.
2. Identify specific activities to be employed in accomplishing specific objectives.
3. Sequence and schedule selected activities.
4. Assign responsibilities for implementing each activity.
5. Designate a monitoring and review process.

As simple as this sounds, it requires careful structuring as an integral part of the evaluation process. This planning should be collaborative.

Others should be involved who have special expertise to contribute. A written plan should be produced and utilized for monitoring purposes.

Exhibit 9.2 provides an illustration of one growth plan utilizing a structured instrument. Not only are activities carefully designated for each diagnosed need for improvement, but specific collaborators are identified and target dates designated.

In a similar illustration by Harris, et al. (1985), a section is provided in a growth plan for designating "Measurement of Outcomes." These same authors illustrate a highly simplified form of "Teacher's Growth Plan" for use when only a single objective is clearly designated.

Several variations of the basic concept of a formal plan for growth are discussed and illustrated by McGreal (1983) in his chapter 4: "Goal Setting as the Major Activity of Evaluation." In fact, goal setting is the point of departure for nearly all growth planning. McGreal reviews Redfern's (1980) model, emphasizing a very specific set of "responsibility criteria" for use in developing an action plan. Morgan and Champagne (1971) elaborated on the five or six clinical supervision cycle steps to include three aspects of planning for growth.

The disadvantages of formal, structured growth planning are emphasized by Iwanicki (1981). Such plans run the risk of being unrealistic in time and resource requirements. They can be needlessly mechanistic. They are difficult to evaluate and, hence, encourge emphasis on the overly simplistic.

Design

A growth plan is no more effective in implementation than the activities selected to provide meaningful, relevant learning opportunities for the teacher. The personalized, collaborative character of the growth plan has both assets and liabilities related to it. The activities must be relevant to the specific improvement need or objective, but they must also be readily available, stimulating, varied, and experienced in a context of support and encouragement.

A vast array of widely recognized training activities is in current use (Harris, 1985: 70–87), but many are not readily useful on an individual basis. Games, role playing, discussion, and brainstorming are among those that require a group. However, reading, observing, film viewing, and guided practice are clearly suitable for use with a single person or a pair of collaborators.

The activities named above are especially important for growth planning purposes because they are adaptable to use with a wide array of learning outcomes. However, care must be taken to plan for such activities with the specific need of the teacher in mind. Readings provided must really contain relevant information. Visits to observe other teachers at work must be planned to assure that the "good" practices will be in evidence.

EXHIBIT 9.2 DeTEK instrument VI: professional growth plan

Teacher _Helen Mathis_ ____ School _J. F. Kennedy_ ____ Date _Jan. 18, 198-_

Teaching Assignment: Grade _3rd_ ___ Subject(s) _All except music and physa. ed._

FIRST — REFERENCE ACCOMPLISHMENTS:
(Designate behavior and indicator numbers accomplished.
Refer to Data Analysis Worksheet, Instrument V)

Behavior # _3c_

Indicators Accomplished
_3c(1)_ ___ # _____
_____ # _____

SECOND—DESIGNATE BEHAVIORS AND INDICATORS AS NEEDS (Refer to Instrument V)		THIRD—LIST ACTIVITIES TO BE UNDERTAKEN (Describe specific activities for each indicator. Refer to Resource File and Activities List for suggestions of activities, materials and sources.)	FOURTH—MAKE DECISIONS	
Number	DEVELOPMENTAL LEVEL		Collaborator Responsible	Date to Complete
3c(3)	Uses an array of question types: recognition, comprehension, analysis, and evaluation.	K Review kinds of questions and questioning techniques in Classroom Questions by Sanders.	Mathis	1/28
		E Work through Learning module "Analysis of Classroom Questions" in Professional Library.	Mathis	2/5
		E Observe Mary Megan's use of class discussions of stories, poems, or plays.	J. A. Bryan and Mathis	2/1-2 2/20-28
		T Tape a discussion in own classroom, and categorize questions using Teacher Question Inventory.	Mathis and Bryan	3/2-5

*INDICATE the proposed date for STEP 10-REVIEW DIALOG SESSION.   Time: _9_ : _30_ to _10 : 15_   Date _Mar. 9, 198-_

Teacher's Signature _Helen Mathis_ ____ Principal's Signature _J. A. Bryan_

Films or video-tapes, too, must be selected with care to be sure that they are truly illustrative of relevant practice.

Guided practice is almost always an essential part of helping teachers implement new, improved practices; hence, it should be considered for any growth plan. This also highlights one of the serious limitations of individual growth planning. Individualized or personalized approaches are very costly (Harris, 1980). Nonetheless, there is no substitute for carefully guided efforts to transfer new skills and concepts into applications (Joyce and Showers, 1984).

A strategy for selecting and sequencing growth plan activities involves estimating the teacher readiness status. We assume that to some degree new practices are learned in a sequence from knowledge, to understanding, to skill development, to application, and then internalized over time (see Exhibit 9.3). The growth planning process includes exploring the status of the teacher with regard to these stages of learning. If the teacher is fully knowledgeable about practice diagnosed as need, then activities designed for advanced levels of learning are more appropriate. Conceivably a teacher may only need assistance with application. Others may start with emphasis on skill training, while others need to start at the beginning.

EXHIBIT 9.3   Stages of learning and activity sequence*

Stages	Usual Sequence	Types of Activities
Knowledge Do I know about it?	1	Reading. Discussing. Brainstorming. Lecturing.
Understanding Do I understand how it works and why?	2	Observing. Film Viewing. Gaming. Demonstrating.
Skill Can I do what is required?	3	Micro-teaching. Gaming. Guided practice. Role-playing.
Application Can I make it all work in the real world?	4	Guided practice. Analyzing. Observing.
Internalization Can I adapt it, refine it, make it a basic part of my teaching "style"?	5	Firsthand experience. Analyzing. Reading. Discussing. Brainstorming.

*Adapted from "Growth Planning, Development and Review (Steps 8–10); Records," In *The DeTEK Handbook*, by Ben M. Harris and Jane Hill. Austin, TX: Southwest Educational Development Laboratory, 1982. pp. 54–58.

Related Group Training

The cost of guiding, directing, and facilitating individual growth activities is high. Such purely individual efforts may also be less effective than they might be. Working together with others to improve teaching practices has benefits in both efficiency and effectiveness. Teachers and evaluators need to interact with groups of practitioners and scholars who have common interests and diverse experiences to contribute.

Individual growth planning should reflect the potential for individual needs to be met in the context of group training. Intervisitation plans for an individual who needs to observe a teacher making skillful use of class discussions or bulletin boards can be implemented for a small group if others have common needs. Similarly, when planning for an individual, group activities such as role playing, discussion, lecture, and field trips can be utilized if the probability of other individuals with common needs is recognized and arrangements made to bring such individuals together.

Using group training activities for implementing individual growth plans is a distinctly different approach from that in common use. The distinctions need to be clearly understood. Many training programs for groups start with (1) future time and resources allocated in fixed amounts. (2) A survey of opinions about presumed needs is conducted. (3) The most commonly reported opinions are assumed to reflect real specific needs. (4) An activity is selected to relate to the most popular needs. Then (5) all teachers, even those not expressing a need are encouraged to attend.

When individual growth plans utilize group training activities, they are tailored to the diagnosed needs of known individuals. The group is organized around individuals. Time and resources are allocated according to individual considerations. Diagnostic analysis replaces the survey of opinions. Needs of diverse kinds are given attention; the individual is the client not a hypothetical, unknown group. Group activity is used only for a portion of the training. Only invited guests are admitted according to plan.

Autonomy and Flexibility

The foregoing discussion of group training for the implementation of individual growth plans clearly suggests the need for rather flexible approaches. Tailoring for both individual and group training activities in response to the unique needs of individual teachers is not likely to be realized with any single plan of action. Each plan will be different in the activities selected, the schedule utilized, and the responsibilities assumed by teacher and others.

The autonomy that the individual teacher can exercise in both planning and implementing a growth plan is crucial to its success. Collaboration in previous steps of the evaluation process pays great dividends in motivating teachers to assume personal responsibility for their professional growth. When needs have been diagnosed in a collaborative way, and growth planning is explicit about the activties and sequences that seem appropriate, individual teachers are often energized to a surprising degree. They find time and energy for doing what is prescribed. They seek out resources for implementing the planned activities. They often find it difficult to wait for assistance.

A caution is in order regarding flexibility, autonomy, and teacher initiatives. While teachers may be motivated by good planning, it is not realistic to ask them to go it alone. The school district and its leadership staff have an ethical responsibility to assist teachers to improve in those areas of performance diagnostically analyzed. Furthermore, collaborators must be thoughtful in encouraging initiatives that have a high probability of success. "Nothing succeeds like success." Nothing fails like lack of success when one has really tried hard.

Reciprocity

An outgrowth of diagnostic analysis techniques as discussed in Chapter 8 is clearly defined accomplishments. These have a special place in effective growth planning. Just as diagnosed needs call for commitment to improvement plans, diagnosed accomplishments represent identified resources for use in improving another person's practices. Schools that have utilized truly diagnostic evaluation systems with all teachers find that the faculty becomes its own most valuable resource pool for implementing growth plans. The teacher who needs assistance in learning better ways to "(3) Adjusts time frames to fit needs of students, allowing time, shifting to new activities more quickly . . . rescheduling . . ." (see Exhibit 9.1) is, in turn, an "expert" for some teacher who needs suggestions or assistance in learning to "(4) Provides tutorial assistance or guides small groups to assist with task accomplishment on schedule." Every school is full of human resources waiting to be better diagnosed and more fully utilized for its strengths.

The system of diagnostic analysis and collaborative planning sets the stage for the emergence of a multitude of symbiotic relationships among faculty members, administrators, and supervisors. The struggle to promote growth implementation gives way to coordination and facilitation of helping relationships.

SUMMARY

The latter steps in the sequence of an evaluation effort require interpretation, valuing, and decisions for action. In a developmental system of teacher evaluation, feedback conferences and growth planning are the primary vehicles for making full use of the evaluation process.

Conferences are much more complicated than is generally realized. There are many differing approaches to the evaluation conference and all seem to have serious limitations. Conferences can rarely be effective in a highly authoritarian mode—tell and expect compliance. But neither is a laissez faire mode likely to produce results. Even nondirective techniques, borrowed from clinical counseling, seem to have only limited utility. Much more attention is needed for alternative strategies that build on principles of good human relations but also emphasize task, a focus on data, and shared responsibility.

Collaboration is a concept that has special importance in the context of both feedback and growth planning. Collaborative efforts can be emphasized in every aspect of the evaluation process. But collaborative behavior must be modeled and learned by all personnel involved in evaluation. Evaluation systems that are designed to emphasize collaboration make it easier for both evaluator and teacher to refine their skills.

Growth planning is an essential in making developmental evaluation productive. Accordingly, it is argued that such planning should be an integral part of the evaluation process. Plans should be detailed, individualized, and carefully tailored to assure individual change in behavior, even though group activities may also be employed.

SELECTED STUDY SOURCES

Anderson, Robert H. and Karolyn J. Snyder (1981). *Clinical Supervision: A Coaching Technology.* Lubbock, TX: Pedamorphosis, Inc.

A brief illustrated treatment of some of the main concepts of clinical supervision that emphasizes the five stage observation cycle. Page 13 details "the supervisory conference."

Blumberg, Arthur (1980). *Supervisors and Teachers: A Private Cold War. 2nd Ed.* Berkeley, CA: McCutchan Publishing Corporation.

A very critical review of a few studies showing supervisors to be employing rather crude, often unstructured or authoritarian approaches in their face-to-face conferences with teachers. A concept of social-contract is explored as a possible approach to improving the teacher-supervisor relationship.

Carrollton-Farmers Branch Schools (no date). "Observing, Conferring, Assisting, Assessing Guide." Carrollton, TX: Personnel Office, mimeographed.

A detailed description of one school district's teacher appraisal system. Much of the instrumentation illustrated is less than ideal but the section on "Appraisal Conference Tips" (p. 24–32) is an excellent source of specifics.

Garman, Noreen B. (1982). "The Clinical Approach to Supervision," in *Supervision of Teaching*, Thomas J. Sergiovanni, editor. Arlington, VA: Association for Supervision and Curriculum Development.

An update on basic concepts and practices associated with clinical supervision is presented. The author gives special emphasis to the pre- and post-conference techniques.

Glatthorn, Allan A. (1984). *Differentiated Supervision.* Alexandria, VA: Association for Supervision and Curriculum Development.

A proposal for differentiating supervisory strategies on the basis of developmental levels of teaching. Implications for feedback strategies are imbedded in the alternatives suggested, even though the schemes seem too simplistic for many purposes.

Glickman, Carl (1980). *Developmental Supervision.* Alexandria, VA: Association for Supervision and Curriculum Development.

A rigorous effort to relate studies on the stages of professional development to supervisory strategies. The various supervisory strategies are worthy of consideration in feedback conferences.

Harris, Ben M. (1975). *Supervisory Behavior in Education,* 2nd Ed.: Englewood Cliffs, NJ: Prentice-Hall, Inc.

Chapters 13, 14, and 15 present case material depicting supervisory conferences and growth planning techniques.

Harris, Ben M. (1980). *Improving Staff Performance Through Inservice Education.* Boston, MA: Allyn and Bacon, Inc.

Chapter VI includes a discussion of a variety of "personalized" approaches to professional growth. Individual growth plans are detailed on pages 229–233.

Harris, Ben M. and Jane Hill (1982). *Developmental Teacher Evaluation Kit.* Austin, TX: Southwest Educational Development Laboratory.

A "DeTEK Handbook" is included in this kit. Chapter 5 discusses growth planning in some detail.

Harris, Ben M., Kenneth E. McIntyre, Vance Littleton, and Dan Long (1985). *Personnel Administration in Education.* 2nd ed. Boston, MA: Allyn and Bacon, Inc.

Management by objectives is discussed and illustrated on pages 236-239. Appendix F illustrates a growth planning format of interest.

Hunter, Madeline (1980). "Six Types of Supervisory Conferences." *Educational Leadership* (February):404–12.

A set of generalizations is presented about teacher evaluation emphasizing evaluation for "improvement" as distinguished from summative purposes or "functions." Five improvement-focused conferences are discussed and illustrated.

Joyce, Bruce and Beverly Showers (1982). "The Coaching of Teaching." *Educational Leadership* 40 (October):4–10.

"Coaching" is discussed as it relates to the problems of transfer of training. The authors discuss the importance of recognizing transfer problems and overtraining in the skills required prior to implementation.

Kaplan, Don (1980). "Feedback: Using Video to Measure Teacher Performance," in *Video in the Classroom: A Guide to Creative Television.* White Plains, NY: Knowledge Industry Publications, Inc., pp. 133–34.

The author provides a list of the kinds of questions that can be used to focus attention on specific aspects of the recorded teacher performance. The author does not suggest analytical techniques, but does pose questions from which analyses may follow.

Kindsvatter, Richard and William Wilen (1981). "A Systematic Approach to Improving Conference Skills." *Educational Leadership* 38 (April):525–29.

The *Conference Category System* is presented as a tool for analyzing conferences. Nine aspects of the conference are scaled.

McGreal, Thomas L. (1983). "Improved Classroom Observation Skills," in *Successful Teacher Evaluation*. Alexandria, VA: Association for Supervision and Curriculum Development.

Starting with the assumption that collecting descriptive data is the essential purpose of classroom observation, the author addresses reliability, accuracy, recording, and feedback techniques in considerable detail. A variety of recording instruments are illustrated. The misuse of rating scales is also addressed.

Pac-Urar, Ian G. and Jo Anne L. Vacca (1984). "Working Toward Collegiality: If at First You Don't Succeed . . ." *Thresholds in Education* 10 (May):36–38.

These authors report the failure of an effort at peer evaluation. A single school in Ohio involved teachers in observing each other and providing feedback on how ". . . the goals of the school were being practiced and met . . ." Reasons for failure are discussed.

Redfern, George B. (1980). *Evaluating Teachers and Administrators: A Performance Objectives Approach*. Boulder, CO: Westview Press.

The most recent work of a pioneer in the field of developmental evaluation. This book emphasizes a five step cycle that stresses "responsibility criteria."

Simon, A. E. (1977). "Analyzing Educational Platforms: A Supervisory Strategy" *Educational Leadership* 34:580–84.

The espoused and operational "platforms" on which the teacher operates are discussed. Methods for identifying both and comparing them are described.

Valverde, Leonard A. (1982). "The Self-Evolving Supervisor," in *Supervision of Teaching*, Thomas J. Sergiovanni, editor. Arlington, VA: Association for Supervision and Curriculum Development. p. 81–89.

Emphasis is given to informal, self-directed learning of supervisors. Many of the same principles apply to teacher growth.

Warner, Allen R. (1981). "Conferencing: The Heart of the (Supervisory) Matter," in *Improving Classroom Practice Through Supervision*, Robert H. Anderson, editor. Dallas: Texas Association for Supervision and Curriculum Development.

An excellent discussion regarding when, where, and how to conduct conferences. "What not to talk about . . ." (p. 31) may be the best contribution of this piece.

10

Linkages to Summative Awards and Terminations

Distinctions between summative and formative evaluation are widely recognized (Harris et al., 1985; McIntyre, 1979; Bloom et al., 1971; Borich and Fenton, 1977). Nonetheless, many efforts at teacher evaluations make little or no distinction between practices. Many, if not most, school systems emphasize the importance of improving teaching through evaluation in policy statements, but structure their instruments and procedures for summative purposes.

This book has emphasized the developmental evaluation of teaching practices. Developmental evaluation is characterized by systematic, objective, data-based efforts to clearly analyze current practice and to diagnose both strengths and needs for improvement. Such evaluation is clearly formative (see Chapter 2 for discussion of these concepts).

Both formative and summative evaluation can serve a variety of purposes. Foley (1981) distinguishes at least three purposes for teacher evaluation: (1) Individual teacher improvement. (2) Evaluation for dismissal of the incompetent. (3) Evaluation for merit. Harris and Hill (1982) suggest a broader array of purposes on a continuum from summative to formative. Nine such purposes include:

1. Promotions
2. Dismissals
3. Merit Awards

4. Accounting to Authorities
5. Public information.
6. Reassignments.
7. Improving administration
8. Improving program operations
9. Improving individual performance.

The South Carolina Act No. 197 (1979), as amended in 1981, illustrates legal emphasis on a variety of more or less developmental purposes:

> It is the intent of this act to provide for a fair and comprehensive program for training, certification, initial employment and evaluation of public educators . . .

Many state legislatures have recently mandated teacher evaluation with emphasis on improvement of performance. While rather broad in scope, the South Carolina law specifies formative evaluation in a variety of ways:

1. . . . each student teacher shall be evaluated . . . The college or university . . . shall make available assistance, training and counseling . . . to overcome deficiencies. (Section 2(i))
2. Develop an observational instrument to be used by the local school district to evaluate . . . during (the) provisional year . . . to inform a teacher of his strengths and weaknesses. (Section 3(b) (7))
3. Establish procedures whereby each school district shall periodically evaluate in the classroom all certified personnel . . . School districts shall give the results to the teacher and shall counsel him . . . (And) shall use . . . the evaluations as a guide to . . . staff development programs. (Section 3(j))

All of this emphasis on formative, developmental uses of evaluation procedures and instruments is followed in this act by Section 4, which provides: "If the evaluations indicate the provisional teacher is deficient in teaching ability the school district shall not continue to employ him . . ." (Section 4, p. 7). In effect, assumptions are being made regarding the utility of formative, diagnostic evaluation procedures for making summative decisions of extremely serious kinds.

McIntyre warns about the differences in formative and summative efforts. "Although both formative and summative evaluation of teacher performance are necessary, and much of the information used to help teachers is also useful in making decisions about teachers, *the two processes are quite different*" (McIntyre, 1979:14). (italics added)

Nearly all scholars and practitioners who address formative and summative evaluations as distinctive types have some distinguishing features to note. Purposes that vary widely have been discussed. Processes involved are recognized as quite different. Instrumentation differences are acknowledged by Borich and Fenton (1977), Seldin (1984), and Medley, et al. (1984). Procedural differences abound with due process, standardization, and external sources of control emphasized for summative evaluation, while collaboration, self-analysis, and individualization are more appropriate for formative efforts. Sharp differences in purpose, process, instrumentation, and procedural characteristics give urgency to the notion that summative and formative evaluation cannot be undertaken as a single undifferentiated task. Either two different evaluation systems must be employed or a more complex system developed with separate and distinct subsystems.

If essentially separate teacher evaluation efforts are required, then the linking of one to the other in productive ways is a special problem. This chapter explores in greater depth the problems of linking formative, developmental evaluation to other evaluation purposes and systems not essentially developmental in nature.

NEED FOR CONTROLLED LINKAGES

Since a high quality developmental evaluation system is not like a summative evaluation system in purpose, process, instrumentation, or procedures, it clearly cannot also be a summative system. The contrary is also true. To the extent that a system of teacher evaluation is truly effective in guiding administrative decisions regarding promotion, dismissal, and merit, it cannot be effective as a guide to individual teacher improvement and program revision.

Conditions for Linking

But there are useful relationships that can be exploited by linking formative systems to summative decision making. Such linkages are possible when several conditions are met:

1. The sequence of procedures is from developmental to summative. The fullest utilization of data in the developmental process is completed before being linked to (used in) a summative effort.
2. Insulation is provided to assure that the linkage from formative to summative does not create a backflow of summative influences on the formative process. This is most commonly recognized in the form of anxieties about future consequences.
3. Selective use is made of developmental data, with caution exercised to avoid misinterpretations or violations of confidences. Data from developmental systems may not have adequate reliability and is often too diagnostic for summative decisioning.

4. Supplemental data and processes are utilized to assure informed decision making of summative kinds.
5. Unnecessary summative processes are eliminated. Summative evalutation efforts are limited to those teachers at those times when a summative decision is clearly required.
6. Procedural and substantive due processes are provided for in the system to protect the vast majority of teachers not subject to summative review.

Assuming that these conditions for linking two rather distinct systems or subsystems are met, six stages or components of the total system need to be clearly developed (Barber and Klein, 1983). Exhibit 10.1 presents a systems diagram for such a total evaluation system.

Component I indicates a subsystem giving direction to all staff development and evaluation efforts. This component is directed by laws, policy, and regulation at whatever levels. Components II, V and VI relate directly to the teacher evaluation program as a formative/developmental subsystem (II), a summative/administrative decision making subsystem (VI), and a linking subsystem (V). Components III and IV are not truly evaluation systems. They are follow-up activity subsystems guided by and supportive of the evaluation efforts in the other subsystems.

It is important to note that Exhibit 10.1 suggests no direct linkages between subsystem II and VI. They are related to each other only through the linking system (V), except for the use of demonstrated improvements as inputs for considering awards, promotions, or reassignments. The specific steps for providing such linkages are discussed below and illustrated in Exhibit 10.2.

It is also important to recognize that there are three different sets of outcomes—X, Y, and Z—shown to the far right in Exhibit 10.1. Not only are they different outcomes, but they also derive from different sequences of events. Still another point must be made that is not so clearly reflected in the systems diagram. Teacher evaluatees are the focus of attention in components I through VI. However, all teacher evaluatees are not involved in all components! At least they need not all be involved. It is wasteful of evaluation resources to involve any evaluatee in stages V and VI unless there is some specific need to make decisions—Y or Z—about each individual.

Unless individual deficiencies are suspected, no systematic effort to identify them is needed because diagnostic analysis efforts in the developmental system are constantly attending to needs for improvement through growth planning. Unless growth planning and improvement efforts (IV) prove ineffective or inadequate, there is no need to move from the developmental system into the summative.

Even the use of summative evaluation efforts to reward, reassign, and promote are selectively applied and must not be allowed to usurp scarce evaluation resources.

EXHIBIT 10.1 A systems view of linkages

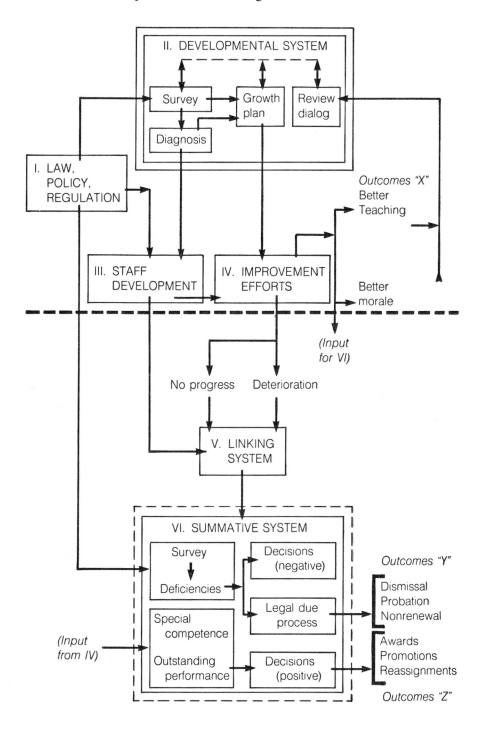

The developmental teacher evaluation system (component II) should remain preeminent in a total system of evaluation because it serves all teachers, all children, and youth in all programs. Furthermore, it is the most productive evalutaion effort that can be undertaken in a school or college setting because it directly affects the quality of teaching and learning, has positive side effects on both students and teachers, has few negative effects, and is relatively less expensive.

Steps from Developmental to Summative

When individual teacher progress is not being demonstrated as the result of developmental efforts, summative evaluation may be in order. Furthermore, when teaching practices are deteriorating despite developmental efforts, then a summative evaluation alternative is even more clearly appropriate. Fortunately, these are rare circumstances, given careful teacher selection and assignment (Harris et al., 1985). Nonetheless, a step-by-step sequence for terminating the developmental sequence and intitiating the summative stage is shown in Exhibit 10.2.

Steps 1a and 1b represent the two kinds of decisions that might lead from developmental to summative evaluation for any individual teacher based on less than fully satisfactory performance. Decision making is not likely to be collaborative in nature. It is a responsibility assumed by an administrator or supervisor who is working closely with the teacher in the developmental evaluation/growth planning process. Such decisions are based on these close working relationships and the understandings that emerge from prior collaborative efforts. The collaborative relationship is necessarily abandoned in these instances.

The linking system (Exhibit 10.1, component V) is purposefully designed to assure all parties to the evaluation process, including the individual teacher, that every effort is being made to promote staff development. Individual growth of the teacher remains a top priority within the linking system, even when there is serious concern about the capacity of the evaluatee to respond in a satisfactory manner.

The steps that safeguard the individual teacher and the welfare of his or her students are specified as a series of questions following a judgment of "lack of progress." Question 2a follows logically, asking for a judgment regarding the need for more time to demonstrate progress toward growth plan improvements. If the judgments are "yes," meaning more time is needed, then the teacher is guided back into the developmental system. If more time is not judged to be necessary, then the next question is considered. Question 3a asks about another growth plan. If such an option is judged appropriate, the teacher is guided back into the developmental system for that purpose. If such an action is not deemed appropriate, a final question asks about the seriousness of the lack of progress. Once again,

EXHIBIT 10.2   Steps in the linking system

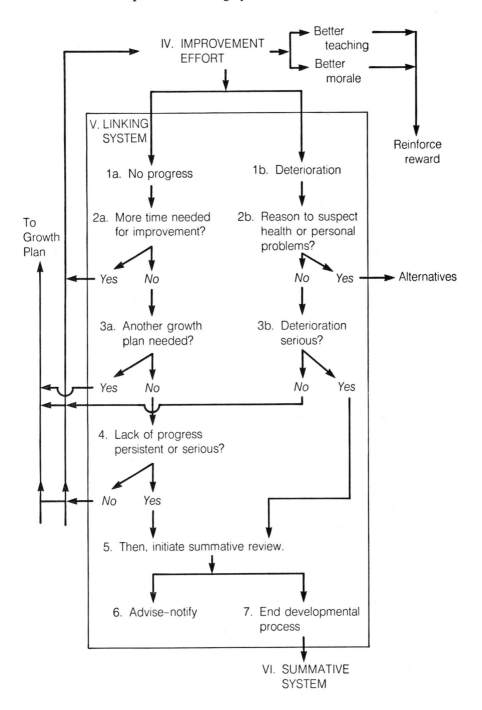

unless the deficiency is judged serious or persistent or both, the teacher returns to developmental alternatives.

A similar series of steps within the linking system is utilized when the judgment is 1b— "deteriorating practice." Question 2b asks about possible causes of the unsatisfactory performance that might be related to health or personal affairs. If such factors are related to the problem then neither developmental nor summative procedures are most appropriate and other alternatives for help need to be considered. However, when there is no reason to suspect such causes, step 3b calls for a judgment about the seriousness of the deteriorating performance. If not yet serious, then a return to developmental processes is in order. If the deterioration in performance is judged truly serious, then step 5 is in order.

The linking system steps, when utilized in the manner suggested above, offer assurances that unsatisfactory performance of two potentially serious kinds will be addressed systematically, humanely, yet with serious intent to protect the quality of instructional opportunity offered to children and youth. Because these linking steps can be taken prior to any summative process being initiated, mistakes are avoided, and anxieties are held in check until a truly serious condition is thoughtfully verified. The linking system also forestalls becoming involved with the legal technicalities of procedural due process until they are clearly a necessity. In fact, the steps in the linking process, while not collaborative in nature, do offer time and opportunity for principals and supervisors to counsel with unsatisfactory teachers regarding career changes. Summative evaluation procedures can be bypassed in many, if not most, instances.

Positive Summative Linkages

Emphasis in the discussion above is on unsatisfactory teacher performance. Both Exhibits 10.1 and 10.2 suggest a link between the outcomes of improvement activities—better teaching and morale—and summative evaluation. The linkage in this instance is related to positive decisions about awards, promotions, or reassignments. While such decisions call for summative evaluation processes, they clearly are not the same as those involving negative decisions.

The summative system depicted in Exhibit 10.1 is actually a dual system. While summative decisions are required for both positive and negative purposes, they have little in common with each other. A special linking system is clearly not required when awards and promotions are involved. The inputs that initiate and guide such positive evaluation efforts are derived from the developmental system as positive outcomes—better teaching and morale. Only selected individuals are usually involved in this positive evaluation process. Furthermore, the anxieties involved are of a different character, and legal due process is less critical.

Awards are based on decisions that may involve evaluation of specialized competencies or outstanding performance of standard kinds. Similarly, either special competence, outstanding performance, or both may need to be evaluated for promotions or reassignments.

Exhibit 10.3 suggests an array of decision outcomes for which summative evaluation of positive kinds might be desirable. The foci for evaluations of these kinds are all summative but address quite different questions:

A. Basic Performance Expectations To what extent can the teacher demonstrate minimum levels of satisfactory performance in all areas that are basic expectations for the position?

B. Superior Levels of Performance To what extent can the teacher demonstrate superior levels of performance in all areas that are basic expectations for the position?

C. Specialized Performance Capability To what extent can the teacher demonstrate (or shows good potential for) performances that are of special importance to the position or some new position?

When *basic performance expectations* are met by an individual, it might lead to any one or more of the following decisions, depending on the intent or purpose for evaluation. An incentive grant of money, a prize, privilege, or other recognition might be conferred. For new teachers, such decisions might lead to granting certification, or a promotion from probationary to full teaching status. In effect, such summative evaluation efforts might serve to guide (1) awards or (2) promotions. It seems unlikely that (3) reassignment decisions could profit from such evaluation efforts.

When *superior levels of performance* are met all three types of decisions might be served. Merit awards to give individuals recognition for their superior performance are possible. Promotions are also possible decisions

EXHIBIT 10.3 Performance evaluation foci for awards, promotions, and reassignments

Focus of Evaluation	1. Award (Recognition)	2. Promotion (Higher Status)	3. Reassignment (New Responsibility)
A. Basic performance expectation	Incentive grant	Certification, probationary review	N/A
B. Superior level of performance	Merit award	Tenure, continuing contract	New assignment (upgrading a program)
C. Specialized performance capability	Merit award	New position	New assignment (not a promotion)

from such a focus on performance levels, if the promotions involve the same basic responsibilities. Tenure, continuing contract, or "career ladder" promotions may be illustrations of these kinds of decisions. Obviously, recognizing superior performance in basic teaching skills might be important for reassignment purposes, especially when a new program is being implemented.

When questions about *specialized performance capability* are answered positively, again all three types of decisions might be served. Merit awards could be offered for specialized competencies over and above the basic expectations of the job. More clearly, new positions will require careful assessment of special capabilities not required at all for teaching. Hence, a promotion from teacher to department head will require evidence of special competence, such as working with adult groups, curriculum coordination, or program evaluation, which might have only marginal importance to most teachers. New assignments are not always promotions in the sense that they may be special but temporary assignments or new assignments without incentives or status associated with promotions. These, too, require the attention of summative evaluation to assure that appropriate specialized capabilities are demonstrable.

MERIT AND INCENTIVE AWARDS

Various systems for rewarding the exemplary teacher have been advocated over the years, in contrast with the dominant trend of the past fifty years to develop standardized salary schedules and restrict promotions through certification. Most systems involving merit awards of some kind have not survived (Schneider 1983). Incentive programs offering support for extra duties, released time, or recognition have continued over the years, but with spotty records. Promotions, on the other hand, are usually responses to institutional needs rather than planned efforts to provide opportunities to deserving teachers.

Confusion abounds and appears to be increasing over just what terms like "merit pay" or "incentives" mean as related to the school and teachers (Bellon and Bellon, 1983). Evaluation procedures for designating meritorious teachers is equally full of uncertainty. Criteria of "excellence" have not generally been developed to the point of differentiating degrees of effectiveness. Evaluation procedures for making fine discriminations between levels of overall performance have not been validated. In fact, it is quite clear that different kinds of performance produce valued outcomes (Joyce and Weil, 1980).

Merit Evaluation

Merit awards of one kind or another pose several problems for evaluation (Silverman, 1983). The criteria of meritoriousness must be clearly defined

(Schneider, 1983). In Exhibit 10.3, it is suggested that a teacher might be designated as meriting an award if (a) some clearly superior level of basic performance expectations, or (b) some specialized performance capability, not readily available in the peer group, can be determined. These two kinds of merit will need to be evaluated differently, even though both are summative in nature.

The time frame for considering merit awards is important unless resources are unrestricted. When merit awards are continuing supplements to salary, each one granted tends to restrict opportunities to offer others found to be equally or more meritorious. If merit awards are restricted to a year or other short time frame, then a morale problem may be in the making as the "merit teacher," whose performance continues to be high, expects continuing recognition and reward. Furthermore, awards for small amounts or limited periods may fail to motivate.

One way to consider the various problems of merit evaluation is in terms of open vs. closed systems. Closed systems in which only a few individuals can be recognized have serious defects. Competition increases and cooperation declines. Invidious comparisons are encouraged. Those with strong feelings of self-confidence may or may not be reinforced, but those needing encouragement and confidence building have only limited opportunities for support from the merit system. Herzberg's (1976) studies in business and industry are clearly not supportive of restricted reward systems based on merit as motivating high performance.

Evaluation efforts for merit award purposes, if required, will have fewer problems if specialized competencies are in focus. Other evaluation endeavors that deal with basic teaching practices and their steady upgrading can and should continue without efforts to identify the superior teacher for recognition and reward. However, special program requirements might readily be identified periodically, and individual teachers rewarded for developing appropriate new competencies, providing a special service, or making a unique contribution. The "Second Mile Plan" adopted in the Houston, Texas, schools (1977) has several features of these kinds.

Awards of merit that do not require more than clearly validating a special competency, service, or contribution do not require elaborate evaluation efforts. An open nominations process which encourages self-nominations can also use self-reports for initial screening purposes. If specifications are precisely drawn, then final selections of awardees can be made via a variety of procedures. Voting, interviewing, and final committee review are possibly useful.

Merit Pay Plans

It is important to recognize that the evaluation requirements for merit pay differentiations are very different from special awards for special purposes. When the same job carries very different salaries for position occupants, some very solid evidence of differentiated need or productivity must be available. Most merit pay plans are concerned with productivity, not need. To date, we have no clear methodology for making such differentiations, except at the crudest level. It may be that new evaluation methods will be able to deal with this problem in the future. It seems doubtful, however, for the following reasons:

1. Teaching is so complex and multi-dimensional that any effort to separate the superior few will be fairly arbitrary.
2. The causal relationships between individual teaching practices and student group learning are highly confounded by student abilities, home influences, prior teacher influence, concurrent teacher influence, curricular constraints, etc.
3. Learning outcomes appropriately considered in measuring productivity are very diverse, very individual, difficult to assess, and without any criteria of comparability.

The greatest argument against merit pay plans that goes beyond the technical problems of evaluation method is low cost/benefit ratio. It is curious that some of the vested interest groups in our society that are most outspoken and critical of schools in terms of accountability, cost containment, and economic efficiency in education, also advocate merit pay plans that are very costly and clearly do not show any evidence of improving instruction (Stufflebeam and Webster, 1980). Merit pay plans are expensive because they must employ elaborate data gathering and analysis techniques.* Data must be highly reliable. Data must be highly objective. Data must sample many aspects of performance and be highly representative of all of them. Observations, interviews tests, anecdotal records, opinionnaires, and other forms of data gathering will be essential. Even with such an array of high cost data, elaborate analytical schemes will be required to properly make sense out of it all.

Benefits derived from merit pay plans have not been demonstrated (Lortie, 1975). At best there appear to be responses among a few of the already good, self-confident, and more independent teachers to improve their teaching and make it more clearly visible. But negative effects also are reported in nearly all merit pay situations (Deci, 1976). Less striving for excellence among the less competitive or less self-confident and beginning teachers is common (Meyer, 1975). Lowered morale among faculty groups, less cooperation in the use of materials, and less sharing of problems and concerns are often reported.

An elementary principal with 37 teachers reports:

---

*A school district official reporting informally to this author on their "merit pay" plan in operation, relates the need to use three outside observers for a total of 20 observations annually at a cost of approximately $2,000 per teacher evaluated and nearly $5,000 per awardee.

I've worked for years to build teams and encourage my teachers to work together. I've been at this for 12 years. I've never had an assistant. I knew I couldn't possibly work with all my teachers as closely as needed; so we've been making progress working together. Everyone of my teachers has something to offer and we share.

Now, with this new order (a mandated law requiring evaluations that identify the outstanding teachers and give them a higher salary while the others are necessarily denied such salaries because funding is sharply restricted) . . . we are already in trouble. They are keeping things to themselves, don't volunteer unless assured it will *count* on the evaluation. I'm spending my time arguing with teachers about why they got a single "satisfactory" rating instead of all ratings of "outstanding."

Merit pay plans are costly in evaluation time and effort, in morale problems, and even interpersonal conflict. The benefits at best seem to be limited to improving the performance of a few. Negative effects may reduce teacher effectiveness more often than not. A further hidden cost, is the diversion of all personnel from concern for students, for instruction, and for professional growth. Instead, emphasis is on teacher profit and survival.

The ERIC Clearinghouse on Educational Management summarizes about merit pay plans:

These findings appear to raise the possibility that merit pay in education is neither practical nor desirable. . . . paying teachers on the basis of performance may actually be counterproductive . . . (1981:3)

Incentives

More open systems for offering incentives for improving performance are generally believed to offer more promise and fewer negative side effects than the merit pay plans. They are also more readily subject to evaluation process. Incentive programs provide rewards for "different kinds or amounts" of performance (Duckett, 1984:4). Incentives can be monetary or not and should not be thought of as pay plans so much as award and recognition programs.

Programs offering incentives of various kinds are practical even when funds are limited, if creative use is made of nonmonetary awards. Exhibit 10.4 lists a rather wide variety of monetary, and nonmonetary incentive awards that have been utilized.

One of the secrets to success of incentive programs appears to be their nonexclusionary or open-ended characteristics. When many awards are used and many kinds of talents, interests, and contributions are recognized, the effects on morale are wide-spread. To what extent they actually enhance productivity is less clear.

The DeTEK system is one of the few that utilizes a certificate of accomplishment as a part of the developmental evaluation program (Hill and Harris, 1982). Only new accomplishments, clearly demonstrated and vali-

EXHIBIT 10.4   List of possible incentive awards

Monetary
- Grant for years of service.
- Grant for new certificate earned.
- Grant for X hours of approved advanced inservice training.
- Grant for new advanced degree.
- Grant for tuition expenses for summer courses completed.
- Travel reimbursement grant for attendance and reporting on a workshop or institute.

Nonmonetary
- Appointment to report to Board on program plan or pilot project.
- Invitation to Rotary, Kiwanis, Chamber of Commerce, etc. to report on new development in classroom.
- Publication of news report in local paper (joint authorships?).
- Publication in a professional journal with editorial assistance.
- Certificate of accomplishment for 10, 20, 30, years of service.
- Certificate of recognition for completing excess hours of approved inservice education.
- Certificate of growth in specialized competency area.
- Leave with pay to attend approved conference, seminar etc.
- Released time to serve on advisory committee, curriculum study, or project.
- Appointment to pilot project evaluation team.
- Assignment on accreditation team.
- Selection as Primary Teacher of the Month (or Secondary, or Vocational).
- Selected to have your own VIT parking place near the building (Very Important Teacher).

dated through observation are certified. The authors urge that earned certificates be conferred at graduation ceremonies, P.T.A. meetings, or some other special occasion.

CAREER LADDERS AND PROMOTIONS

The evaluation of teachers for purposes of assignment to new, different, or more prestigious positions is still another kind of summative evaluation purpose. As emphasized before, when purpose changes, some important aspects of the design for evaluation must also change to be effective. Summative evaluation efforts depicted in Exhibit 10.1 are oversimplified in suggesting that awards and promotions can be served in similar ways within the summative system. In fact, promotions represent one of the most demanding of evaluation tasks, requiring attention to a whole host of new criteria of performance.

The so-called "career ladder" has become a popular term for a variety of schemes for increasing classroom teachers' opportunities for promotions, usually with only limited reassignment of responsibilities. The career ladder concept, while currently taking many forms, had its origins in the collegiate personnel practices of promoting from instructor to assistant professor to associate and full professor. In the public school sector, career ladders have been associated in the past with "differentiated staffing" (English, 1972) and "team teaching" (Shaplin and Olds, 1964), as well as with recruitment, selection, and on-the-job training of minority personnel for teaching (Harris, et al., 1985).

Career ladders as they are now being promoted and mandated are curious mixtures of old staffing concepts and political concerns for fiscal restraint on salaries, control of educational policy, and the continuation of teacher shortages into a new century. With such diversity of forms, evaluations of quality for making individual promotional decisions will be very difficult.

Common Promotions

Evaluation of teaching personnel for promotional purposes logically calls for the following sequence of events:

1. Identify individuals with prerequisites: competencies, experiences, motivations, and personal characteristics.
2. Select individuals with the optimum pattern of prerequisities in numbers appropriate to anticipated openings.
3. Provide advanced and specialized training for positions where openings are anticipated.
4. Assess specialized competencies of individuals in relation to potential new position assignments.
5. Decide on individuals to be promoted (reassigned).

In the best-ordered, well-planned organization these steps will assure opportunities for the most able and the availability of qualified personnel when needed. In reality, this sequence of steps rarely can be followed. Nonetheless, the five steps outlined above are all essential to effective evaluation for promotions.

The problems associated with implementing a systematic evaluation plan for promotion should cause us to plan and design more carefully rather than to capitulate. Problems to recognize and cope with include:

1. Uncertainty about future positions.
2. Legal restrictions (certification, seniority, etc.) on selection and assignment.
3. Political pressures to give preferences to "local" applicants.
4. Civil rights obligations to affirmative action for women and minorities.

5. Retaining qualified personnel until promotional opportunities emerge.
6. Creating a group of "heirs apparent" who wait to be "annointed."

None of these problems are completely intractable, but all tend to be present in most situations and are often persistent. As such, the evaluation plan must be designed to respond systematically to each problem while avoiding capitulation to unsound procedures.

Nearly all problems listed above can be ameliorated if a proactive, on-going staffing plan is utilized. All too often, a position becomes open with suddenness (retirement, child birth, illness, or moving away), and the evaluation process begins at that point in time. This ad hoc approach leaves little room for a quality sequence of identification, selection, training, assessment, and decision-making.

An on-going program of teacher evaluation can be identifying individuals, documenting their interests and prerequisites as a regular part of the personnel management program of the school or district. Periodic selection exercises can be scheduled regardless of imminent appointments, with incentives provided—released time, tuition awards, extra duty assignments, etc.—encouraging the selected teachers to seek advanced and specialized training experiences.

A proactive program of teacher evaluation will initiate staffing decisions that increase and regularize opportunities to promote qualified individuals. Reassignments of personnel as opportunities to gain new experiences are urgently needed by many staff members. Principals and supervisors need to return to teaching periodically, assistant principals need central staff supervisory experiences, elementary teachers need exposure to secondary curriculum. As reassignment policies and plans are implemented, opportunities can be opened for promotions to new positions, either temporarily or permanently.

A whole series of reassignments can be initiated when a position becomes vacant, thereby securing a variety of teachers seeking opportunities for promotion and new experiences. For instance, the impending retirement of a principal and a supervisor can be the stimulus for various promotions. Consider moving both older officials into temporary assignments as advisors to the Superintendent and Board; move the assistant principal into a principalship in another school, reassigning that principal to temporary teaching duty; then move a young assistant principal to the original principals' position; select a teacher to become assistant principal, etc., etc. Exhibit 10.5 illustrates a series of reassignments stimulated by two retirements. Eight reassignments are produced, involving three selected teachers, assistant principals, and principals in three different schools. Obviously, these retirement openings could have been handled more traditionally. But the potential for creating a variety of appropriate new openings exists with every resignation and new position (Harris et al., 1979).

EXHIBIT 10.5 Illustration of planned reassignments to promotions

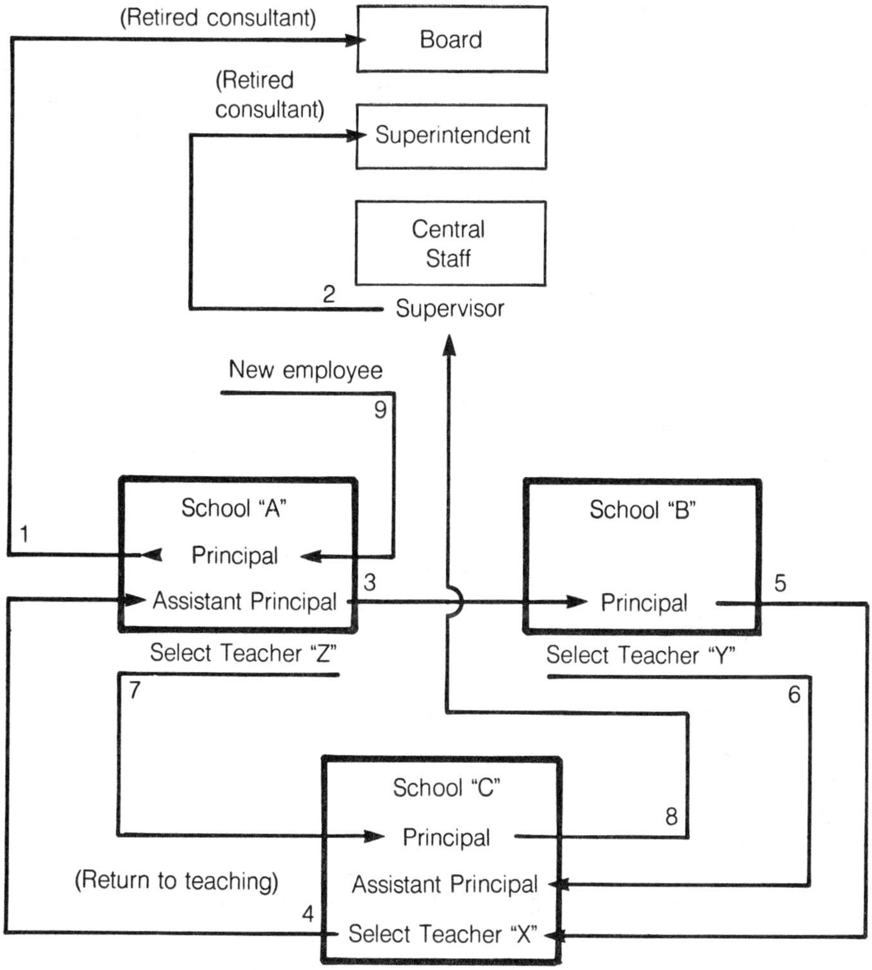

The challenge to evaluation in creative assignments is that the assessment and advanced training of teachers for various positions must be a continuing process. When it is time to make promotional decisions, the specialized competencies of individual teachers must already be verified.

The Career Ladder

A Congressional task force makes an interesting distinction between merit pay and career ladders. The term "performance-based pay" is used to depict a variety of systems (Merit Pay Task Force Report, 1983:37). This same task force, in its recommendations to Congress included the following:

3. Despite mixed and inconclusive results with performance-based pay in the private sector and in education, we support and encourage experiments with performance-based pay. (p. 39)

Despite the cautions raised in this statement, state legislatures are mandating career ladder plans, while numerous school districts are launching them on their own. Unfortunately, these are rarely experimental programs as recommended to Congress.

The intent of career ladders as currently advocated relate to (1) more adequately rewarding selected teachers and (2) differentiating assignments and roles. The rationale by which these outcomes are expected from a career ladder plan include the following:
Higher salaries will:

- Attract more able people to teaching.
- Entice able teachers to remain in the classroom, instead of seeking other jobs.
- Enhance morale and reduce "burnout."

Differentiated roles and *responsibilities* will do all of the above, plus:

- Improve the quality of the instructional program by using classroom teacher talents more fully.

This rationale has much to support it from a purely logical point of view. The recruitment potential is both long-range and heavily dependent upon reducing rather substantial differentials in salary. Furthermore, higher starting salaries might be more powerful in recruitment effects. The holding power of the classroom may be enhanced if adequate funding is available to assure that all qualified teachers get timely promotions. On the other hand, if money is not readily available (a certainty in many schools and states), then negative consequences may flow from career ladder procedures and plans. In fact, morale problems may be increased unless timely promotions are made using highly objective and humane evaluation procedures.

The probability of success or failure in career ladder plans cannot be predicted. Charters and Pelegrin (1972) studied the problems of four differentiated staffing programs in action in 1970–71 and identified many factors constraining implementation. They stress the strain in conflicting ideas about teaching, the lack of clarity in conceptualization, unrealistic time perspective, lack of training, severity of overloads, and failure to provide resources as some of the fatal flaws. These hard realities are likely to persist in the near future. Yet they are ignored in many mandated proposals.

The Texas plan for career ladder implementation clearly illustrates many of the evaluation problems associated with most of those mandated by

State law (House Bill 72, 1984). Four levels of career assignment are provided, with promotions dependent upon certification, teaching experience, advanced training, and annual evaluations of performance on prescribed criteria of classroom teaching. This presents to evaluators a seemingly straightforward problem of instrumentation, data gathering, and analysis. Unfortunately, the task is complicated by a mandated, outmoded scale, by a requirement to evaluate every teacher every year, by funding levels supporting no more than one-third of the faculty at higher levels of assignment, and by provisions that give teachers no security in their assignments.

Legal issues are complicating career ladder evaluation efforts in several states already. A teachers' union in Florida has filed suit against the State Board, attempting to have a "master-teacher plan" declared unconstitutional (*Education Week* 1985 (January 9): 4). The right to collective bargaining, as distinguished from performance evaluation as the basis for decisions, is apparently at issue in this case. However, the Florida plan uses both performance data and scores on tests to determine master-teacher status, thereby raising many other issues regarding predictive validity of pencil and paper tests (Popham, 1974).

North Carolina is one state that has taken a more systematic approach to career ladder planning (Heard, 1982). A plan will be tested in 1985–86 in 16 school systems (Lowery, 1984). This plan calls for five steps with a 10 percent salary increase for every step. Since teachers would be required to spend two years at each step, the increases seem rather nominal. The chances that this incentive will recruit and retain quality personnel and enhance morale seem remote. Furthermore, as a plan requiring rigorous summative evaluation, promotion decisions on all teachers every two years presents districts with a costly challenge.

The Tennessee Master Teacher program provides four levels of assignment including "apprentice teacher" (Klein, 1983). It, too, provides for systematic evaluation at every level, using state mandated criteria and procedures. As in the Texas plan, each promotion requires additional years of experiences and appropriate certification as well as evaluations relating to "student achievement" . . . "knowledge of subject matter," "classroom practice," "willingness to assume additional duties," and "classroom effectiveness." A rather elaborate evaluation system is suggested by all of these mandates.

The salary increments for each level are graduated in the Tennessee plan from $1,000 to $2,000 to $3,000. Further refinements include provisions for "senior teachers" and "master teachers" to earn additional income by extending their contracts from 200 days to 220 days. These provisions offer, perhaps, greater flexibility in meeting individual teacher needs. They may also enhance contributions to morale and improvement of instruction.

These career ladder plans reflect both promising efforts to enhance teaching as a productive career and the complexities of evaluation. The ease with which legislators mandate new evaluation responsibilities is deceptive. One might assume that legislators either have great faith in educators as evaluators, or are terribly naive about the complexities and costs of high quality evaluation. The latter is a more conservative assumption. It should caution us not to be equally naive.

Current efforts to implement career ladder plans on state-wide mandates are almost certain to be less than effective and in many cases will simply fade away or be corrupted out of existence. The constant mixing of merit pay, incentives, salary scales, certification, and performance evaluation produces plans with too much complexity for survival. The diversity of situations facing schools in every state make it unlikely for any mandated plan to be implemented state-wide or to produce comparable results. Finally, a rising cost of living, the upcoming new "baby boom," and the oppressive cost of military, medical, old age, and poverty programs will make resources for career ladders too scarce for success.

Dramatically different kinds of career development plans could be quite promising in the near future. Differentiated staffing patterns would be emphasized. Lower rungs on the ladder would be developed for student-service workers, aides, part-time specialists, and parents. Expansion of the numbers and variety of personnel in our schools would not reduce costs but would greatly increase personnel at little or no added cost, as the ratio of low-cost personnel to high-cost personnel increases. Teachers' careers would be individualized, with flexible opportunities to tailor job descriptions and change them when needs of the school or the individual teacher altered.

By deemphasizing hierarchy and reward, the emphasis can be placed on cultivating teacher interests and capabilities to perform. Designing staffing patterns to optimize the use of teacher resources would gain new significance. Cooperation among equals with differentiated talents and interest would replace the competitiveness of merit pay and career ladders. Job enrichment to assure each individual opportunities for growth satisfaction, variety, and relief would replace emphasis on higher and lower status positions. Above all, perhaps, such a movement toward creative staffing would not consume resources in summative, nonproductive evaluations ad infinitum. Instead, developmental evaluation efforts could largely suffice. Court costs would also be reduced.

SUMMARY

Merit pay, incentive, promotion, and career ladder programs all have different characteristics and some things in common. The current scene is such a confusing mixture of these programs that systematic evaluation efforts are almost impossible to implement without seriously sacrificing quality.

To the extent that they can be distinguished from each other, merit pay has the least promise of success, is likely to be very demanding of evaluation efforts, and will produce serious legal challenges. Incentive awards, by contrast, if varied and open to all, are likely to be quite successful, relatively inexpensive, and require very little formal evaluation.

Promotions and career ladder plans are both very complex. The promise in each plan is the hope that competent individual teachers will be recognized and offered opportunities to assume greater responsibilities. More flexible, proactive, continuing efforts to help individual teachers grow in competence and develop specialized competencies are essential to sound promotions. Such a program requires more emphasis on developmental evaluation than on summative decision making.

A career ladder as a vehicle for creating a hierarchy within the teaching position seems to have a dubious future. Many alternatives, a greater diversity in job descriptions, and more flexibility in career patterns is what the schools need. Rigidly bureaucratic promotional schemes are for bygone times and circumstances.

SELECTED STUDY SOURCES

Barber, L. W. and K. Klein (1983). "Merit Pay and Teacher Evaluation," *Phi Delta Kappan* (December):247–251.

> Illustrates the need for "parallel systems" with teacher collaboration in formative efforts while summative reviews are kept separate.

Bellon, Elmer C. and J. H. Bellon (1983). "Merit Pay and Other Incentive Programs," *Tennessee Educational Leadership* 10 (Fall):64–75.

> A thoughtful discussion of various plans and proposals for both merit pay and other incentive programs.

Clearinghouse on Educational Management (1981). "Merit Pay," *Research Action Brief,* 15 (February):1–4. Eugene, OR: ERIC Clearinghouse, University of Oregon.

> A brief but pointed summary of both research and theory on intrinsic and extrinsic motivation in education leads to clear implications for educational policy and practice.

Ellsberry, Jim (1982). "What are the Jury's Findings? . . . A Judicial Model for Program Evaluation," *Discrepancy Digest* 5 (April):2–3. The Evaluation Training Consortium Newsletter. Western Michigan University, Kalamazoo, Michigan.

> An interview is reported between the editor and the author who report on the use of Wolfe's judicial review model of evaluation applied to educational program components at North Central High School in Indianapolis, Indiana. The implications for summative program decisions may be even more relevant for summative personnel decisions.

Harris, Ben M., Vance Littleton, Dan Long, and Kenneth E. McIntyre (1985). *Personnel Administration in Education,* 2nd ed. Boston: Allyn and Bacon, Inc.

Chapters 6 and 11 deal with recruitment, selection, and evaluation of personnel. Chapter 9 addresses a variety of due process and legal requirements, especially as they relate to summative assessment to assignment and balancing teacher personnel.

Hawley, Robert C. (1984). *How to Improve the Evaluation of Teacher Performance.* Amherst, MA: Educational Research Associates.

A brief overview of several alternative efforts to deal with both summative and formative evaluation.

Klein, Karen, editor (1983–84). *Merit Pay and Evaluation.* Bloomington, IN: Phi Delta Kappa.

A compendium of reprints, and selected materials reflecting a broad variety of state, local, and national action relating to merit pay plans and various teacher evaluation systems.

Duckett, Willard R. (1984). "Learning About Merit Pay from Business and Industry," *Research Bulletin,* Center on Evaluation, Development and Research, April 1984. Bloomington, IN: Phi Delta Kappa.

A succinct summary report on business and industrial experiences as well as experts' views on these practices and their effects.

McGreal, Thomas L. (1983). "Separation of Administrative and Supervisory Behavior," in *Successful Teacher Evaluation.* Alexandria, VA: Association for Supervision and Curriculum Development.

Arguments are reviewed for clearly separating improvement effort from administratively-oriented evaluation. The author discusses the Monticello system, which clearly defines and separates improvement processes from attention to serious problems.

Medley, Donald J., et al. (1984). *Measurement-Based Evaluation of Teacher Performmance.* New York: Longman.

A very systematic, comprehensive treatment of the measurement aspects of teacher evaluation. The authors analyze problems with present practices. Chapter 9— "Measurement-Based Teacher Evaluation in Operation"—is especially useful in the context of trying to operationalize a system that works.

Merit Pay Task Force Report (1983). Report No. 98, 98th Congress, 1st Session. A report prepared for the use of the Committee on Education and Labor, House of Representatives. (October 1983). Washington, D.C.: U.S. Government Printing Office.

An objective review of both merit pay and career ladder proposals. Most interesting, perhaps, is a wide-ranging array of recommendations for Federal legislation as well as state and local action. Interestingly, the Task Force is very cautious about "performance-based" pay plans.

Principles and Guidelines for Teacher Evaluation Systems. (1979). Austin, TX: The Texas Cooperative Committee on Teacher Evaluation, Texas Classroom Teachers' Association.

A detailed listing of 36 specific guidelines within eight categories of "principles" is presented. These ideas, developed by representatives of teachers' associations and those of administrative groups, reflect wide-spread agreement on good practices in one diverse state.

Schneider, Frank (1983). "Merit Pay for Teachers." Mobile, AL: Division of General Services, Research and Evaluation, Mobile County Public Schools, June 1983. Mimeographed.

A carefully detailed analysis of merit pay practices in U.S. Schools. Historical trends are reviewed, alternatives suggested, pros and cons delineated. Industrial experiences are identified along with some current efforts in local schools.

Silverman, Buddy R. S. (1983). "Why the Merit Pay System Failed in the Federal Government." *Personnel Journal,* 62 (1983):294–97.

A detailed analysis of merit pay efforts among federal civil service employees.

11

Organizing, Staffing, and Training

An organized system of teacher evaluation requires staff whose assigned responsibilities are clearly understood and who have been properly trained. Previous chapters have emphasized performance specifications, instrument development, observation, and data analysis, with obvious implications for a well organized system, adequately staffed. Chapter 9 stresses collaboration on a scale that has special implications for training. Chapter 10 gives clear evidence of the need to organize for a variety of related, yet distinct evaluation purposes.

This chapter identifies organizational arrangements to be considered in developing new or restructured systems of teacher evaluation. Staffing considerations for quality implementation and maintenance of developmental evaluation efforts are considered. Special attention is paid to training for evaluation. Clearly, this is not only crucial, but has been most widely neglected (Stipnieks, 1981).

ORGANIZATION

Despite extensive growth and increasing school district complexity in recent decades, there is little centralization or coordination of teacher evaluation in most local schools. State-mandated evaluation systems are changing this in a few states, but to date the organization for evaluation of teachers is extremely limited. Policy and instrumentation are simplistic, and principals are generally designated as the only implementers.

Policy, Law, and Courts

The emphasis of state laws in recent years has been on summative evaluations relating to licensure, probation, nonrenewal, and dismissal. Court decisions are clearly related to summative decision making. However, the practice of intermingling developmental and summative purposes has had serious effects. Recent legislation in Texas (H.B. 72, 1984) and in North Carolina (Heard, 1984) are only two of many illustrations of growing legal influence on developmental evaluation. The Georgia (1983) new teacher certification program remains in many ways unique as a set of legal mandates acknowledging developmental realities and treating them in special ways.

Court decisions have become concerned with developmental teacher evaluation too. Judicial opinions, in some such cases, have called for developmental efforts to precede summative judgments. This no doubt has influenced the American Association of School Personnel Administrators (1978) to adopt explicit standards regarding emphasis on developmental efforts first.

Centralization Needs

Developmental teacher evaluation must be decentralized in many ways. Each school principal will inevitably carry much of the responsibility for maintaining the system in operation. However, the entire process cannot realistically be delegated to the lone principal. Implementation of new program efforts requires policy revisions, training, and coordination across schools and programs. Personnel officers and instructional supervisors will need to be closely associated with the developmental teacher evaluation system during an implementation phase and beyond.

Continuing training of new teachers, principals, and others will generally be more economical and effective if directed by those not assigned to an individual school. Quality control efforts are crucial in maintaining sensitive evaluation processes. Hence, periodic retraining and reliability analysis are important efforts best handled in more centralized ways.

Instrument development is still another aspect of teacher evaluation that is better directed in more centralized ways. Individual schools and faculty members should be involved, but overall responsibility for revisions or adaptations and testing of instruments can be readily undertaken in central offices or even contracted through a college or other agency.

Staff development related to developmental evaluation of teaching has to be a shared responsibility. In Chapter 9 the importance of both personalized and group approaches to professional growth were emphasized. Hence, much of the organization for in-service education opportunities can and should be highly decentralized. However, a district-wide or regional system for delivery of training should be closely coordinated with the operations within the individual schools (Hagen, 1981).

Coordination

The most important changes in perspective and organizational arrangements needed in most schools relate to making developmental teacher evaluation a system rather than an event. This requires coordination efforts of a variety of kinds and the acceptance of shared responsibilities by a variety of individuals. Training, scheduling, observing, conferencing, and planning activities need to be organized programmatically, as is true of any important effort. However, developmental teacher evaluation, because of its collaborative nature and the involvement of all professional personnel, will need special attention to be sure that schedules do not conflict, resources (time and energy) are available, and decisions are actually implemented.

INSTALLING A SYSTEM

New developmental teacher evaluation systems or dramatically revised systems need to be formally installed. At least three phases for installation precede the actual operations of data gathering, analysis, etc. An orientation and planning phase creates readiness on the part of all who need to be concerned. Training, while continuing beyond early implementation, is essential in the earliest stages. Organizational arrangements made prior to any actual implementing efforts are crucial to the success of a new program.

Orientation

All persons associated with a new developmental evaluation system should become familiar with its purposes, general procedures, materials, and unique features. Orientation clients include school board members, citizen groups, and all professional personnel to be directly affected. It is important that policy makers and the public be aware of new efforts in teacher evaluation in order to gain their support and build confidence.

Orientation activities may include brief visual presentations. If a pilot program testing of a new system has been utilized, reports from these pilot participants can serve to make orientation presentations more meaningful.

It is important to recognize orientation as different from planning and training. Participants in orientation sessions are being informed but are not being asked to decide or participate in the evaluation process itself. School boards may be in decision making roles before and after orientation presentations have been presented to them. Teachers and other staff will need to be trained to assume their responsibilities in a new evaluation system. Orientation sessions are precursors to such training efforts.

Planning

Developing detailed plans for a new developmental teacher evaluation system may be relatively simple if an already fully developed system is adopted. More commonly, planning for a new system involves studying alternative systems, testing, selecting, adapting, and pilot testing.

Once a system is ready to be implemented and groups are properly oriented, the plans must be carefully developed for training programs, making organizational changes, and monitoring progress. Ultimately, an evaluation plan will be employed to assess the quality of the operating system.

Organizational Alternatives

Most new, complex systems will have greater chances for success if some gradual or incremental plan for implementation is utilized. Wholesale adoptions on school-wide or system-wide bases are rarely effective. Any complex operation calls for many changes and time must be allowed for making them with minimum cost, pain, and distress.

Pilot projects have been mentioned as a desirable precursor of fuller implementation efforts. Pilot projects are usually small scale programs. They have access to more resources than might otherwise be available. They can serve as demonstrations, build leadership, and give confidence to others implementing at later times.

Study groups may be important to an implementation plan. They are especially useful when the new system is a controversial departure and when group commitment is essential to success. Even though developmental teacher evaluation is a highly personal affair, it can profit from system-wide support and group commitment.

Volunteer implementation is still another useful mechanism for gradually involving individuals or groups in the new system. Since developmental teacher evaluation is individualized, it is possible to involve volunteers while others abstain, even when a school or program is committed as a whole.

Most school systems utilize an array of these alternatives in implementing a new developmental system. Three years is generally a minimum time period for implementation. Five-year implementation programs are not unusual.

Staffing and Support

Extended time frames and fairly elaborate plans for implementation are required for success with complex new systems. They require that institutional commitments be clear, unequivocal, and adequate. Policy changes should clearly reflect the intent to install a new system. The superintendent of schools and other key officials must be clearly and visibly associated with the effort. But staff and supporting resources also must be clearly allocated and sustained over time.

Coordination for implementation should be vested in some individual or group that can assume district-wide responsibility for planning, training, monitoring, and evaluating. An advisory committee or council can be used to good advantage. But an instructional or personnel officer needs to be named director for implementation purposes.

Training plans are discussed in more detail later in this chapter. It is important for training needs to be clearly designated in early planning efforts. Then responsibilities for training can be delegated and resources allocated.

Supporting service needs should never be underestimated. Any new program calling for new modes of behavior, reallocation of time, and new responsibilities will struggle to become a reality. Communications among principals, teachers, trainers, and others will need increased attention. People involved will need more opportunity to "blow off steam." Released time, protection from diversions, and even more frequent reinforcement efforts are essential in early phases of implementation.

TRAINING PLANS

The need for both education and training about teacher evaluation has been stressed throughout this book. This chapter is concerned primarily with the kinds of training activities that are essential to the implementation of more sophisticated and effective developmental teacher evaluation systems. In emphasizing basic training requirements for implementation, the educational impact of the developmental evaluation processes themselves will be taken for granted. However, it is important to face reality about the technical competence required for any kind of quality evaluation effort, to recognize that basic understandings and skills may need to be developed, and to recognize that every new instrument and procedure requires some training.

Training plans for implementing new developmental teacher evaluation systems should focus on the needs of each type of participant in the evaluation process. The training needs of teachers and principals will be paramount. However, if students are providing data, they, too, must be given some attention. When large scale programs are being implemented, the training of trainers will need special attention.

Each distinct instrument and procedure will require some training. While classroom observations and feedback conferences are two of the most demanding aspects of teacher evaluation requiring training, each instrument—questionnaire, checklist, inventory, worksheet—will require some formal training to assure that users understand and are skilled in its use. Even a set of procedures, policies, and performance criteria will need systematic review to assure proper understandings.

Goals and Objectives

Four sets of objectives might be considered in developing a training plan for a school or district implementing a developmental teacher evaluation system. Participants generally need:

1. To understand the principles, purposes, and techniques that are most directly related to the system.
2. To understand the specific system's rationale, characteristics, and implementing procedures.
3. To actually use the instruments and procedures with reliability, fidelity, and economy.

These three general goals should guide planning to assure that the specific needs of different participants are recognized. Training in the actual use of instruments and procedures will necessarily be quite different for teachers than for principals or supervisors.

A fourth goal for a training plan includes attention to systematic implementation procedures within school and classroom settings. If several observers are to be employed, for instance, the thoughtful coordination of their efforts needs to be planned. If only volunteers are to be evaluated initially, then the transitional schedules and selection procedures will need special attention. Procedures for handlings problems will also need attention as part of the training program.

Exhibit 11.1 illustrates a set of goals and objectives developed and used to guide a training program for a pilot program implementing the DeTek system in an array of schools in Australia. The objectives for training are detailed to address the specifics of this particular system. Similar detail will need to be addressed in implementing any system.

Some objectives will be appropriate for all participants in the evaluation process, others will not. Generally, the objectives illustrated under I and II in Exhibit 11.1 will be included in training plans for all. However, special training plans will be needed to differentiate between the skills required for evaluators and evaluatees. There is some advantage in developing as much common understanding and skill as possible, to enhance the basis for collaboration. There are limits, however. Teachers may have neither time nor interest in developing sophisticated observation-recording skills. The costs may also be prohibitive. Nonetheless, the more common experiences that are provided the better.

Program Design

A program designed to develop an extensive array of understandings and skills will require a series of formal sessions as well as independent study activities. Attempts to implement new systems of any kind with a few

EXHIBIT 11.1 Illustration: Goals and objectives for extended training for DeTEK disseminators

I. *To understand teacher evaluation principles, purposes, and techniques*
   1.1 To distinguish among current, past, and emerging practices and concepts related to teacher evaluation.
   1.2 To recall a variety of purposes to be served.
   1.3 To recognize essential features of developmental vs. administrative evaluation.
   1.4 To recognize the importance of research-based criteria.

II. *To understand the DeTEK system, its rationale, design characteristics, and implementation procedures*
   2.1 To distinguish the four-phases and ten steps in the system.
   2.2 To identify the contribution of each of the ten steps to a logical, developmental sequence of collaboration.
   2.3 To recall each of the six performance areas.
   2.4 To identify a variety of alternatives for utilizing the system.

III. *To use DeTEK instruments and procedures with reliability, effectiveness, and economy of time*
   3.1 To relate each instrument to a specific step and procedure in the system.
   3.2 To recall the specific procedures essential to proper utilization of each DeTEK instrument.
   3.3 To recognize each of the twenty-two behaviors as associated with performance areas.
   3.5 To produce observation records which are detailed, descriptive, and void of judgments and opinions.
   3.6 To observe, record, and report performance estimates with high levels of interobserver reliability.
   3.7 To utilize three sets of data to produce diagnoses, utilizing congruence analysis techniques.
   3.8 To confer with teachers, using collaborative procedures, to produce a growth plan likely to be responsive to a diagnosed need for improvement.

IV. *To plan for implementation of DeTEK in school settings using training methods and materials provided*
   4.1 To identify four or five alternative implementation strategies.
   4.2 To designate support services to be developed for implementation purposes.
   4.3 To schedule training and orientation activities.
   4.4 To recognize phasing-in possibilities for saving time and avoiding problems.

brief "awareness" sessions are virtually useless. Joyce and Showers (1983) have demonstrated the importance of going through a sequence that emphasizes both laboratory practice and "coaching" for application. Harris (1980) has provided a framework for selecting training activities to assure variety, high "experience impact," and sequence in appropriate group or individual arrangements.

A program designed for implementing a developmental system is shown schematically in Exhibit 11.2. This particular program involved 15 sessions scheduled for approximately 40 hours of activity. Activities included lectures, demonstration, discussion, laboratory training, and on-site observation practice in small subgroups. Independent study, general orientation, and follow-up consultation during implementation were planned in addition to the formal training sequence. The sessions varied from one to three hours in length and were scheduled over a two week period. A longer time frame would be possible, with some loss of time for required review of prior sessions.

Classroom observation training is often the most demanding. In the program illustrated in Exhibit 11.2, 25 to 30 hours were utilized for each subgroup participating in the on-site activities. This particular program still does not address another essential aspect of training for developmental teacher evaluation. Training in basic feedback conference techniques is often required in addition to sessions addressing specific diagnostic and growth planning procedures.

Another training program designed for classroom observation is presented in Exhibit 11.3 to illustrate a scheme for training trainers (local teams) to work within individual schools. In this particular situation, all classroom teachers were utilized as observers, so a major training effort was required in each school.

Laboratory Training

Actual techniques and procedures can often be simulated for training purposes (Harris, Bessent and McIntyre 1969). By simulating reality for a group of trainees, it is possible to build initial skills and complex understandings for an entire group. Time is utilized more efficiently in a group setting. Mistakes can be corrected more readily. Self-confidence can be nurtured.

Simulated laboratory training for developmental teacher evaluation can be utilized without elaborate designs. A group of principals can be asked to pretend they are teachers as they utilize the teacher self-report instrument and score it to produce a profile. In role playing, these principals become intimately acquainted with the nature of the instrument and its scoring procedures.

Role playing is a useful form of simulation for feedback conferences involving diagnostic analysis and growth planning. Such a laboratory training session might be planned as follows:

EXHIBIT 11.2 A system diagram disseminators' extended training program

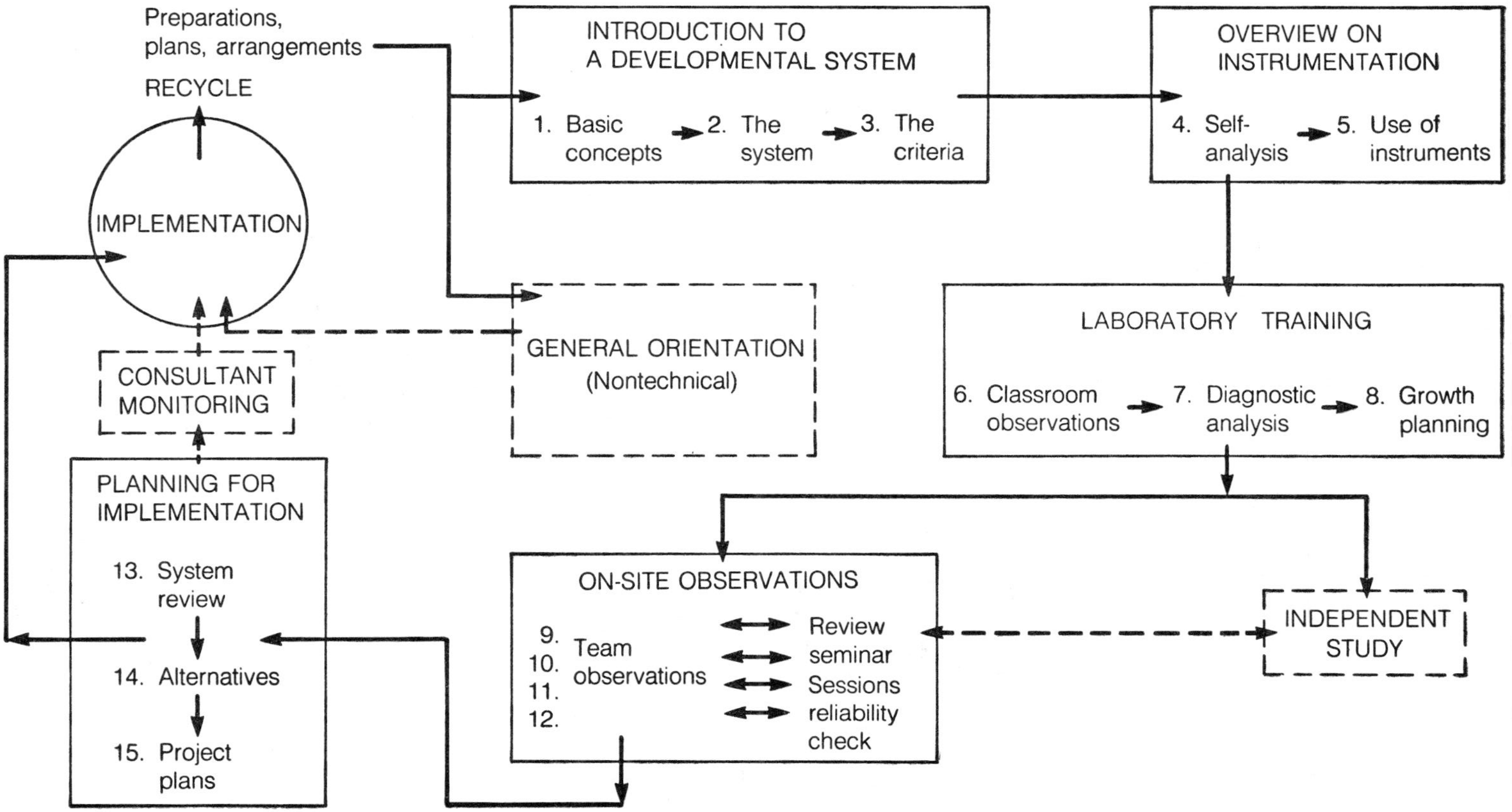

EXHIBIT 11.3   A training plan flowchart for classroom observers

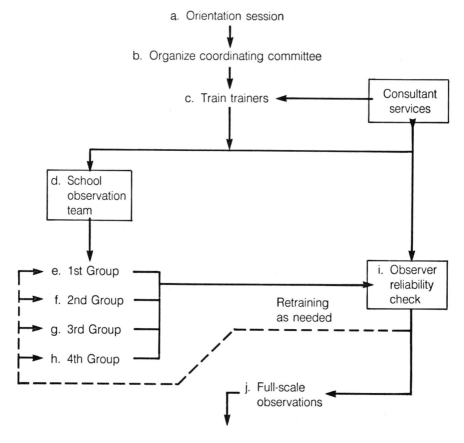

*Adapted from *Improving Staff Performance Through In-Service Education* by Ben M. Harris (1980:117).

1. Introduce a lesson and its teacher with a film or lesson protocol.
2. Present the instruments reporting the data on the lesson.
3. Review procedures for using the simulated data in a feedback conference. Distribute materials for diagnostic analysis, etc.
4. Organize role playing T-groups. Designate a work place for each group of three. Direct them to take roles as (a) teacher, (b) principal or supervisor, and (c) listener.
5. Allow time for each T-group to role play the use of simulated data in a simulated conference.
6. Discuss role playing experiences. Suggest improvements. Caution against certain practices. Urge using approved procedures.
7. Repeat role playing in T-groups having each person take on a new role.

8. Repeat discussion.
9. Repeat role playing, rotating role assignment again.
10. Restructure T-groups and continue role playing.
11. Take video-camera and record portions of several role playing groups in action.
12. Reassemble groups for viewing of video-tape and discussion of results.

This sequence of activities would likely take 2 to 3 hours and require a break or rest period. Similar laboratory sessions would be quite useful for simulated experiences in growth planning, use of student report instruments in classrooms, and for classroom observation.

Classroom Observation Training

Since classroom observation is such a crucial aspect of data gathering for developmental teacher evaluation, it deserves special attention in a training program. Chapter 7 goes into detail regarding observation-recording-analysis techniques and problems. Exhibit 7.1 details a whole array of "characteristics" of professional, systematic classroom observation. These are also requirements for training when they are not already among the skills possessed.

Basic observation skills, once developed, will be adaptable to a variety of instruments. However, every instrument requires training to assure that the specific techniques required are skillfully employed. Laboratory training is useful initially to familiarize observer trainees with instrument characteristics and special techniques. Films, video-tapes, and typescripts (protocols) are useful in such a laboratory session, where observing and recording are simulated.

The observation-recording process is so complex that only limited progress can be expected in a laboratory situation. Training plans should provide for on-site classroom observations after only a very few hours of simulation and discussion. The sequence of standardized procedures required for use of any instrument should be incorporated into the training sequence.

A basic training sequence for on-site classroom observations provides for the following activities:

1. Make arrangements for observing in a selected classroom as a group of 3 to 10 trainees.
2. Observe in classroom according to prescribed procedures for a full class period. (All trainees record independently, but use common procedures.)
3. Training group leaves classroom to revise recordings, analyze, compare, discuss, and critique their efforts.

This three-phase plan is detailed in Appendix D-2. It has been utilized extensively for training in rather complex procedures and is effective in producing needed skills and understandings. Generally, four or five such on-site observation training sessions are needed to produce minimum levels of performance.

Testing Reliability

All data utilized in teacher evaluations should be as reliable as possible. Data that are not reliable cannot be valid. Carefully developed instruments, rigorously utilized by well trained individuals can assure all collaborators that the data utilized are at least reasonably reliable and have probable validity too. A part of a well-designed training program should be designated for checking on the reliability of the data gathered.

Instruments of different kinds will vary in the level of reliability that can be expected. For all instruments, however, training is a prerequisite and fidelity in the use of procedures is essential. Reliability levels of roughly 80 percent agreement, or 0.75 and better as a coefficient, are desirable and realistic.

Procedures for testing observer agreement are discussed and illustrated by Medley et al. (1984) and in the Harris and Hill *Trainers Manual* (1982) in nontechnical terms. In general terms, a test of reliability conducted between two observers involves scoring the observation records independently, calculating a difference score for every item or criterion, summing the difference scores (ignoring the plus or minus nature of the differences), and calculating the percent of disagreement between the two sets of observations. A percent agreement can then readily be obtained.

Reliability reports on a small group of observer trainees use performance estimates. For a set of behaviors based on a three-point scale, the computations used are illustrated in abbreviated form in Exhibit 11.4. A trainee and an experienced observer both observed the same lesson and made performance estimates independent of each other. Their total scores for the lesson were very similar. This could be used to deceive ourselves about reliability. Difference scores are shown on nearly one-half of all items. Since there are 22 behaviors scaled, each one could have produced a maximum difference score of 2 points (+2). Hence, if our two observers were in complete disagreement the sum of all difference scores could have been as great as 44, instead of the actual 11 point sum of differences. Differences amount, then, to 25 percent of possible differences and the observers are in agreement on 75 percent of the total possible scaled values. This is a simple estimate of reliability.

A more rigorous estimate of reliability should often be used. Since it is possible for any two observers to agree purely by chance we should eliminate this chance score from our estimate. The formula for this is:

$$\text{Reliability} = \frac{\% \text{ Agreement} - \% \text{ Chance}}{100\% - \% \text{ Chance}}$$

In the illustration in Exhibit 11.4 this equation gives the following coefficient of reliability:

$$\text{Reliability} = \frac{75\% - 33\%}{100 - 33\%} = \frac{42\%}{67\%} = \underline{0.63}$$

As you can see, the two observers are not really as reliable as the simple percentage estimate seemed to indicate.

In our work with observation training over the years, it has been possible to get reliability coefficients of 0.75 and better for nearly all experienced trained observers who use sound instruments with fidelity. Those

EXHIBIT 11.4 Illustration of basic computations for testing observer reliability

Criterion Behavior	Observers' Estimates		Difference Scores
	"X" Trainee	"Y" Expert	
1a	2	3	−1
1b	2	2	0
1c	2	2	0
1d	2	2	0
2a	3	3	0
2b	3	2	+1
2c	2	3	−1
2d	2	3	−1
3a	3	3	0
3b	3	3	0
3c	3	3	0
4a	2	1	+1
4b	2	3	−1
4c	1	1	0
4d	3	1	+2
5a	1	1	0
5b	1	2	−1
5c	2	2	0
5d	2	2	0
6a	2	1	+1
6b	1	1	0
6c	2	1	+1
Total (Actual)	46	45	11
	÷	÷	÷
Maximum Scores	66	66	44
	70%	68%	25%

untrained observers who use poorly structured instruments in haphazard ways are rarely reliable above the 0.25 level.

The practical implications of reliability checking are several. It tells us when training has been sufficient or needs to be resumed. It assures teachers that they can trust the data generated. Finally, it assures that analyses and diagnoses can be respected for use in decision making.

A word about generalizability is necessary. An observation that is reliable can be trusted in cautious degree to produce data worthy of analysis and interpretation. But generalizability about the full range of teaching in a classroom requires more than testing one observation against another (Shavelson and Atwood, 1977). To generalize on the total performance of a teacher over time requires reliable observations over time. All aspects of the teaching must be sampled—mornings, afternoons, fall, winter, spring, Mondays, Wednesdays, Fridays, fast groups, slow groups, favorite subjects, etc. It should come as no surprise, then, that most quick and simple efforts at summative evaluation of teaching are not defensible. Several studies suggest that about a dozen highly reliable observations, properly sampling the total teaching year, can lead to generalizations of some certainty.

SUMMARY

Organizing, planning, training for, and implementing an evaluation system needs the same policy, staffing, and resource considerations of any program or project. When developmental evaluation of teaching is undertaken, special care must be exercised to assure high quality implementation. Such evaluation is too important and involves too many people to be approached haphazardly.

The myth lives on that planning for teacher evaluation is simply creating a new instrument. Obviously instrumentation is always important. Chapter after chapter in this book is devoted to emphasizing evaluation as a process, with instrumentation only one part of the sequence. Every aspect of the eight-step sequence—criteria, instrumentation, data gathering, etc.—must be considered in organizing, planning, training, and implementing developmental teacher evaluation.

In addition to the many specific suggestions presented here, such things as having a director, installing with an incremental approach, or detailing training plan, a few broad-gauged considerations are also warranted.

Collaboration is as important in the planning, organizing, and training as it is in the actual operating of the developmental system.

Resource allocations are crucial to the success of any quality endeavor. In the case of developmental teacher evaluation most of the resources required are the hours of professional time and the intellectual and emotional energies of teachers, administrators, and supervisors. These resources are already allocated. They must be reallocated from less important, less productive endeavors. That is part of the organizing, training, and implementation process.

Satisfactions are the only sure motivators for most of us. Developmental teacher evaluation can increase satisfactions and motivate for greater effectiveness, but it takes time for such results.

SELECTED STUDY SOURCES

Boehm, Ann E. and Richard A. Weinberg (1977). *The Classroom Observer: A Guide for Developing Observation Skills.* New York: Teachers College Press.

One of the very few sources that addresses the problem of training observers. Thoughtful and useful ideas. Discusses objectivity, biases, and other distortions. Urges focus of observer guided by question or problem statements.

Frick, Ted and M. I. Semmel (1978). "Observer Agreement and Reliabilities of Classroom Observational Measures," *Review of Educational Research* 48 (Winter):157–84.

Discusses observer agreement measures. Urges using an expert coder for comparisons.

Hagen, Nancy Joyce (1981). "A Comparative Analysis of Selected Inservice Education Delivery Systems." Unpublished doctoral dissertation, The University of Texas at Austin, Austin, Texas.

Case studies show strong evidence for highly structured training programs to assure implementation of new practices.

Harris, Ben M. (1980). *Improving Staff Performance Through In-Service Education.* Boston: Allyn and Bacon, Inc.

Chapters on use of activities with high experience impact, the design of training sessions, and personalized approaches to training are useful guides for planning training for evaluation.

Harris, Ben M., Louise Goodlet, and C. M. Sloan (1975). *A Manual for Observing with the New Comprehensive Observation Guide.* Austin, TX: Instructional Leadership Training Materials, Department of Educational Administration, The University of Texas. Mimeographed.

An example of a manual for using a particular instrument. Details of procedures are provided for users. Illustration of completed observation records are shown.

Harris, Ben M. and Jane Hill (1982). "The DeTEK Handbook" and "Trainer's Manual," in the *Developmental Teacher Evaluation Kit.* Austin TX: Southwest Educational Development Laboratory.

Both documents illustrate the use of materials and plans for assuring training for all participants in an evaluation effort.

Joyce, Bruce and Beverly Showers (1983). *Power in Staff Development Through Research on Training*. Alexandria, VA: Association for Supervision and Curriculum Development.

A review of several studies leading to renewed emphasis on the training sequence and process for assuring change in behavior. The authors emphasize laboratory activities followed by "coaching" and warn against expecting easy transfer.

Medley, Don et al (1984). *Measurement-Based Evaluation of Teacher Performance*. New York: Longman, Inc.

The last of a long line of contributions to this field with much technical detail on reliability and validity as well as other related topics.

Shavelson, Richard and Nancy Attwood (1977). "Generalizability of Measures of Teaching Process," in *The Appraisal of Teaching: Concepts and Process* by Gary D. Borich and Kathleen S. Fenton, editors. Reading, MA: Addison-Wesley Publishing Co. pp. 351–67.

The authors discuss "stability coefficients" for various measures, emphasize distinctions between reliability and generalizability, and discuss problems with very short observation periods.

APPENDIX

Guidelines for Good Practice

A. PRE-CONDITIONS FOR TEACHER EVALUATION

1. *The teaching/learning situation* should be one which maximizes student learning. An effective and realistic teacher evaluation system can only be developed if student learning remains the primary activity of the school.

2. *The teacher-pupil ratio* should be such that teachers will not be placed in the position of simply acting as student custodians.

3. *The time limits for instruction* should be flexible in order that teachers may meet the individual learning rates, styles, and capabilities of all students.

4. *The basic learning goals* should be clearly stated· and be understood by students and teachers.

B. GENERAL PRINCIPLES

5. *Purpose.* The primary purpose of teacher evaluation is the improvement of instruction for student learning. Thus, the integrity of the *developmental* character of the evaluation system should be safeguarded at all times to assure the ability of the system to *guide* and *stimulate* improvement efforts.

6. *Policy Development.* The essential features of the total personnel evaluation system should be carefully specified in local school board policy.

7. *All Personnel Evaluated.* The evaluation system should provide for developmental evaluation of all personnel, not just teachers.

---

*Source: *Principles and Guidelines for Teacher Evaluation Systems* (Austin, TX: The Texas Cooperative Committee on Teacher Evaluations, 1979).

8. *Research, Theory, Practice, and Artistry.* The teacher evaluation system must clearly reflect the best state of knowledge (research, theory, practice, and artistry) relating to teaching and learning.

C. SOURCES AND USES OF DATA

9. *Recognition of Diversity.* Data collection procedures should be flexible enough to accommodate and give recognition to a variety of teaching styles, learning modes, and unknowns in the teaching/learning process.

10. *Description and Diagnosis.* Data gathering should emphasize description and diagnostic analysis of teacher performance on-the-job, as distinguished from opinions and judgments.

11. *Communication of Expectations.* Employees should be informed concerning all aspects of the evaluation system *prior* to the implementation of any contractual or employment status determinations.

12. *Separation of the Formative and Summative.* Both developmental (formative) and employment status (summative) evaluation should be provided. However, the developmental purpose must be safeguarded by clearly separating formative and summative data processing and analysis procedures. Employees should understand the difference between the two.

13. *Sequence of Formative and Summative.* The formative evaluation system should be utilized to the fullest to improve teacher performance *prior* to any contractual or employment status determinations.

14. *Instructional Relevance.* All data selected for use should be clearly relevant to instructional improvement and student learning.

15. *Pupil Learning Focus.* Measures of pupil achievement should be used in the evaluation process only as they can be clearly related to improving teacher performance.

D. INSTRUMENTATION

16. *Reliability and Objectivity.* Data secured from whatever source should be as highly reliable (consistent) and objective (non-judgmental) as possible.

17. *Qualitative Analysis.* Data should be collected which recognizes those important aspects of teacher performance which are not readily measured.

18. *Instrument Design.* Instruments should be developed, selected, or adapted to reflect local needs as well as the best available technology of instrumentation to insure objectivity, reliability and relevance in data provided.

19. *Instrument Diversity.* Different kinds of instrumentation should be employed whenever necessary to assure data that best serves developmental needs.

20. *Cooperative Selection.* Instruments should be cooperatively reviewed and accepted for use only on the basis of demonstrated capability to produce data of proper quality.

E. COLLABORATION

21. *Collaboration.* All aspects of the evaluation system should be developed and implemented with the fullest possible collaboration among all persons affected. Individuals, the district and the organized professional groups involved should be clearly committed to being guided by the outcomes from the evaluation process.

22. *Individual Responsibility.* The individual being evaluated should share responsibility with administrators and others for all aspects of the process as possible.

23. *Peer Responsibility and Reciprocity.* In the use of developmental, objective evaluation systems, all personnel should serve in various roles—evaluatee, observer, analyst, improvement planner, etc.

F. TRAINING FOR EVALUATION

24. *Specialized Training.* Special training should be provided to all staff involved to assure general understandings and skills necessary for use of instruments and procedures adopted.

25. *Differentiating Training.* Training programs should be responsive to the different needs of individuals, schools and programs.

26. *Competence.* Each person utilizing a data gathering instrument or diagnostic process in connection with teacher evaluation should be able to demonstrate competence in its use.

27. *Competent Leadership.* At least one person with specialized competencies and commitment to developmental evaluation purposes should be available within each school district to assist with developing and implementing the evaluation system.

G. DUE PROCESS

28. *Due Process and Rights.* All evaluation procedures should conform to well established principles of due process and respect for the rights of people.

29. *Pre- and Post-Evaluation Events.* Each individual being evaluated should be assured of opportunities to participate in pre-evaluation planning, clarifying objectives, criteria, and procedures. Similarly, post-evaluation opportunities should be assured to review data, assist in its analysis and/or interpretation, and make plans for improvement activities.

30. *Systems Operation.* The evaluation system should be designed with clearly designated sequences of events which preclude ad hoc, unilateral, or unfair procedures.

31. *Continuity of Process.* For each individual the evaluation process should be one with continuity which assures periodic performance review, diagnosis of growth, and decisions for improvement.

32. *Diagnostic Decision-Making.* The process of evaluation should begin with individual diagnosis, based on objective performance records (including observation records). These records should be the basis for reaching agreements about what is/are the appropriate objectives for growth, how they will be objectively assessed, and setting target dates.

33. *Disagreements.* Individual teachers should have opportunities to disagree with diagnoses or decisions for improvement being presented. Procedures for handling such disagreements in a constructive, collaborative way should be clearly a part of the evaluation system.

H. IMPROVEMENT ACTIVITIES

34. *In-service Training.* In-service training and other support systems should be fully developed to assure maximum possible benefits to persons being evaluated as well as to students and the community served.

35. *Limited Expectations.* Individual plans for growth developed in the evaluation process should be clearly limitied to those improvement objectives that the school district can and will support.

36. *Resource Allocations.* Resources provided for the total evaluation system operaton should be *clearly* supplemented with resources for supporting the improvement efforts of the individual teachers.

APPENDIX

B

DeTEK
Criteria List

Appendix B

1

DeTEK Criteria List

Performance Area	Behaviors and Indicators

1. BUSINESSLIKE
The teacher is organized, systematic, goal oriented, and prepared.

The teacher performs in a variety of ways that clearly reflect planning, goal orientation, prioritization, and detailed consideration of relationships between purpose, activity, sequence, materials, delegation, time constraints, and space utilization. In essence, the teacher clearly knows what is intended and facilitates its realization.

1a. *Organizes classroom activities to produce a smooth flow of events with a minimum of confusion or waste of time.*

1a (1)—Gives clear, simple directions for shifting from one activity to another.

1a (2)—Initiates changes in activity for individuals who are ready while others are still busy with prior assignments.

1a (3)—Arranges all materials for easy distribution as needed during activity.

1a (4)—Makes prompt use of supplemental activities or plan modifications to assure full use of all available time.

1a (5)—Organizes and directs clerical and housekeeping chores to prevent waste by time by teacher and students.

1b. *Informs students of objectives, sequence of events, the rationale, and responsibilities well in advance of lesson or activity.*

1b (1)—Displays and/or verbalizes the planned sequence of events for the lesson or period.

1b (2)—Specifies objectives in clear, explicit terms before students are given directions, and refers to such objectives as needed for clarification and evaluation purposes.

1b (3)—Discusses the rationale for assignments in terms of objectives, course goals, and the realities of student life.

1b (4)—Defines student responsibilities, emphasizing expectations, growth, progress, excellence, and effort.

1c. *Delegates responsibilities to students, aides, and others in ways that keep them involved and conserve teacher time and energy for the most demanding responsibilities.*

1c (1)—Assigns routine clerical and housekeeping chores to students (and aides) on a scheduled basis, dispersing the workload and conserving time.

1c (2)—Arranges for students to work individually or in small groups, defining the responsibilities of all students.

1c (3)—Leads students in evaluating their own assignments, providing all necessary materials and directions to assure objectivity.

1c (4)—Stimulates students to seek assistance from other school personnel, parents, and others in conjunction with regular course assignments.

1d. *Paces activities to assure task accomplishment, arranging for assistance for those who need it to make progress and reach goals.*

1d (1)—Surveys the progress of students toward task accomplishment, and reminds students of time allocations, urging greater speed as needed.

1d (2)—Adjusts time frames to fit needs of students, allowing time, shifting to new activities more quickly, or rescheduling target dates.

1d (3)—Provides tutorial assistance or guides small groups to assist with task accomplishment on schedule.

1d (4)—Encourages and directs students in assisting each other to assure task completion.

2. FRIENDLY
The teacher is warm, empathetic, outgoing, positive, and personal.

The teacher displays warm, friendly, personal relationships with all pupils by emphasizing the positive, avoiding negativism, being accessible to students, considering their feelings and problems, recognizing differences in interests, abilities, and experiences. In essence, the teacher clearly regards every individual and the student group as persons who are likeable, worthy, interesting, and capable.

2a. *Speaks to students in positive, praising, encouraging ways.*

2a (1)—Acknowledges student comments or responses verbally without interrupting or reducing focus on the student.

2a (2)—Praises student efforts, using phrases, sentences, and tonal inflections which are meaningful to the student(s) involved.

2a (3)—Frees students from embarrassment by using reassuring and supportive statements.

2a (4)—Avoids giving negative reactions, criticisms, threats, sarcasm, etc.

2a (5)—Interacts personally with all students, balancing the attention given the more aggressive and the less aggressive students.

2b. *Expresses interest in individuals as persons over and above being students.*

2b (1)—Seeks out individual students and groups of students for informal personal contacts.

2b (2)—Encourages students to share thoughts and feelings, reflecting and clarifying in ways that help students assess the effectiveness of their behavior patterns.

3b (5)—Utilizes activities which allow for a high degree of student interac-

Appendix B-1

Performance Area	Behaviors and Indicators

2b (3)—Inquires about students' personal accomplishments or interests.

2b (4)—Assists students in defining realistic self-development goals.

2c. *Reflects empathy, concern, and warm liking of students as related to both school and other aspects of life.*

2c (1)—Comments sympathetically on feelings of students.

2c (2)—Asks about and comments with acceptance on family and personal affairs.

2c (3)—Shares personal experiences.

2c (4)—Encourages students to recognize peer accomplishments.

2c (5)—Tells and listens to jokes, puns, or amusing incidents.

2d. *Demonstrates interest and concern for students nonverbally in a variety of ways.*

2d (1)—Maintains eye contact with students when interacting verbally with them.

2d (2)—Listens attentively when students are talking or presenting.

2d (3)—Smiles openly, broadly, and frequently; and laughs freely when appropriate.

2d (4)—Moves close to students when assisting them, leaning, stooping, sitting, etc., as needed.

2d (5)—Uses with, and accepts from, students such physical contacts as handshakes, pats on the back, or embraces.

3. VERBALLY INTERACTIVE
The teacher listens, accepts, probes, questions, and encourages.

The teacher utilizes a variety of verbal interaction techniques to enhance clarity of communication, stimulate verbalizations by students, and provoke higher-level thought processes; and encourages students to relate talk, listening, and thinking to their various classroom learning experiences.

3a. *Communicates clearly and concisely.*

3a (1)—Gives directions or comments as needed to assure progress.

3a (2)—Avoids directions or comments which disrupt students and waste their time.

3a (3)—Uses a level of language students can understand.

3b. *Encourages and guides student responses and teacher-student interactions.*

3b (1)—Gives and asks for information and suggestions.

3b (2)—Encourages alternative answers, rephrasing to suggest responses from different students.

3b (3)—Prompts, reflects, accepts disagreements, and waits extended periods of time for students' thoughts to emerge.

3b (4)—Listens thoughtfully to students' ideas, incorporating them into the lesson and recognizing their worth.

3b (5)—Utilizes activities which allow for a high degree of student interaction—discussion, simulation, experiments, problem solving, games, inquiries.

3c. *Utilizes a variety of questioning techniques which provoke different levels of thinking on the part of all students.*

3c (1)—Uses open-ended questions to stimulate discussion, probing in ways that keep the question open-ended and enhance student thinking.

3c (2)—Adjusts pace of questioning to allow periods of silence so all students may engage in higher-level thinking.

3c (3)—Uses an array of question types, ranging from simple recognition and recall to analysis, synthesis, and evaluation.

4. STIMULATING
The teacher is imaginative, stimulating, exciting, provocative, interesting, avoiding dull routine.

The teacher expresses interest in the subject matter and activities of the class. The teacher avoids dull routines in favor of many variations in procedures, materials, and activities. The teacher utilizes student interests.

4a. *Expresses interest, enthusiasm, and curiosity about subject matter and other events.*

4a (1)—Decorates or arranges the classroom in ways which reinforce the theme of the lesson or the subject.

4a (2)—Shares personal books, artifacts, experiences, reading, or other materials with the students.

4a (3)—Uses self-invented written materials, models, drawings, or processes.

4a (4)—Improvises furniture, objects, costumes, or sets to meet unique or spontaneous needs.

4a (5)—Raises questions about others' thoughts, opinions, or ideas in ways which reinforce the theme of the lesson or event.

4a (6)—Communicates excitement, surprise, wonder about lesson or event by inflection and by varying speaking rate, gestures, and body movement.

4a (7)—Elaborates on subject matter by drawing from a personal knowledge base which is accurate, up-to-date, and of significant depth.

Appendix B-2

3

Performance Area	Behaviors and Indicators

4b. *Uses a variety of styles, techniques, and approaches to present subject matter.*

4b (1)—Organizes subject matter presentations to show relationships between disciplines and connections of subject matter to the real world.

4b (2)—Uses shifts in sensory modes, levels of thinking, interaction styles, or in location of teacher/learners to keep the lesson flowing and student interest and attention high.

4b (3)—Models, and guides students in using, a wide array of higher cognitive operations, e.g., classifying, comparing, evaluating, inferring, generalizing, hypothesizing.

4b (4)—Plans and executes presentations which are surprising, out of the ordinary, and memorable, increasing active response of the students and motivating them toward further participation.

4b (5)—Sets up and provides resources for a wide variety of challenging learning acivities, e.g., inquiries, experiments, simulations, case studies, interviews, brainstorming.

4c. *Draws upon students' interests and current events for content, illustrations, and applications within the classroom.*

4c (1)—Substitutes current problems, issues, or happenings of interest to students for those offered in commercial materials or texts, when doing so makes for lively and efficient learning.

4c (2)—Refers to up-to-date bulletin boards, exhibits, interest centers, newspapers, periodicals, books, or other selected sources of information.

4c (3)—Provides students with choices in topics for study, in activities, or in coworkers.

4c (4)—Encourages students to reveal their interests by facilitating such student-centered activities within the classroom as sharing books of particular interest, displaying artifacts, or talking about experiences or current issues.

4c (5)—Invites students to initiate projects, experiments, or other learning activities, assisting them directly when called upon.

4d. *Responds spontaneously to unplanned events, using them as reinforcers or illustrations.*

4d (1)—Maintains a planned but flexible learning environment in which unplanned events *can* emerge.

4d (2)—Cues students that the event is important by recognizing the event and calling attention to it.

4d (3)—Guides students in relating the event to past, present, or future learning, tying the event to specific learnings, materials, or processes.

4d (4)—Introduces extension activities as a followup to the event when doing so aids significantly in accomplishing the learning objectives set up prior to the event's occurrence.

5. INDIVIDUAL ORIENTED
The teacher treats each individual as a unique learner.

The teacher makes learning different for individuals in many ways. Intraclass groupings are utilized routinely, as well as for special occasions, along with total group instruction. Assignments are routinely differentiated to provide for individual needs with respect to objectives, time allocations, and mode of learning. Materials assigned for use are varied. Individual students are provided freedom to pursue learning tasks differently, to progress more rapidly, and to go beyond basic requirements. Teachers and students are both tutors in formal one-to-one relationships.

5a. *Collects, organizes, and analyzes diagnostic data about individual students' current learning needs.*

5a (1)—Develops and administers tests and other evaluative procedures which are diagnostically scored to indicate what individuals *have* learned and what they *need* to learn.

5a (2)—Observes students' learning styles, recording individuals' rates of learning and use of time and their preferred study skills, sensory modes, and working relationships.

5a (3)—Maintains cumulative profiles of individuals' learning behaviors, highlighting those needs which *can* and *will* be met through the school program.

5b. *Plans an instructional program which meets the unique needs and learning styles of individual students.*

5b (1)—Uses diagnostic information about individuals' current needs in lesson planning.

5b (2)—Departs from standard curricular expectations to respond more directly to urgent individual needs.

5b (3)—Differentiates experiences by providing objectives, varied assignments, materials, activities, working relationships, time on task, and teacher assistance tailored to the needs of individual students.

5b (4)—Organizes materials and resources for student use so that individual learners have what they need when they need it.

Appendix B-3

Performance Area	Behaviors and Indicators

5c. *Directs instruction in response to the unique needs and learning styles of individual students.*

    5c (1)—Guides the work of student groups whose membership, tasks, location, and size change periodically in response to individual learning needs.

    5c (2)—Provides for and processes feedback to and from individuals about class activities and homework assignments, adjusting instructional modes, materials, or time on task if needed.

    5c (3)—Encourages individual initiative in pursuing learning, reinforcing such actions as seeking help from other students, bringing materials from home, moving about the room to get resources, going to the library independently, or suggesting alternatives.

5d. *Responds to individuals in ways that assist them in accomplishing their objectives.*

    5d (1)—Encourages and guides students in finding their own "best" way of learning.

    5d (2)—Makes self available to individual students and groups, conferring during independent study time, arranging for peer tutoring, reteaching, checking to see work is done correctly, or clarifying.

    5d (3)—Recognizes and responds positively to efforts and approximate performance of learning objectives.

    5d (4)—Grades papers and projects with diagnostic notations clearly indicating strengths *and* needs of students.

    5d (5)—Leads students in checking and correcting their own work diagnostically.

    5d (6)—Discusses graded work with individual students and small groups, assuring their recognition of ways of improving performance or overcoming difficulties.

    5d (7)—Shares diagnostic profile data with individual students, helping them to set specific, realistic learning objectives.

6. MULTI-MEDIA INTEGRATIVE
The teacher provides, through diverse media, for visualization, dramatization, demonstration, manipulation, reading, and listening.

6a. *Uses a variety of audio-visual and manipulative aids regularly as integral parts of lessons and assignments.*

    6a (1)—Utilizes print materials which are illustrated and colorful.

    6a (2)—Uses chalkboards, charts, bulletin boards, displays, photographs, posters, slides, and transparencies to portray content visually.

    6a (3)—Makes audio materials such as records and tapes a regular part of lessons.

    6a (4)—Incorporates audio-visual materials such as television, videotape, sound film, etc., regularly in lessons.

    6a (5)—Provides manipulative experiences through games, puzzles, clay, painting, drawing, construction, etc.

6b. *Involves students actively and regularly in such multi-sensory experiences as dramatizations, verbal interactions, games, drawings, and field studies.*

    6b (1)—Directs students in using role-plays or socio-dramas in connection with their assignments.

    6b (2)—Structures discussion groups to provide extended opportunities for students to verbalize and share knowledge with each other.

    6b (3)—Encourages students to illustrate learning in graphic or artistic forms.

    6b (4)—Utilizes games in ways which stimulate interest and participation without excessive competition.

    6b (5)—Provides for out-of-classroom learning in school and community settings.

    6b (6)—Arranges for laboratory experiments, special projects, or action research studies as a part of regular assignments.

6c. *Participates with students in multi-media, multi-sensory activities—demonstrating, helping, and extending learning.*

    6c (1)—Utilizes teacher-made as well as commercial and student-made materials in the classroom.

    6c (2)—Serves as participant as well as leader or observer in role-playing, discussion, or game activities.

    6c (3)—Demonstrates and helps students understand ways of using multi-media.

    6c (4)—Introduces multi-media carefully to assure student awareness of their purpose in the lessons.

    6c (5)—Follows use of multi-media/sensory activities with discussion, testing, or other planned activity.

APPENDIX

C

Illustrations of Completed Instruments

The DeTEK System*

Ben M. Harris
and
Jane Hill

Appendix C-1

DeTEK INSTRUMENT I

TEACHER PERFORMANCE SCREENING INVENTORY

A Self-Analysis Survey Profile

Teacher _Helen Wills_ School _High Line City_ Date _9/8/8 –_

Teaching Assignment: Grade _9th_ Subject(s) _Science_

DIRECTIONS:

After completion of sections **A** and **B**
- A. TALLY choices from Section A to column A below.
- B. Transfer check marks (✓) from Section B to column B below.
- C. Check HIGH Performance clusters.
  (4 or 5 choices and 3 or 4 checks)
- D. Check LOW performance clusters.
  (0, 1, or 2 choices and 0 or 1 check)
- E. SELECT a performance and one or more of its behaviors for study.

	A. Performance Choices	B. Behaviors a	b	c	d	Performance Clusters C. High	D. Low
1. Businesslike	卌	(✓)	(✓)	( )	(✓)	X	
2. Friendly	IIII	(✓)	(✓)	(✓)	(✓)	X	
3. Verbally Interactive	III	(✓)	( )	(✓)	( )		
4. Stimulating	I	( )	( )	(✓)	(✓)		
5. Individual Oriented	II	( )	(✓)	( )	( )		X
6. Multi-Media Integrative		(✓)	( )	( )	( )		X
7. Other		( )	( )	( )	( )		
8. Other		( )	( )	( )	( )		

E. SUMMARY

Selected Performance (1 only): **(6)**

Selected Behaviors (1, 2 or 3): **b** **c**

Comments: _I'm not clear on my abilities in area 4-Stimulating._

Appendix C-2

A DeTEK INSTRUMENT
COMPREHENSIVE OBSERVATION OF PERFORMANCE

Teacher *Helen Wills*   Grade *9th*   Subject *Science-Math*

School *Highline City High*   Observer *H.E. Ellis* Date *9/8/8 -*

Lesson and Topic *Relating equations to science-* Time *9:40* to *10:30*
Chemical reactions.

General Directions:

This instrument is intended as a guide for observing and recording the full array of twenty-two behaviors in the DeTEK system of teacher evaluation. The observer is to record in objective, descriptive notations any and all observed evidence which might be relevant to each listed behavior. No opinions or judgments are to be noted. Detailed directions for use of this instrument are provided in the DeTEK Handbook, chapter 3.

ROOM DIAGRAM:

Draw a sketch of the floor plan and physical arrangements in the instructional space being observed. Show the location of groups and the number in each group. Show seating arrangements, displays, equipment, windows, doors, cabinets, etc.

Prepare this sketch on first entering the room, prior to beginning to record on-going events.

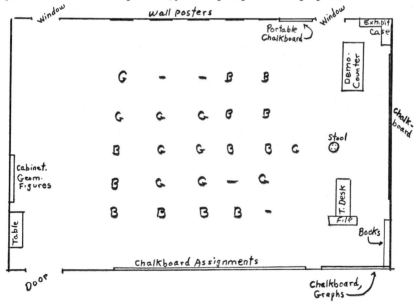

Performance Area #1 — Businesslike
The teacher is organized, systematic, goal oriented, and prepared.

No
Evidence

____1a — Organizes classroom activities to produce a smooth flow of events with a minimum of confusion or waste of time.

- T. announces the things students should do before the bell rings: "Check the assignment on the board... get out your work... check it over..."
- T. records grades in a record book as papers are being passed out (by T.).
- T. stays up front at all times after distributing papers...
- T. works rapidly, drawing on board and explaining simultaneously... asks... questions while drawing.
- T. runs out of time. Bell rings as last exercise underway... T. holds class... Then gives

____1b — Informs students of objectives, sequence of events, the rationale, and responsibilities well in advance of lesson or activity.

- T. refers to purpose: "... we're going to use those..."
- T. reviews sequence ... "we're going to go over that (homework) then ..."
- T. "remember ...It's one you don't have to memorize... " T. gives reminders: "Don't forget... " "...memorize those..." "...write it down..." "Ask!" "Take it one step at a time ..." "Tonight you should finish this problem..." "Go back and be sure you have it right..."

____1c — Delegates responsibilities to students, aides, and others in ways that keep them involved and conserves teacher time and energy for the most demanding responsibilities.

T. urges students to "...be sure to ask questions..."
T. take roll orally by self as students review homework.
T. passes materials. T. puts all material on board.

____1d — Paces activities to assure task accomplishment, arranging for assistance to those who need it to make progress and reach goals.

T. distributes materials to individuals (their homework?) as students work on board assignments.
T. starts giving directions before the bell rings.
T. shifts... "Now we have to find this other unknown..."
T. shifts to work on the board. "OK... I'm going to show this on the board..."
T. says, "Now, let's do the last..." Boy says, "I did it already." T. hesitates. Says "OK".

____ Other Behaviors (specify):

1d continued
T. runs out of time --- Tries to hold class past the bell. Realizes problem --- restlessness --- dismisses class.

Performance Summary:

Observed evidence is:				Behaviors				
	1a	1b	1c	1d		Others		
Highly descriptive	HD	(HD)	HD	HD	HD	HD	HD	HD
Moderately descriptive	(MD)	MD	MD	(MD)	MD	MD	MD	MD
Not very descriptive	ND	ND	(ND)	ND	ND	ND	ND	ND

Appendix C-2 (continued)

Performance Area #4 — Stimulating

The teacher is imaginative, stimulating, exciting, provocative, interesting, avoiding dull routine.

No
Evidence

_____4a —Expresses interest, enthusiasm, and curiosity about subject matter and other events.

T. illustrates with diagrams on the board.
T. strongly responds to student answer. "Keep up that good work!"
T. exclaims: "That's not fair!" as a student beats teacher to the answer.
T. tells girl - "Nothing wrong with those little creatures...They're fun!"

_____4b —Uses a variety of styles, techniques, and approaches to present subject matter.

T. seeks choral responses. T. probes for individual responses. T. illustrates
T. gets up on a box to work at chalkboard -- making sketches.
T. uses colored chalk to accentuate part of a sketch.
T. asks for discovery. "Do you see it?" T. waits. Students respond. T. says,
"That's interesting. How we are cooking with gas..." Students begin
to elaborate.

_____4c —Draws upon students' interests and current events for content, illustrations, and applications within
the classroom.

T. says, "I don't think it is fair to you...I'll work some of those examples
for you to get you going."
student asks question. T. starts to illustrate, says, "Someone help me."
T. refers to size - need to get up on a box to use top of chalkboard.
T. makes no references to out-of-school realities. All examples are bookish.

_____4d —Responds spontaneously to unplanned events, using them as reinforcers or illustrations.

- Students ask about problems. T. says "I'm sorry...I called it out wrong.
I'm sorry. Thank you for telling me".
- Boy insists on sharing his answer even though it isn't due until next
class period. T. gives in. "OK...Tell us what you have". Bell rings.
T. has to interrupt. "ok... we'll finish it tomorrow..."

_____ _____Other Behaviors (specify):

Performance Summary:

Observed evidence is:				Behaviors				
	4a	4b	4c	4d		Others		
Highly descriptive	(HD)	HD	HD	HD	HD	HD	HD	HD
Moderately descriptive	MD	(MD)	MD	(MD)	MD	MD	MD	MD
Not very descriptive	ND	ND	(ND)	ND	ND	ND	ND	ND

Appendix C-2 (continued)

A DeTEK INSTRUMENT
COMPREHENSIVE OBSERVATION OF PERFORMANCE

Teacher _Helen Wills_ Grade _9th_ Subject _Science-Math._
School _Highline City High_ Observer _H. E. Ellis_ Date _9/8/8-_
Lesson and Topic _Relating equations to_ Time _9:40_ to _10:30_
Science — chemical reactions.

THE PROFILE

Performance	a	b	c	d	Other
			Behaviors: Summary of Observed Evidence		
1. Businesslike	(M)	(H)	(N)	(M)	(−)
2. Friendly	(H)	(M)	(N)	(M)	(−)
3. Verbally Interactive	(H)	(M)	(M)		(−)
4. Stimulating	(H)	(M)	(N)	(M)	(−)
5. Individual Oriented	(N)	(N)	(M)	(M)	(−)
6. Multi-Media Integrative	(M)	(N)	(N)		(−)
Other_____	( )	( )	( )	( )	( )

OBSERVED ACCOMPLISHMENTS: Performance areas _#1 #2 #3 #4_

SUGGESTED FOR FURTHER ANALYSIS: Performance Areas: _#6 #5_

Behaviors: #_6b_ #_6c_ #_5a_ #_5b_ #____

Comments:

Four strong performance areas in evidence this lesson. Businesslike 1c needs review? Also, 2c? Areas #5 and #6 seem likely targets for more attention?

APPENDIX C-3

DeTEK INSTRUMENT II   6b

TEACHER BEHAVIOR SELF REPORT

Teacher _Helen Wills_____ Grade _9th__ Subject _Science_

School _High Line City High_____ Date _9/18/8-_____

| PERFORMANCE # | 6 MULTI-MEDIA INTEGRATIVE |

BEHAVIOR #

6b - Involves students actively and regularly in such multi-sensory experiences as dramatizations, verbal interactions, games, drawings, and field studies.

Directions: Show the extent to which each indicator is descriptive of your teaching by circling the appropriate designation in the space to the right.	Highly	Moderately	Not Very
6b(1) Directs students in using role-plays or socio-dramas in connection with their assignments.	(HD)	MD	ND
6b(2) Structures discussion groups to provide extended opportunities for students to verbalize and share knowledge with each other.	HD	(MD)	ND
6b(3) Encourages students to illustrate learning in graphic or artistic forms.	(HD)	MD	ND
6b(4) Utilizes games in ways which stimulate interest and participation without excessive competition.	HD	(MD)	ND
6b(5) Provides for out-of-classroom learning in school and community settings.	(HD)	MD	ND
6b(6) Arranges for laboratory experiments, special projects, or action research studies as a part of regular assignments.	HD	(MD)	ND
	HD	MD	ND
	HD	MD	ND

Conference Notes:

Appendix C-4

DeTEK INSTRUMENT III   6b

CLASSROOM OBSERVER REPORT

Teacher _Helen Wills_____ Grade _9th_ Subject _Science._

School _Highline City High_ Observer: Prin. ( ) Supv. (X) Other ( ) Date _9/22/8-_

Time: _8:40_ to _9:25_ Lesson Topic _Leaking Bottle Lesson — Where condensation_
comes from and why?

PERFORMANCE #	BEHAVIOR #	6b - Involves students actively and
MULTI-MEDIA INTEGRATIVE		regularly in such multi-sensory experiences as dramatizations, verbal interactions, games, drawings, and field studies.

INDICATORS AND DESCRIPTIONS OF OBSERVED EVENTS

6b(1) Directs students in using role-plays or socio-dramas in connection with their assignments.

- T. asks students to be like scientists "... being very critical, ... avoid making assumptions ... "

- T. encourages continuing speculation about the condensation, pressures in the bottle, leaking, ice formation. But no real structured, "scientific" approach is provided.

- T. role of scientists not really structured ... students allowed to freely speculate instead.

6b(2) Structures discussion groups to provide extended opportunities for students to verbalize and share knowledge with each other.

- Opens discussion following presentation with "core" bottle. "What do you think of my explanation?" .. "
- T. repeats students' words. "It's 'thawing out' .... 'sweating ...'" Say it again Pam." Next student answers: "It's condensing." T. say "It's condensing" Alright. Do you all agree?" Students just nod. T. says, "Is that what Pam means?" Keith tries to explain "sweating" as moisture in the air. Kenneth and Mike add similar ideas.
- T. cuts off student reactions as interest mounts. Only 5 students made comments.
- T. rarely probes or challenges. Speculations accepted just as are facts. Misconceptions never challenged.

6b(3) Encourages students to illustrate learning in graphic or artistic forms.

T. illustrates ideas of students on the board as they talk. T. uses a cause and effect sequence (diagrams it on the board).

T. does not encourage use of board or other illustrate modes. When Tim and others are struggling for words: T. "... the pressure forced the cap up ... Is that what you mean?" Tim. "well ... sort of ... around the sides ..." Students begin to argue over ice, pressure, leaks, etc. but no use of illustrations suggested.

Appendix C-4 (continued)

6b(4) Utilizes games in ways which stimulate interest and participation without
excessive competition.
  —T. introduces lesson by taking a bottle of coke from a thermos.
  —T. interrupts logical explanations being given to say: "How do you
know that bottle is cold? How do you know the beads of liquid are water?
How do you know the bottle is even glass?" students respond eaagerly
with logical test. "... taste it!", "fee it", "tap it with a pencil."
T. starts to talk about "assumptions".
  —T. asks for student to explain. "Roxanne had an idea that... Well, let's
have her explain." Later. Kenneth- "Well. I agree with Michael cause----"
Keith: "well I want him to explain it to me --- why?" Teacher acts as
facilitator. "Go ahead." Go ahead, I don't have to call on you." Four others make comments.
  —T. encourages others.
6b(5) Provides for out-of-classroom learning in school and community settings.

  (No evidence)

6b(6) Arranges for laboratory experiments, special projects, or action research
studies as a part of regular assignments.
  —T. asks "... what's happening to our coke?" after wiping it dry and
placing it on a stool for all to see.
  —T. has coke in thermos on entering the room, using ice(?) to assure
that it will be very cold --- moisture forms quickly on the bottle.
  —T. does not submit student ideas to tests. Students not involved
in feeling, measuring, testing. Emphasis is on talking above
visual observations and related known facts (some not correct).

SUMMARIZE YOUR OBSERVATIONS. Circle the appropriate designation for each indicator.

Indicator is:	Indicator Numbers							
	6b(1)	6b(2)	6b(3)	6b(4)	6b(5)	6b(6)		
Highly Descriptive	HD	HD	HD	HD	HD	HD	HD	HD
Moderately Descriptive	MD	(MD)	MD	MD	MD	(MD)	MD	MD
Not very Descriptive	(ND)	ND	(ND)	(ND)	(ND)	ND	ND	ND

Appendix C-5

DeTEK INSTRUMENT IV   6b

SUPPLEMENTAL STUDENT REPORT

Teacher's Name _Helen Mills_   Grade _9th_

Subject _Science_   Boy _✓_ Girl _____ Date _9/18/8-_

Put a check mark in the box after every statement below that *tells something your teacher does.*   Example: [✓]

(1) Shows us how to act out ideas or things we are learning. [✓]

(2) Sets up groups where we really talk to each other as a part of the lesson. [ ]

(3) Likes for us to show what we have learned by drawing or using some other kind of art. [ ]

(4) Uses games which are interesting and help us learn. [✓]

(5) Takes us to places outside the classroom as a part of out lessons. [ ]

(6) Has us do experiments and special projects as a part of our regular work. [✓]

Appendix C-6

DeTEK INSTRUMENT V
DATA ANALYSIS WORKSHEET *

Teacher: Helen Mills   Grade: 9th   Subject: Science   Date: 9/22/8-

School: High Vista City High   Collaborator(s): _____   Prin. ( ) Supv. (X) Other ( )

PERFORMANCE: 6   BEHAVIOR: 6b - Involves students actively and regularly in such multi-sensory experiences as dramatizations, verbal interplay, etc.

(1) Indicators (Write abbreviated description of indicators)	(2) Self-Report II	(3) Observation Report III	(4) Agree or Disagree	(5) Supplemental Student Report IV	(6) Accomplishments (Circle)	(7) NEEDS Yes-Uncertain
6b(1) - Uses role-play.	HD	ND	Disagree	⁊H+ III	*	Uncertain
6b(2) - function disc.	MD	MD	Agree	II	*	Yes
6b(3) - Encourage art	HD	ND	Disagree	IIII	*	Uncertain
6b(4) - Uses games	MD	ND	Disagree	⁊H+	*	Uncertain
6b(5) - Provides out	HD	ND	Disagree	II	*	Uncertain
6b(6) - arranges lab and projects	MD	MD	Agree	⁊H+ ⁊H+ II	*	Uncertain

Number of Student Reports = 15

(8) If "uncertain" is designated in col. 7, set date for an observation here.
Day: Wed.
Date: 10/23/7-
Time: 9:45

Diagnostic comments:
Collaborators agree to growth planning on 6 b(2).
Observer and teacher need to review 6b(1), (3) and (5) carefully.
Teacher agrees to upgrade 6b(6) on her own.

Appendix C-7

DeTEK INSTRUMENT VI
PROFESSIONAL GROWTH PLAN

Teacher _Helen Wills_   School _Highline City High_   Date _9/26/8–_

Teaching Assignment: Grade _9th_   Subject(s) _Science and Math._

FIRST — REFERENCE ACCOMPLISHMENTS: Behavior # _6a_
(Designate behavior and indicator numbers accomplished.
Refer to Data Analysis Worksheet, Instrument V)

Indicators Accomplished
#_1_ #____ #____
#____ #____ #____

SECOND-DESIGNATE BEHAVIORS AND INDICATORS AS NEEDS (Refer to Instrument V) Number DEVELOPMENTAL LEVEL	THIRD-LIST ACTIVITIES TO BE UNDERTAKEN (Describe specific activities for each indicator. Refer to Resource File and Activities List for suggestions of activities, materials and sources.)	FOURTH-MAKE DECISIONS	
		Collaborator Responsible	Date to Complete
6b(2) Structures discussions groups to provide extended opportunities	K – Secure one of several books on group discussion leading. See Cantor or Hogg foundation pamphlet	Ellis	10/1
	– Read journal article in module by Lawrence	Wills	10/1
for students to verbalize and share knowledge with each other.	E "Promoting Total Member Participation" (1972.) – Read in one or more books provided.	Wills	10/7
	E – Arrange for viewing of Glasser film.	Ellis	10/2
	"Questions for thinking" – View film and discuss use of ideas.	Wills and Ellis	10/7
	E – Prepare lesson with discussion involved	Wills	10/5
	T – Present trial discussion lesson, and tape record it for review.	Wills	10/23
	– Observe trial lesson	Ellis	10/23
	e – Discuss trial discussion. Review tape. Re-plan for new lesson	Wills and Ellis	10/23
	– Observe follow-up lesson	Ellis	11/1

*INDICATE the proposed date for STEP 10-REVIEW DIALOG SESSION.   Time: _8:10_ to _8:30_   Date _Nov. 4, 198–_

Teacher's Signature _Helen Wills_   Principal's Signature _H. E. Ellis_

APPENDIX

D-1

Introductory Workshop Sessions

Agenda

DeTEK Workshop

OBJECTIVES

1. To know the DeTEK system as a distinctive approach to developmental teacher evaluation.
2. To develop skill in using comprehensive, descriptive observation techniques.
3. To develop skill in using congruence analysis techniques for diagnosing teaching practice.
4. To understand the rationale and procedures for collaboration using the 10-step sequence.
5. To plan for implementation of DeTEK in 198--198-.

ACTIVITY SEQUENCE

August 7
    9:00 a.m.—Opening. Introductions
          —Overview on Evaluation Problems and Concepts
          —The DeTEK System in Review
          —An Exercise in Self-Analysis

  Break

    10:45 a.m.—A Simulation: Evaluating C. Henry, Fifth Grade Teacher
           —Discussion

Lunch

1:30 p.m. —Observation Techniques
          —Review of Performance Criteria. Descriptive Recording. Practicing with Film and Video
4:00 p.m. —Adjourn

August 8

8:30 a.m. —Review of DeTEK Instrumentation
9:00 a.m. —Diagnostic Analysis Practice

Break

10:30 a.m. —Growth Planning with Resource File
11:30 a.m. —Record Keeping and Recycling Alternatives
11:50 a.m. —Summation
12:00 noon—Adjourn

(Post-session after lunch for administrators to consider plans and procedures for fall implementation and pilot project possibilities.)

Appendix

D-2

Outline of Topics for Extended Training

The DeTEK System

Day/ Date	Session Number	Topic	Time Est. (hrs.)
		OVERVIEW AND INTRODUCTION	
One 11/30			
	1.	Basic Concepts: Issues, Problems, Processes	1 ½
	2.	The System: Design and the 10-Step Sequence	1 ½
	3.	The Criteria: Specifications, Scope and Research Bases	2
	4.	Simulated Self-Analysis: Instrument I, Collaboration, and Uniqueness in Use	1
	5.	Simulated Use of Instruments: The 10-Step Sequence with C. Henry, A Teacher	2
Two 12/3		LABORATORY EXERCISES	
	6.	Classroom Observation: Comprehensive Observing Using Tapes and Films	3
	7.	Diagnostic Analysis: Congruence Analysis Using Diagnostic Data	2
	8.	Growth Planning: Role-Playing, the Use of Growth Plans, Resource Guide, Other Activities	1 ½

ON-SITE CLASSROOM OBSERVATION TRAINING

Three
12/4

| | 9. | Team Observation #1: Classroom Observation Practice with Follow-Up Seminar | 3 |
| | 10. | Team Observation #2: Classroom Observation Practice with Follow-Up Seminar | 3 |

Four
12/5

| | 11. thru 13. | Small Group Observations, Practicing Observation Techniques, Refining Skills. | 5–8 |

Five
12/6

| | 14. | Team Observation/ Reliability Checking | 3 |

PLANNING FOR IMPLEMENTATION

| | 15. | Review of DeTEK System, Projecting Alternative | 3 |
| ADJOURN | | | |

Appendix
D-3

Description of Training Procedures for Faculty-Wide Involvement

Component I:
Observing and Analyzing Classroom Practices

a. The entire faculty will have an opportunity to become familiar with the purposes to be served by classroom observations, the instruments to be utilized, and the training and other procedures planned. A general faculty meeting will be planned. This will be followed by school-level discussions.

b. A coordinating committee for component I will be organized. Each building and grade level will have an elected teacher representative on the committee. Each building will have an administrative representative. The central staff will be represented by an instructional supervisor from each of the elementary and secondary divisions, and the superintendent will serve as chairman at least for the first year.

c. A local training team will be organized and trained as observation trainers in each building. Most if not all of these trainers will also be members of the Coordinating Committee. At least three trainers in each building wil be selected, provided with released time, and trained in the use of systematic classroom observation techniques. They will also be given training in the use of standardized training procedures and provided with consulting services from a visiting consultant.

d. As training teams are ready, they will proceed to work with one fourth of

Source: *Improving Staff Performance Through In-Service Education* by Ben M. Harris (1980). Allyn and Bacon, Inc. pp. 374–375.

the faculty in each building to train them in the use of classroom observation procedrues.

e-h-j. As each group of the faculty gains skill in the use of observation techniques, interobserver reliability checks will be scheduled to secure agreements of high order. Training will be conducted in workshop settings but quickly move to classrooms, where small groups will practice on each other.

i. A visiting consultant will be holding regular conferences with training team leaders (trainers) to discuss problems, reactions, and concerns they may be encountering.

k. Demonstrations will be planned and presented to provide opportunities for observers to see specific practices under high-quality conditions. If necessary, some of these demonstrations will be scheduled in schools in other districts to assure only top-quality displays of practices.

f. As trainers certify a substantial portion of the faculty as qualified observers, routine observations with individual feedback will be scheduled. Observations will provide each faculty member no less than five feedback reports by five different observers, one for each of an array of lessons.

n. Principals will have debriefing sessions with small faculty groups to determine concerns and problems and obtain suggestions for revisions in procedures during the following year.

Procedures for subsequent years will be much like those described here, with only a few exceptions: (1) new teachers will be trained as soon as possible; (2) rechecking of reliability levels will be provided; (3) growth planning wil be related to observation and feedback processes beginning early in the second year as a part of Component III.

Bibliography

Archilles, Charles M., and R. L. French (1977). *Inside Classrooms: Studies in Verbal and Non-Verbal Communication.* A Report of the University of Tennessee, IDER Studies (1970–75). Danville, IL: The Interstate Printers and Publishers, Inc.

Alfonso, R. J., and L. Goldsberry (1982). "Colleagueship in Supervision," in *Supervision of Teaching.* Alexandria, VA: Association for Supervision and Curriculum Development.

Alkin, Marvin C., Richard Daillak, and Peter White (1979). *Using Evaluations: Does Evaluation Make a Difference,* Sage Library of Social Research, Volume 76. Beverly Hills, CA: Sage Publications.

Allen, Dwight W. (1966). "Microteaching: A New Framework for Inservice Education," *High School Journal* 49: (May): 355–362.

American Association of School Administrators (1978). *The Competency Movement: Problems and Solutions.* Arlington, VA: American Association of School Administrators.

American Association of School Administrators (1979). *Staff Dismissal: Problems and Solutions.* Reston, VA: American Association of School Administrators.

American Association of School Personnel Administrators (1972). *Standards for School Personnel Administration,* 2nd ed. Walnut Creek, CA: The Association.

American Association of School Personnel Administrators (1978). *Standards, Policies and Practices for School Personnel Administration,* 3rd ed. Seven Hills, OH: The Association.

Anderson, Jonathan, and B. C. Hansford (1974). "An Information Processing Procedure for Scoring Flanders' Interaction Analysis Categories," *Journal of Experimental Education* 43 (Fall 1974):6–10.

Anderson, Robert H., editor (1981). *Improving Classroom Practice Through Supervision.* Dallas, TX: Texas Association for Supervision and Curriculum Development.

Anderson, Robert H., and Karolyn J. Snyder (1981). *Clinical Supervision: A Coaching Technology.* Lubbock, TX: Pedamorphosis, Inc.

Anderson, Scarvia B., and Samuel Ball (1978). *The Profession and Practice of Program Evaluation.* San Francisco: Jossey-Bass.

Andre, Thomas (1979). "Does Answering Higher Level Questions While Reading Facilitate Productive Learning?" *Review of Educational Research* 49 (Spring): 280–318.

Annadale, Dave (1980). "Teacher Accountability in Higher Education," Unpublished paper. Tempe, AZ: Arizona State University.

Archer, Margaret S. (1979). *Social Origins of Educational Systems.* Beverly Hills, CA: Sage Publications.

Armes, Nancy (1980). "Teaching Effectiveness: A Research-Based Analysis," in the *Newsletter* of the Center for Teaching Effectiveness, The University of Texas at Austin. 2 (October): 2–3.

Ashton, Patricia M. E., Evan S. Henderson, John E. Merritt, and Derek J. Mortimer (1983). *Teacher Education in the Classroom: Initial and In-Service.* London: Croom Helm.

Avidan, Moshe (1984). "Can A School Principal with Bureaucratic Authority be a Pedagogic Leader of Teachers in Subjects that Require Specific Professional Judgments?" *Studies in Educational Administration and Organization.* No. 11, (Summer): VI–VII, University of Haifa, School of Education.

Bailey, Gerald Douglas (1974). "A Study of Classroom Interaction Patterns from Student Teaching to Independent Classroom Teaching," *Educational Leadership* 32 (December): 225–230.

Bailey, G. D. (1979). "Maximizing the Potential of the Videotape Recorder in Teacher Self-Assessment," *Educational Technology* 19 (September): 39–44.

Barber, Larry W., and Karen Klein (1983). "Merit Pay and Teacher Evaluation," *Phi Delta Kappan* 4 (December): 247–251.

Barnes, Susan (1983). "Observer Training Manual for the Changing Teacher Practice Study." Revised Manual, Report No. 9050, Austin, TX: Research and Development Center for Teacher Education, The University of Texas at Austin.

Barro, Stephen M. (1970). "An Approach to Developing Accountability Measures for the Public Schools," *Phi Delta Kappan* 52 (December): 196–205.

Beegle, Charles W., and Richard M. Brandt (1973). *Observational Methods in the Classroom.* Washington, D.C.: Association for Supervision and Curriculum Development.

Bellon, Elmer C., and Jerry H. Bellon (1983). "Merit Pay and Other Incentive Programs," *Tennessee Educational Leadership* 1 (Fall): 64–75.

Benham, Barbara J., Phil Giesen, and Jeannie Cokes (1980). "A Study of Schooling: Students' Experiences in Schools," *Phi Delta Kappan* 61 (January) 337.

Bennett, Neville, and David McNamara (1979). *Focus on Teaching: Readings in the Observation and Conceptualization of Teaching.* London: Longman.

Berliner, David C. (1975). "Impediments to the Study of Teacher Effectiveness." A Paper presented at the Conference on Research on Teacher Effects, November 2–4, 1975. Austin, TX: Research and Development Center for Teacher Education, The University of Texas at Austin.

Biddle, B. J., and Ellena, W. J., editors (1964). *Contemporary Research on Teacher Effectiveness.* NY: Holt, Rinehart and Winston.

Blease, Derek (1983). "Observer Effects on Teachers and Pupils in Classroom Research;" *Educational Review* 35 (November):2–17.

Blackbourn, Richard (1983). "The Relationship Between Teachers' Perceptions of Supervisory Behaviors and Their Attitudes Toward the Supervisory Conference Following Classroom Observation." Unpublished paper. Columbus, MS: Loundes County Schools.

Block, James H. (1978). "The "C" in CBE," *Educational Researcher* 4 (May): 13–16.

Bloom, Benjamin S. (1976). *Human Characteristics and School Learning.* New York: McGraw-Hill.

Bloom, Benjamin S. (1980). "The New Direction in Educational Research: Alterable Variables," *Phi Delta Kappan* 61 (February): 382–385.

Bloom, Benjamin, et al. (1956). *Taxonomy of Educational Objectives: Handbook I Cognitive Domain,* New York: McKay.

Bloom, Benjamin S., J. Thomas Hastings, and George F. Madaus (1971). *Handbook on Formative and Summative Evaluation of Student Learning.* New York: McGraw-Hill.

Blumberg, Arthur (1980). *Supervisors and Teachers: A Private Cold War,* 2nd ed. Berkeley, CA: McCutchan Publishing Corporation.

Boehm, Anne E., and R. A. Weinberg (1977). *The Classroom Observer: A Guide for Developing Observation Skills.* New York: Teachers College Press.

Bolton, Dale L. (1973). *Selection and Evaluation of Teachers.* Berkeley, CA: McCutchan Publishers.

Bolvin, John O. (1967). "Evaluating Teacher Functions," Working Paper 17, presented at the American Educational Research Association Annual Meeting, February 1967. Pittsburg, PA: Learning Research and Development Center, University of Pittsburg.

Borich, Gary D., and K. S. Fenton (1977). *The Appraisal of Teaching: Concepts and Process.* Reading, MA: Addison-Wesley.

Borich, Gary D., and Susan K. Madden (1977). *Evaluating Classroom Instruction: A Source Book of Instruments.* Reading, MA: Addison-Wesley.

Borich, Gary D., and R. P. Jemelka (1981). *Programs and Systems: An Evaluation Perspective.* New York: Academic Press.

Boulding, Kenneth E. (1980). "Yes, the World Is Winding Down, but Is the Sky Really Falling, Too,?" *The Christian Science Monitor* (November 16): 34–35.

Bridges, Edwin M. (1984). *Managing the Incompetent Teacher.* Eugene, OR: Eric Clearinghouse on Educational Management, University of Oregon.

Brookover, Wilbur B., (1980). *Measuring and Attaining Goals of Education.* Alexandria, VA: Association for Supervision and Curriculum Development.

Brophy, Jerre E., and Carolyn M. Evertson (1976). *Learning from Teaching: A Developmental Perspective.* Boston: Allyn and Bacon.

Brophy, Jere E., and T. H. Good (1974). *Teacher-Student Relationship.* NY: Holt, Rinehart and Winston.

Brown, J. A., and W. C. Kameen (1975). "Focused Video-tape Feedback: A Consultative Approach with Teachers," *Elementary School Guidance and Counseling* 10 (October): 4–12.

Bruininks, Virginia (1978). "Assessing and Influencing Teachers' Affective Interactions in the Classroom," *Educational Technology* 18 (July): 10–14.

Bruner, Jerome S. (1966). *Toward a Theory of Instruction.* Cambridge, MA: Belknap Press of Harvard University.

Burlingame, Martin (1978). "A Modest Proposal About Accountability," *Educational Researcher* 7 (December): 1–2.

Buros, Oscar K. (1978). *The Eighth Mental Measurements Yearbook.* Highland Park, NJ: The Gryphon Press.

Burtt, E. A. (1967). *In Search of Philosophic Understanding.* New York: New American Library.

Byham, William C., and Pentacost, Regina (1970). "The Assessment Center: Identifying Tomorrow's Managers," *Personnel* 47:17–28.

California Teachers Association (1964). *Six Areas of Teacher Competence.* Burlingame, CA: California Teachers Association.

Campbell, Richard J., and Bray, Douglas (1967). "Assessment Centers: An Aid in Managerial Selection," *Personnel Administration* 30:6–13.

Capie, William, et al. (1978). "The Objectivity of Classroom Observation Scales," A Paper presented at the Annual Meeting of the Southern Association for the Education of Teachers of Science. New Orleans, LA (November 29) 182–306.

Carey, Lou M. (1980). "State-Level Teacher Performance Evaluation Policies," *NCSIE Inservice* (February). Syracuse, NY: National Council of States on Inservice Education, Syracuse University, School of Education, pp. 9–14.

Carrollton-Farmers Branch Schools (1980). "Observing, Conferring, Assisting, Assessing Guide." Carrollton, TX: Personnel Office. Mimeographed.

Carthel, James T. (1973). "An Application of a Systems Analysis Model to the Evaluation of an Instructional Improvement Program," Unpublished Ph.D. dissertation. Austin, TX: The University of Texas at Austin.

Cartwright, C., and P. Cartwright (1974). *Developing Observation Skills.* NY: McGraw-Hill.

Castetter, William B. (1971). *The Personnel Function in Educational Administration.* NY: The Macmillan Company.

Ceballos, Elva G. (1980). "Analysis of Teacher Evaluation Practices and Instruments in South Texas School Districts." Unpublished report.

Center on Evaluation, Development, and Research (1980). "On Mixing and Matching Teaching and Learning Styles," *Practical Applications of Research.* Newletter of Phi Delta Kappa, Bloomington, IN 3 (December):1–4.

Centra, John A., and David A. Potter (1980). "School and Teacher Effects: An Interrelational Model," *Review of Educational Research* 50 (Summer): 273–291.

Charters, W. W., Jr. and Roland J. Pellegrin (1972). "Barriers to the Innovation Process: Four Case Studies of Differentiated Staffing," *Educational Administration Quarterly* 9 (Winter): 3–14.

Christensen, Douglas D. (1978). "The Professional Performance File," *NASSP Bulletin* 62 (December): 27–33.

Christner, C. A., D. Malitz, C. L. Kugle, and D. S. Calkins (1979). "Competency-Based Teacher Evaluation in a School District: Validation of Competencies' Importance by District Administrators, Professionals, Students and Parents." A paper presented at the Annual Meeting of the American Educational Research Association.

Clark, Vernon L., Offilie Hightower, and Frances Randolph (1978). "The Maintap Inventory of Teacher Competencies." Norfolk, VA: Norfolk State College, ED 182 004.

Clearinghouse on Educational Management (1981). "Merit Pay," *Research Action Brief* 15 (February): 1–4. Eugene, OR: ERIC Clearinghouse, University of Oregon.

Clift, John C., and B. W. Imrie (1981). *Assessing Students, Appraising Teaching.* NY: Halsted Press, John Wiley and Sons.

Clive, Fletcher (1984). "What's New in Performance Appraisal?" *Personnel Management* (February): 20–23.

Coody, Betty, and Ben M. Harris (1971). *Individualization of Instruction Inventory.* Austin, TX: Instructional Leadership Training Materials, Department of Educational Administration, The University of Texas at Austin.

Cogan, Morris (1973). *Clinical Supervision.* Boston: Houghton Mifflin.

Cohen, Peter A., and James A. Kulik (1981). "Synthesis of Research on the Effects of Tutoring," *Educational Leadership* 39 (December):227.

Colbert, C. Dianne (1978). "A Process for Identifying, Observing and Describing Classroom Teacher Behavior." A paper presented at the Annual Meeting of the Association of Teacher Educators. (February) ED 177 165.

Cole, Robert W., Jr. (1979). "Minimum Competency Tests for Teachers: Confusion Compounded," *Phi Delta Kappan* 61 (December):233.

Coleman, Donald G. (1979). "Barnard's Effectiveness and Efficiency Applied to a Leader Style Model," (May) ED 173 946.

Commission on Elementary Schools (1970). *Guides to Conducting Programs of School Improvement.* Atlanta, GA: Southern Association of Colleges and Schools.

Cooley, William W. (1983). "Improving the Performance of an Educational System." Unpublished paper. Pittsburgh: Learning Research and Development Center, University of Pittsburgh. Mimeographed

Costa, Arthur L. (1977). "Recent Research on the Analysis of Instruction," *NN and Q* 21 (May–June). Bloomington, IN: Phi Delta Kappa.

Crane, A. R. (1980). "Anxiety in Organizations: Explorations of an Idea," *The Journal of Educational Administration* 18 (October):202–212.

Cronbach, L. J. (1963). "Course Improvement Through Evaluation," *Teachers College Record* 64: 672–683.

Cronbach, L. J., and R. E. Snow (1977). *Aptitudes and Instructional Methods: A Handbook of Research on Interactions.* NY: Irvington.

Cronbach, Lee J., and Associates (1980). *Toward Reform of Program Evaluation.* San Francisco: Jossey-Bass.

Damerall, David (1981). "Survey of Teacher Evaluation Instruments Used in a Sampling of Texas School Districts." Unpublished paper.

Davidson, Charles W., and Michael L. Bell (1975). "Relationships between Pupil-on Task Performance and Teacher Behaviors," *Southern Journal of Educational Research* 9 (Fall): 223–235.

Deci, Edward L. (1976). "The Hidden Costs of Rewards," *Organizational Dynamics* 4 (Winter): 61–72. ED 168 137.

DeKalb County Schools (1975). *PCB/SS Observational Record.* Doraville, GA: DeKalb County Schools, New Teacher Certification Project.

DeKalb County Schools 1975). *Performance-Based Certification/ Supportive Supervision Model.* Doraville, GA: DeKalb County Schools.

Denmark, George, and E. Nelli (1980). "Emerging Patterns of Initial Preparation for Teachers: Generic Teaching Domains." A paper presented at the Conference on Operation PROTEACH. Gainsville: College of Education, University of Florida, Report No. 11 (October).

Denham, Carolyn, and Ann Lieberman, editors (1980). *Time to Learn.* Sacramento, CA: California Commission for Preparation and Licensing (May).

Denton, William T. (1982). "Time on Task: What Does Research Say About Promoting Student Learning," *TASCD Newsletter* 18 (Spring): 7, 10.

Descamps, Jorge A., and Norma G. Hernandez (1981). "Constructing Classroom Observation Instruments," in *Improving Classroom Practice Through Supervision.*

Robert H. Anderson, editor. Dallas, TX: Texas Association for Supervision and Curriculum Development.

DeVault, M. Vere, W. R. Houston, and C. C. Boyd (1962). "Television and Consultant Services as Methods of In-Service Education for Elementary School Teachers of Mathematics." Bureau of Laboratory Schools, Publication 15. Austin: The University of Texas Press.

Diamond, Stanley C. (1978). "Toward Effective Supervision of Classroom Instruction," *NASSP Bulletin* 6 (May):89–97.

Dillon, J. T. (1981). "To Question and Not to Question During Discussion. II Non-Questioning Techniques," *Journal of Teacher Education* 32 (November–December):15–20.

Dillon, J. T. (1984). "Research on Questioning and Discussion," *Educational Leadership* 42 (November): 50–56.

Dodl, Norman R. (1972). *Florida Catalog of Teacher Competencies.* Tallahassee, FL: Florida State University.

Donahue, Thomas J., and Mary Ann Donahue (1983). "Understanding Interactive Video," *Training and Development Journal* 37 (December 1983): 27–30.

Doyle, Kenneth O., Jr. (1983). *Evaluating Teaching.* Lexington, MA: Lexington Books, D.C. Heath.

Doyle, W. (1977). "Paradigms for Research on Teacher Effectiveness," *Review of Research in Education,* L. S. Shulman, editor. Itasca, IL: Peacock Press.

Doyle, Walter (1981). "Research on Classroom Contexts," *Journal of Teacher Education* 32 (November–December):3–6.

Dranov, Paula (1980). *Video in the 80s: Emerging Uses for Television in Business, Education, Medicine and Government.* White Plains, NY: Knowledge Industry Publications.

Duckett, Willard R. (1984). "Learning About Merit Pay from Business and Industry," *Research Bulletin,* Center on Evaluation Development and Research. (April). Bloomington, IN: Phi Delta Kappa.

Dunkerton, John (1981). "Should Classroom Observation Be Quantitative?" *Educational Research* 23 (February): 144–150.

Dunkin, Michael J., and Bruce J. Biddle (1974). *The Study of Teaching.* NY: Holt, Rinehart and Winston.

Dunn, Rita, and Kenneth J. Dunn (1977). *Administrator's Guide to New Programs for Faculty Management and Evaluation.* West Nyack, NY: Parker Publishing Co.

Eckard, Pamela J., and James H. McElhinney (1977). "Teacher Evaluation and Educational Accountability," *Educational Leadership* 34 (May): 613–618.

Ector County Schools (1981). *Professional Personnel: Teacher Assessment. Improvement in Learning.* Odessa, TX: Ector County Independent School District, August.

Eder, Michael D. (1971). "A Study of the Effectiveness of Video-tape Recorder with and without Modeling in the Inservice Training of Teachers," College Park, Maryland: University of Maryland, ED 053 547.

Education Service Center (1974). "Competency-Based Staff Assessment Model," Project No. S-3-02-021-1, Title III, ESEA. Corpus Christi, TX: Education Service Center, Region Two, (No date).

Edwards, John, and Perc Marland (1984). "What Are Students Really Thinking?" *Educational Leadership* 42 (November): 63–67.

Eisner, Elliot (1972). "Emerging Models for Educational Evaluation," *School Review,* 80 (1971–72): 573–590.

Eisner, Elliot W. (1977a). "On the Uses of Educational Connoisseurship and Criticism for Evaluating Classroom Life," *Teachers College Record* 78 (February):346.

Eisner, Elliot (1977b). "Thick Description," in *Beyond the Numbers Game.* David Hamilton, editor. Berkeley, CA: McCutchan Publishing.

Eisner, Elliot (1979). *The Educational Imagination.* NY: Macmillan.

Ellis, Elmer C., J. T. Smith, and W. H. Abbott, Jr. (1979). "Peer Observation: A Means for Supervisory Acceptance," *Educational Leadership* 36 (March): 423–426.

Elliott, Chad D. (1980). "Georgia's New Teachers Must Show Talent in the Classroom," in *Report on Education Research* 12 (August 20). Capitol Publications Inc., Washington, D.C.

Ellsberry, Jim (1982). "What are the Jury's Findings?. . . A Judicial Model for Program Evaluation," *Discrepancy Digest.* The Evaluation Training Consortium Newsletter. 5 (April): 2–3. Western Michigan University, Kalamazoo, Michigan.

Emmer, Edmund T. (1978). "Appendix B: Classroom Observation Scales," in *Texas Junior High School Study: Final Report of Process-Outcome Relationships.* R and D Report No. 4061, Research and Development Center for Teacher Education, The University of Texas, Austin, Texas. (April).

Emmer, Edmund T., and B. G. Millett (1968). "An Assessment of Terminal Performance in a Teaching Laboratory: A Pilot Study." Austin, TX: Research and Development Center for Teacher Education, The University of Texas at Austin.

English, Fenwick W. (1969). "Et Tu, Educator: Differentiating Staffing? Rationale and Model for a Differentiated Teaching Staff," TEPS Write-In Papers on Flexible Staffing Patterns No. 4. Washington, D.C.: National Commission on Education and Professional Standards, National Education Association.

English, Fenwick W., and D. K. Sharpes (1972). *Strategies for Differentiated Staffing.* Berkeley, CA: McCutchan Publishing.

English, Fenwick, et al. (1985). *Incentives for Excellence in America's Schools.* A report from the ASCD Task Force on Merit Pay and Career Ladders. Alexandria, VA: Association for Supervision and Curriculum Development.

ERIC Clearinghouse on Educational Management (1977). "Participative Decision-Making," *Research Action Brief* 2 (July). Eugene, OR: University of Oregon.

Evaluating Teacher Performance (1978). Arlington, VA: Educational Research Service.

Evans, Michael C., Ben M. Harris, and Richard L. Palmer (1975). *A Diagnostic Assessment System for Professional Supervisory Competencies.* Special Education Supervisor Training Project, Document No. 11. Austin, TX: University of Texas at Austin.

Farley, Joseph M. (1981). "Student Interviews as an Evaluation Tool," *Educational Leadership* 39 (December): 184–186.

Feldvebel, Alexander M. (1980). "Teacher Evaluation: Ingredients of a Credible Model," *Clearinghouse* 53 (May): 415–420.

Finlayson, Harry J. (1979). "Incompetence and Teacher Dismissal," *Phi Delta Kappan,* 61 (September): 69.

Finn, Chester E., Jr. (1985). "Studying Shakespeare Where It's Taught Best," *Christian Science Monitor* 77 (February 20): 13.

Flanders, Ned (1970). *Analyzing Teaching Behavior.* Reading, MA: Addison-Wesley.

Flanders, Ned A., and Anita Simon (1969). "Teacher Effectiveness," in *Encyclopedia of Educational Research,* 4th ed. Robert L. Ebel, editor. New York: MacMillan.

Florida Department of Education (1973). *The Florida Catalog of Teacher Competencies* Tallahassee: Florida Department of Education, Division of Elementary and Secondary Education.

Floyd, Steve, and Beth Floyd (1982). *Handbook of Interactive Video.* White Plains, NY: Knowledge Industry Publishers.

Foley, Walter J. (1981). "On Evaluation and the Evaluation of Teachers," *The Executive Review.* Institute of School Executives. 1 (April). Iowa City, IA: The University of Iowa.

Fort Worth ISD (1984). "House Bill 72 and Career Ladder Requirements". Fort Worth, TX: Fort Worth Independent School district. Mimeographed.

Frick, Ted, and M. I. Semmel (1978). "Observer Agreement and Reliabilities of Classroom Observational Measures," *Review of Educational Research* 48 (Winter): 157–184.

Fuller, Frances F., et al. (1967). *Creating Climates for Growth.* Austin, TX: The Hogg Foundation for Mental Health, The University of Texas.

Fuller, Frances (1969). "Concerns of Teachers: A Developmental Conceptualization." *American Educational Reserach Journal* 6 (March): 207–226.

Fuller, Frances F. (1969b). "FAIR System Manual: Fuller Affective Interaction Records." Austin: Research and Development Center for Teacher Education, University of Texas at Austin.

Gage, N. L. (1972). *Teacher Effectiveness and Teacher Education: The Search for a Scientific Basis.* Palo Alto, CA: Pacific Books.

Gage, N. L. (1979). "The Generality of Dimensions of Teaching," in Peterson and Dalberg's *Research on Teaching.* Berkeley, CA: McCutcheon Publishing.

French, R. L., and C. M. Galloway (1968). "A Description of Teacher Behavior, Verbal and Non-verbal," ED 028 134.

Gage, N. L., editor (1976). *The Psychology of Teaching Methods.* Part I. 75th Yearbook of the National Society for the Study of Education. Chicago, IL: The National Society for the Study of Education.

Gage, N. L. (1978). *The Scientific Basis of the Art of Teaching.* New York: Columbia University Teachers College Press.

Gage, N. L. (1984). "What Do We Know About Teaching Effectiveness?" *Phi Delta Kappan* 66 (October): 87–93.

Gagne, R. M. (1976). "The Learning Basis of Teaching Methods," in *The Psychology of Teaching Methods,* R. M. Gagne, editor. Part I, 75th Yearbook. National Society for the Study of Education. Chicago: University of Chicago Press.

Gagne, R. M. (1970). *The Conditions of Learning,* 2nd ed. New York: Holt, Rinehart and Winston.

Gallup, George H. (1978). "The 10th Annual Gallup Poll of the Public's Attitudes Toward the Public Schools," *Phi Delta Kappan* 60 (September): 33–45.

Gallup, George H. (1979). "The 11th Annual Gallup Poll of the Public's Attitudes Toward the Public Schools," *Phi Delta Kappan* 61 (September): 33–45.

Gardner, Don E. (1977). "Five Evaluation Frameworks: Implications for Decision Making in Higher Education," *Journal of Higher Education* 48 (September–October): 571–592.

Garman, Noreen B. (1982). "The Clinical Approach to Supervision," in *Supervision of Teaching.* Alexandria, VA: Association for Supervision and Curriculum Development.

Georgia Department of Education (1983). *Guidelines for the Implementation of Perfor-*

mance-Based Certification by the Georgia Department of Education, Regional Assessment Centers, and Local School Systems. Division of Staff Development. Atlanta, GA: (June). Mimeographed.

Gerhard, Ronald J. (1981). "The Organizational Imperative," in Evaluation of Complex Systems, Ronald J. Woolridge, editor. Number 10 in New Directions for Program Evaluation. San Francisco: Jossey-Bass.

Glass, G. V., et al. (1977). Teacher "Indirectness" and Pupil Achievement: An Integration of Findings. Boulder, CO: Laboratory of Educational Research, University of Colorado. Multilith.

Glathorn, Allan A. (1984). Differentiated Supervision. Alexandria, VA: Association for Supervision and Curriculum Development.

Glickman, Carl D. (1980). "The Developmental Approach to Supervision," Educational Leadership 38 (November): 178–180.

Glickman, Carl D. (1983). "Directions for Research on Supervisory Conference Approaches Appropriate to Developmental Levels of Teachers." Unpublished paper presented to the American Educational Research Association, Montreal, April.

Glickman, Carl (1981). Developmental Supervision: Alternative Practices for Helping Teachers Improve. Alexandria, VA: Association for Supervision and Curriculum Development.

Glickman, Carl, and Edward Pajak (n.d.). "Teachers' Discrimination Between Information and Control in Response to Simulated Supervisory Conferences," Unpublished paper. University of Georgia, Athens, GA.

Goldhammer, Robert, Robert Anderson, and Robert Krajewski (1980). Clnical Supervision: Special Methods for the Supervision of Teachers. 2nd ed. New York: Holt, Rinehart and Winston.

Good, Thomas, and Jere Brophy (1984). Looking in Classrooms, 3rd ed. New York: Harper & Row.

Good, T. L., B. J. Biddle, and J. E. Brophy (1975). Teachers Make a Difference. New York: Holt, Rinehart and Winston.

Goodlad, John I., K. E. Sirotnik, and B. C. Overman (1979). "An Overview of 'A Study of Schooling'," Phi Delta Kappan 61 (November):174–178.

Government Employee Relations Report, No. 574 (1974). Washington: Bureau of National Affairs.

Grabinski, Roger N. (1977). "Personnel Evaluation: The State of the Art." A presentation before the National Conference of Professors of Educational Administration, Eugene, OR. Mimeographed.

Grasha, Anthony F. (1977). Assessing and Developing Faculty Performance: Principles and Models. Cincinnati, OH: Communication and Education Associates.

Gregory, Thomas B. (1969). "Teaching for Problem-Solving Development and Testing of a Set of Teaching Laboratory Tasks." Unpublished dissertation, The University of Texas at Austin.

Grouws, Douglas A. (1980). "The Teacher Variable in Mathematics Instruction," in Selected Issues in Mathematics Education, Mary Montgomery Lindquist, editor. Berkeley, CA: McCutchan Publishing.

Guba, Egon G., and Yvonna S. Lincoln (1981). Effective Evaluation. San Francisco: Jossey-Bass.

Gudridge, Beatrice M. (1980). Teacher Competency: Problems and Solutions. AASA Critical Issues Report. Arlington, VA: American Association of School Administrators.

Gupta, Nina (1979). *Some School and Classroom Antecedents of Student Achievement.* Austin, TX: Regional Planning Council, Southwest Educational Development Laboratory.

Gump, Paul V. (1980). "Observation of Persons and Contexts." A paper presented at the American Educational Research Association Meeting, Boston, MA: ED 193 312.

Gurney, David W. (1977). "Judging Effective Teaching," *Phi Delta Kappan* 58 (June): 774–775.

Haefele, Donald L. (1980). "How to Evaluate Thee, Teacher—Let Me Count the Ways," *Phi Delta Kappan* 61 (January): 349–352.

Haffey, B. T. (1979). "Developing the People Who Replace You," *Administrative Management* 6 (March).

Hagen, Nancy Joyce (1981). "A Comparative Analysis of Selected Inservice Education Delivery Systems." Unpublished doctoral dissertation, University of Texas at Austin.

Hall, Gene E., A. A. George, and W. L. Rutherford (1979). *Measuring Stages of Concern About the Innovation: A Manual for the Use of the So C Questionnaire.* Austin, TX: Research and Development Center, The University of Texas.

Hansen, J. Merrell (1979). "The Evaluation of Teaching: No Guppies or Goldfish in My Classroom," *NASSP Bulletin* 62 (March 1979): 11–15.

Hardebeck, Richard J. (1973). "A Comparison of Observed and Self-Reported Individualization of Instruction by Vocational, Academic, and Special Education Teachers in Texas." Unpublished doctoral dissertation. Austin: The University of Texas.

Hardebeck, Rick (1978). "Teacher Observation Evaluation: Needs Anchored Instructors' Learning System." Austin, Tx: Texas Education Agency. Mimeographed.

Harris, Ben M. (1975). *Supervisory Behavior in Education,* 2nd ed. Englewood Cliffs, NJ: Prentice-Hall.

Harris, Ben M. (1979). "Orientation on Branching Diagram Analysis," *Studies in Educational Evaluation* 5:157–162.

Harris, Ben M. (1980). *Improving Staff Performance Through Inservice Education.* Boston: Allyn and Bacon.

Harris, Ben M. (1981). *Pilot Program Evaluation Report, Analysis of Teacher and Principal Reports on the Use of DeTEK.* Austin, TX: The University of Texas, Department of Educational Administration, (June). Mimeographed.

Harris, Ben M. (1984). "A Diagnostic Model of Teaching Performance," *Thresholds in Education* 10 (May): 11–16.

Harris, Ben M. (1985). *Supervisory Behavior in Education,* 3rd ed. Englewood Cliffs, NJ: Prentice-Hall.

Harris, Ben M., E. W. Bessent, and Kenneth E. McIntyre (1969). *Inservice Education: A Guide to Better Practice.* Englewood Cliffs, NJ: Prentice-Hall.

Harris, Ben M., and Sandra Burks (1982). *Describing Good Teaching Practices.* Austin, TX: Texas Cooperative Committee on Teacher Evaluation, Texas Classroom Teachers Association.

Harris, Ben M., and Jane Hill (1982). *Developmental Teacher Evaluation Kit (DeTEK).* Austin, TX: National Educational Laboratory Publishers.

Harris, Ben M., and Jane Hill (1982). "The DeTEK Handbook," in *Developmental Teacher Evaluation Kit.* Austin, TX: Southwest Educational Development Laboratory.

Harris, Ben M., and Jane Hill (1982). "Trainers' Manual," in *Developmental Teacher Evaluation Kit.* Austin, TX: Southwest Educational Development Laboratory.

Harris, Ben M., Louisa Goodlett, and Cynthia M. Sloan (1975). *A Manual for Observing with the New Comprehensive Observation Guide.* Austin, TX: Instructional Leadership Training Materials.

Harris, Ben M., and Kenneth E. McIntyre (1964). *Teacher Question Inventory.* Austin, TX: Instructional Leadership Training Materials, The University of Texas at Austin.

Harris, Ben M., Vance Littleton, Dan Long, and Kenneth E. McIntyre (1979). *Personnel Administration in Education.* Boston, MA: Allyn and Bacon.

Harris, Ben M., Kenneth E. McIntyre, Vance Littleton, and Dan Long (1985). *Personnel Administration in Education.* 2nd ed. Boston, MA: Allyn and Bacon.

Harris, William U. (1981). "Teacher Command of Subject Matter," in *Handbook of Teacher Evaluation.* Jason Millman, editor. Beverly Hills, CA: Sage Publications.

Hartmann, C. (1978). "A Longitudinal Look at Self-Appraisal Strategies," *Journal of Teacher Education* 29 (September–October):11–12.

Heard, Alex (1982). "North Carolina to Begin Statewide Evaluation of Teachers, Principals," *Education Week* 1 (August 25):41.

Hersey, Paul W. (1982). *The NASSP Assessment Center Project: Validation and New Development.* Reston, VA: National Association of Secondary School Principals.

Herzberg, F. (1976). *The Managerial Choice: To Be Efficient and To Be Human.* Homewood, IL: Dow-Jones-Irwin.

Hiatt, Diana B., and J. W. Keesling (1979). "Dependability of Classroom Observations." A paper presented at the Annual Meeting of the American Educational Research Association, San Francisco, CA, April 8–12.

Hildebrand, Milton (1973). "The Character and Skills of the Effective Professor," *Journal of Higher Education* 44 (January):41–50.

Hill, Winfred F. (1964). "Contemporary Developments within Stimulus-Response Learning Theory," in *Theories of Learning and Instruction.* Ernest R. Hilgard, editor. Part I, 63rd Yearbook, National Society for the Study of Education. Chicago: University of Chicago Press.

Hinson, James H., Jr. (1975). *Handbook for Field Testing the Performance Based Certification/Supportive Supervision Model (1975–76).* DeKalb, GA: DeKalb County Schools.

Honzay, Aideen (1983). "Dimensions of Teacher Behavior That Promote Student Engagement." Unpublished doctoral dissertation, Claremont Graduate School, Claremont, California.

Hook, Collin M., and B. V. Rosenshine (1979). "Accuracy of Teacher Reports of Their Classroom Behavior," *Review of Educational Research* 49 (Winter):1–12.

Hough, John B., and James K. Duncan (1970). *Teaching: Description and Analysis.* Reading, MA: Addison-Wesley.

House, Ernest R. (1980). *Evaluating with Validity.* Beverly Hills, CA: Sage Publications.

House Bill No. 72 (1984). "An Act Relating to the Public School System, including Administration, Finance, Personnel, Students, Programs and Teacher Retirement." 2nd Called Session of the 68th Legislature. Austin, TX: June 30, 1984.

Houston Independent School District (1977). *The Second Mile Plan.* Houston, TX: Houston Schools. Mimeographed.

Houston Independent School District (1984). "Proposal for Career Ladder Implementation," Houston, TX: Houston Independent School District. Mimeographed.

Hughes, Larry W., and Gerald C. Ubben (1978). "The Staff Evaluation Cycle," in *The Elementary Principal's Handbook: A Guide to Action.* Boston: Allyn and Bacon.

Hunkins, Francis P. (1980). *Curriculum Development: Program Improvement.* Columbus, OH: Charles E. Merrill.

Hunter, Madeline (1980). "Six Types of Supervisory Conferences," *Educational Leadership* 37 (February): 408–412.

Hunter, Madeline (1983). "Script Taping: An Essential Supervisory Tool," *Educational Leadership* 41:3 (November 1983): 43.

Illich, Ivan D. (1971). *DeSchooling Society* New York: Harper & Row.

Irvine, Jacqueline J. (1983). "The Accuracy of Pre-Service Teachers' Assessments of their Classroom Behaviors," *Journal of Research and Development in Education.*

Iwanicki, E. F. (1981). "Contract Plans: A Professional Growth Oriented Approach to Evaluating Teacher Performance," in *Handbook of Teacher Evaluation.* J. Millman, editor. Beverly Hills, CA: Sage Publications.

Jenrette, David V. (1981). "Feedback and Calibration: Their Significance in Education," *Innovation Abstracts* 3 (May):1–2. Austin, TX: National Institute for Staff and Organizational Development, The University of Texas at Austin.

Johnson, Mauritz (1979). "The Locus of Value Judgments in Educational Program Evaluation," *Studies in Educational Evaluation* 5:109–122.

Johnston, John M., and R. Lewis Hodge (1981). "Self-Evaluation Through Performance Statements—A Basis for Professional Development," *Journal of Teacher Education* 32 (November–December):30–33.

Johnston, S. G., and C. C. Yeaky (1979). "The Supervision of Teacher Evaluation: A Brief Overview," *Journal of Teacher Education* 30 (March/April):17–27.

Jones, Keith, and A. Sherman (1980). "Two Approaches to Evaluation," *Educational Leadership* 37 (April):553–557.

Jones, Linda L. and Andrew E. Hayes (1980). "How Valid Are Surveys of Teacher Needs?" *Educational Leadership* 37 (February):390–392.

Jones, Wayne, Paul A. Sommers, and Lee M. Joiner (1976). "Three Structures for Teacher Evaluation," *Educational Technology* 16 (February):48–50.

Joyce, Bruce, and M. Weil (1980). *Models of Teaching.* 2nd ed. Englewood Cliffs, NJ: Prentice-Hall.

Joyce, Bruce, and Beverly Showers (1982). "The Coaching of Teaching," *Educational Leadership* 40 (October):4–8, 10.

Joyce, Bruce R., and Beverly Showers (1983). *Power in Staff Development Through Research on Training.* Alexandria, VA: Association for Supervision and Curriculum Development.

Kaplan, Don (1980). "Feedback: Using Video to Measure Teacher Performance," in *Video in the Classroom: A Guide to Creative Television.* White Plains, NY: Knowledge Industry Publications.

Kean, Michael H., Anita A. Summers, Mark J. Raivetz, and Irvin J. Farber (1979). *What Works in Reading?* Philadelphia, PA: Office of Research and Evaluation, The School District of Philadelphia.

Kerlinger, Fred N., editor (1975). *Review of Research in Education,* vol. 3. Itasca, IL: F. E. Peacock Publishers.

Kerlinger, Fred N., editor (1973). *Review of Research in Education,* vol. 1. Itasca, IL: F. E. Peacock Publishers.

Kindsvatter, Richard, and William Wilen (1981). "A Systematic Approach to Improving Conference Skills," *Educational Leadership* 38 (April): 525–529.

Klein, Karen, editor (1983–84). *Merit Pay and Evaluation.* Phi Delta Kappa Center on Evaluation, Development and Research, Hot Topics Series: Bloomington, IN: Phi Delta Kappan.

Klein, Stephen P., and Marvin C. Alkin. "Evaluating Teachers for Outcome Accountability," *Evaluation Comment* 3:5–11.

Korth, Bruce (1979). "Relationship of Extraneous Variables to Student Ratings of Instructors," *Journal of Educational Measurement* 16 (Spring):27–38.

Kounin, J. S. (1970). *Discipline and Group Management in Classrooms.* New York: Holt, Rinehart and Winston.

Kowalski, Joan P. Sullivan (1978). *Evaluating Teacher Performance.* Arlington, VA: Educational Research Services.

Kulka, Richard A. (1979). "Interaction as Person-Environment Fit," in *New Directions for Methodology of Behavioral Science.* Lynn R. Kahle, editor. San Francisco: Jossey-Bass.

Laird, Dugan (1978). *Approaches to Training and Development.* Reading, MA: Addison-Wesley.

Lanier, Ted, Bill Bailey, and Ben M. Harris (1978). "Acceptance Levels and Needs for Revision of Guiding Principles for Teacher Evaluation Systems." A progress report. Austin, TX: Joint Committee on Teacher Evaluation in Texas Schools, Texas Classroom Teachers' Association. Mimeographed.

Lawrence, Gordon (1974). "Delineating and Measuring Professional Competencies," *Educational Leadership* 31 (January): 298–302.

Lawrence, Gordon, and Charles Branch (1974). *Guidelines for Developing a Competency-Based Inservice Teacher Education Program.* Tallahassee, FL: Department of Education, Florida Educational Research and Development Program, August.

"Lawsuit Charges Master-Teacher Plan Is Unconstitutional" (1985). *Education Week* IV (January 9):4.

Lessinger, Leon M. (1979). *A Job Description for the School Teacher.* A working draft: for use in the IPEA program. Unpublished paper.

Levin, Benjy (1979). "Teacher Evaluation—A Review of Research," *Educational Leadership* 37 (December):240–245.

Lowery, Raymond (1984). "Teachers' Ladder Enacted in N.C.," *Education Week* IV (September):9.

Lindzey, Jeff (1980). *DeTEK Case Report: Dripping Springs Independent School District.* Austin, TX: An unpublished report, mimeographed, dated May 20.

Lorti, Dan C. 1975). *School Teacher: A Sociological Study.* Chicago: University of Chicago Press.

Lufkin ISD (1980). "Summary Report: Survey of Teacher Reactions to the Use of DeTEK." Lufkin, TX: Lufkin Independent School District. Mimeographed.

MacKay, A. (1979). "Project Quest: Teaching Strategies and Pupil Achievement." Occasional Paper Series, Research Report #79-1-3. Edmonton, Canada: Centre for Research in Teaching, Faculty of Education, University of Alberta. Mimeographed.

Madaus, George F., Thomas Kellaghan, and Ernest A. Rakow (1979). "Within

School Variance in Achievement: School Effects or Error?" *Studies in Educational Evaluation* 5 (1979):101–107.

Mager, Robert F., and Pipes, Peter (1970). "Is Non-Performance Rewarding?" in *Analyzing Performance Problems or "You Really Oughta Wanna"*. Palo Alto, CA: Fearon Publishers.

Mager, Robert F. (1975). *Preparing Instructional Objectives*. Palo Alto, CA: Fearon-Pitman, Publishers.

Maier, Norman R. F. (1976). *The Appraisal Interview: Three Basic Approaches*. La Jolla, CA: University Associates.

Manatt, Richard P. (1979). *Teacher Performance Evaluation*, 3rd ed. Alexandria, VA: Association for Supervision and Curriculum Development.

Manatt, Richard, Kenneth Palmer, and Everett Hidlebaugh (1976). "Teacher Performance Evaluation with Improved Rating Scales," *The Bulletin* 60 (September): 21–24.

Mangano, Nancy G. (1983). "External Validity Issues Associated with Classroom Observational Research." College Station: Texas A and M University, Instructional Research Laboratory.

Marshall, Hermine H. (1977). "Stability of Classroom Variables as Measured by a Broad Range Observational System," *The Journal of Educational Research* 70 (July–August): 304–311.

Martin, Jeanne, Don Veldman and L. Anderson (1980). "Within-Class Relationships Between Student Achievement and Teacher Behaviors," *American Education Research Journal* 17 (Winter): 479–490.

Masling, J., and G. Stern (1969). "The Effect of the Observer in the Classroom," *Journal of Educational Psychology* 60 (October): 351–354.

McConnell, John H. (1971). "The Assessment Center: A Flexible Program for Supervisors," *Personnel* 48 (September/October):35–40.

McDaniel, Ernest (1979). "An Observation Scale for Inquiry Teaching." A paper presented at the Annual Meeting of the American Educational Research Association, San Francisco, California, April 8–12, ED 175 927

McGee, Reece (1979). "Criteria Problems in Assessing Teaching Performance." A paper presented at the annual meeting of the American Sociological Association, ED 179 171.

McGreal, Thomas L. (1982). "Effective Teacher Evaluation Systems," *Educational Leadership* 39 (January): 303–306.

McGreal, Thomas L. (1983). "Improved Classroom Observation Skills," in *Successful Teacher Evaluation*. Alexandria, VA: Association for Supervision and Curriculum Development.

McGreal, Thomas L. (1983). "Separation of Administrative and Supervisory Behavior," 3 in *Successful Teacher Evaluation*. Alexandria, VA: Association for Supervision and Curriculum Development.

McGreal, Thomas L. (1984a). "Artifact Collection," *Educational Leadership* 41 (April): 20–21.

McGreal, Thomas L. (1984b). "Artifacts of Teaching in Teacher Evaluation." An unpublished paper presented to the Council of Professors of Instructional Supervision, Austin, TX, November.

McIntyre, Kenneth E. (1979). "Evaluation of Teaching: Can a Formula Be Found?" *TASB Journal* 5 (September 1979): 12–16.

McKenna, Bernard H. (1981). "Context/Environment Effects in Teacher Evaluation," in *Handbook of Teacher Evaluation*. Jason Millman, editor. Beverly Hills, CA: Sage Publications.

McNergney, Robert F. (1978). "Supervising Different Teachers Differently," *Planning and Changing* 9 (Winter): 224–227.

McNeil, John D., and W. James Popham (1973). "The Assessment of Teacher Competence," in *Second Handbook of Research on Teaching*. R. M. Travers, editor. Chicago, IL: Rand McNally.

McNergney, Robert F., and Carol A. Carrier (1981). *Teacher Development*. New York: Macmillan.

Medley, Donald M. (1973). "Closing the Gap Between Research in Teacher Effectiveness and the Teacher Education Curriculum," *Journal of Research and Development in Education* 7 (Fall): 39–46.

Medley, Donald M. (1977). *Teacher Competence and Teacher Effectiveness*. Washington, D.C.: American Association of Colleges of Teacher Education.

Medley, Donald M. (1979). "The Effectiveness of Teachers," in *Research on Teaching: Concepts Findings and Implications*. Penelope L. Peterson and H. J. Walberg, editors. Berkeley, CA: McCutchan Publishing.

Medley, Donald M., and H. E. Mitzel (1963). "Measuring Classroom Behavior by Systematic Observation," in *Handbook of Research on Teaching*. N. L. Gage, editor. Chicago: Rand McNally.

Medley, Donald, Homer Coker, and Robert S. Soar (1984). *Measurement-Based Evaluation of Teacher Performance*. New York: Longman.

Merit Pay Task Force Report (1983). Report No. 98, 98th Congress, 1st Session. A report prepared for the use of the Committee on Education and Labor, House of Representatives (October). Washington, D.C.: U. S. Government Printing Office.

Merritt, Daniel L. (1973). "The Teacher Assessment Center: A Concept," *Peabody Journal of Education* 50 (July): 309–312.

Merwin, Jack C. (1978). "A Review of the National Teacher Examinations," in the *Eighth Mental Measurements Yearbook*. O.K. Buros, editor. Highland Park NJ: The Gryphon Press.

Miller, Delbert C. (1977). *Handbook of Research Design and Social Measurement* 3rd ed. New York: David McKay.

Millman, Jason, editor (1981). *Handbook of Teacher Evaluation*. Beverly Hills, CA: Sage Publications.

Millman, Jason (1981). "Student Achievement as a Measure of Teacher Competence," in *Handbook of Teacher Evaluation*. Jason Millman editor. Beverly Hills, CA: Sage Publications.

Mills, Johnnie R. (1980). "A Guide for Teaching Systematic Observation to Student Teachers," *Journal of Teacher Education* 31 (November/December): 5–9.

Mitchell, James V. Jr., editor (1983). *Tests in Print III: An Index to Tests, Test Reviews, and the Literature on Specific Tests*. Lincoln, NE: Buros Institute of Mental Measurements, University of Nebraska Press.

Montgomery Schools, Leadership Action Project (1982). *Specification of Teacher Performances—Part A* (draft edition). Mongtgomery, AL: Montgomery County Schools (March).

Moody, Lamar, and Joe Blackbourn (1980). "The Relationship of Race, Sex, Degree Level, Age, Teaching Level and Years of Experience of Teachers to Their Perceptions of the Post-Evaluative Conference Following Classroom Observation". Unpublished report, Mississippi State University, Department of Educational Leaderhsip, Mississippi State, Mississippi.

Morgan, John L., and David W. Champagne (1971). "The Supervisory Conference." Pittsburg, PA: University of Pittsburg, Spring. Mimeographed.

Munnelly, Robert J. (1979). "Dealing with Teacher Incompetence: Supervision and Evaluation in a Due Process Framework." *Contemporary Education* 50 (Summer): 221–225.

Muro, James F. (1983). "Merit Pay for Teachers: A Review." Occasional Paper, Office of Academic Affairs, North Texas State University, Denton, TX. Mimeograhed.

Musella, D. (1970). "Improving Teacher Evaluation," The *Journal of Teacher Education* (Spring): 15–21.

National Association of Elementary School Principals (1979). "Down and Out in the Classroom: Surviving Minimum Competency," *The National Elementary Principal* 58 (January): 11–67.

National Study of School Evaluation (1973). *Elementary School Evaluative Criteria.* Arlington, VA: National Study of School Evaluation.

"NEA Survey Investigates Teacher Attitudes, Practices." *Phi Delta Kappan* 62 (September 1980): 49–50.

Nelli, Elizabeth (1981). "Program Redesign in Teacher Preparation," *Journal of Teacher Education* 32 (November—December): 39–42.

Newfield, John (1980). "Accuracy of Teacher Reports: Reports and Observations of Specific Classroom Behaviors," *Journal of Educational Research* 74 (November/December): 78–82.

Newfield, John (1981). "The Accuracy of Teacher Reports: Reports and Observations on Specific Classroom Behaviors." A paper presented at the American Educational Research Association annual conference, Los Angeles, California, April.

Nixon, George (1973). *People, Evaluation and Achievement.* Houston, TX: Gulf Publishing Co.

O'Neill, Ernest D. (1977). *Teacher Corps Exiting Competencies: A Supervisory Packet for Team Leaders.* Austin, TX: The University of Texas at Austin. Mimeographed.

O'Neill, Ernest D. (1977). "Target Areas/Teacher Exiting Competencies". Unpublished paper. Austin, TX: The University of Texas at Austin.

Ostrander, Kenneth H. (1981). *A Grievance Arbitration Guide for Educators.* Boston, MA: Allyn and Bacon.

Pac-Urar, Ian G., and JoAnne L. Vacca (1984). "Working Toward Collegiality: If at First You Don't Succeed. . .," *Thresholds in Education* 10 (May):36–38.

Paley, Vivian (1979). *White Teacher.* Cambridge, MA: Harvard University Press.

Patterson, James W. (1969). "An Exploratory Study of Selected Supervisor Interviews." Unpublished doctoral dissertation. Austin, TX: The University of Texas.

Patton, Michael Q. (1978). *Utilization of Focused Evaluations.* Beverly Hills, CA: Sage Publishing.

Pearson H. Delmer (1980). "Development of a Forced-Choice Teacher Behavior Rating Scale." Unpublished doctoral dissertation. Austin, TX: The University of Texas at Austin.

Peck, R. F., et al. (1977). "Studying the Effects of Different Kinds of Teaching on Different Students." Austin, TX: Research and Development Center for Teacher Evaluation, University of Texas at Austin.

Penn-Harris-Madison School Corporation (1981). *An Appraisal Plan for Increasing Teacher Effectiveness and Student Learning.* Osceola, IN: The Corporation.

Peterson, P. L., and H. J. Walberg (1979). *Research on Teaching: Concepts, Findings and Implications.* Berkeley, CA: McCutchan Publishing.

Phi Delta Kappa (1979). "Gallup Says Public Wants Greater Productivity," in *News, Notes and Quotes,* Newsletter of Phi Delta Kappa. 24 (November–December):1.

Phi Delta Kappan (1982). "Purposes of Evaluation," in *Practical Applications of Research.* 4 (March):1–4. Bloomington, IN: Center on Evaluation, Development, and Research.

Popham, William James (1971). *Designing Teacher Evaluation Systems.* Los Angeles, CA: The Instructional Objectives Exchange, December.

Popham, W. J. (1971). "Performance Tests of Teaching Proficiency: Rationale, Development, and Validation," *American Educational Research Journal* 8 (January): 5–117.

Popham, W. J. (1975). *Educational Evaluation.* Englewood Cliffs, NJ: Prentice-Hall.

Popham, W. James (1974). "Pitfalls and Pratfalls of Teacher Evaluation," *Educational Leadership* 32 (November): 141–146.

Price, Kingsley (1974). "The Sense of 'Performance' and Its Point," *Educational Theory* 24 (Fall): 313–327.

Principles and Guidelines for Teacher Evaluation Systems (1979). Austin, TX: The Texas Cooperative Committee on Teacher Evaluation, Texas Classroom Teachers' Association.

Quinto, F., and B. McKenna (1977). *Alternatives to Standardized Testing.* Washington, D.C.: National Education Association.

Randall, Robert S. (1969). "An Operational Application of the CIPP Model for Evaluation." *Educational Technology* 9 (July): 40–44.

Raths, James, and Hallie Preskill (1982). "Research Synthesis on Summative Evaluation of Teaching," *Educational Leadership* 39 (January):310–313.

Ratsoy, Eugene, and Leroy V. Sloan (1981). "Effective Teaching as a Focus for Supervisory Activity," *The Canadian Administrator* 20 (April): The University of Alberta, Department of Educational Administration.

Rayder, Nicholas, and Trent Taylor (1979). *One Responsive Supervision for Professional Development Overview of the Process.* San Francisco: Far West Laboratory for Educational Research and Development, ED 175 207.

Redfern, George B. (1980). *Evaluating Teachers and Administrators: A Performance Objectives Approach.* Boulder, CO: Westview Press.

Reyes, Donald J., and Gloria T. Alter (1984). "Research on Learning and Teacher Effectiveness: Implications for Instructional Supervision," *Thresholds in Education* 10 (May):17–20. Northern Illinois University, DeKalb, Illinois.

Richards, I. A. (1968). "The Secret of 'Feed-forward'," *Saturday Review* 51 (February): 14–17.

Rissel, Dorothy (1978). "Videotaping Classes," *Teaching and Learning at Indiana University: An Occasional Newsletter* 3 (February). ED 177–112.

Rodin, Miriam (1975). "Rating the Teachers," *Education Digest* XLI (November):54–57.

Rose, Gale W. (1964). *School Executive's Guide.* Englewood Cliffs, NJ: Prentice-Hall.

Rosenshine, Barak, and N.F. Furst (1971). "Research on Teacher Performance Criteria," in *Research in Teacher Education.* B. O. Smith, editor. Englewood Cliffs, NJ: Prentice-Hall.

Rosenshine, B., and N. Furst (1970). "Research in Teacher Performance Criteria," in *Teacher Training: A Symposium*. B. O. Smith, editor. Englewood Cliffs, NJ: Prentice-Hall.

Rosenshine, Barak (1970). "The Stability of Teacher Effects Upon Student Achievement," *Review of Educational Research* 40 (December):647–662.

Rosenshine, Barak, and Norma Furst (1973). "The Use of Direct Observation to Study Teaching," in *Second Handbook of Research on Teaching*. Robert M. W. Travers, editor. Chicago, IL: Rand-McNally.

Ross, Victor J. (1981). "Here's How Teachers Should Be Evaluated," *American School Board Journal* (August): 25–27.

Rossi, Peter H., and Howard E. Freeman (1982). *Evaluation: A Systematic Approach*, 2nd ed. Beverly Hills, CA: Sage Publications.

Rossmiller, Richard A. (1983). "Resource Allocation and Achievement: A Classroom Analysis," in *School Finance and School Improvement*. Allan Odden and L. Dean Webb, editors. Fourth Annual Yearbook of the American Education Finance Association. Cambridge, MA: Ballinger Publishing.

Rutman, Leonard, editor (1977). *Evaluation Research Methods: A Basic Guide*. Beverly Hills, CA: Sage Publications.

Rutter, Michael (1980). "School Influences on Children's Behavior and Development," *Pediatrics* 65 (February):208–220.

Ryans, David G. (1960). *Characteristics of Teachers*. Washington, D.C.: American Council on Education.

Samph, Thomas (1976). "Observer Effects on Verbal Classroom Behavior," *Journal of Educational Psychology* 68 (December): 736–741.

Sandefur, J. T. (1984). "Teacher Competency Testing: The Public's Mandate," *Teacher Education and Practice* 1 (Spring):11–16.

Schmitt, Neal, Ronni Meritt, Michael P. Fitzgerald, and Raymond A. Noe (1982). "The NASSP Assessment Center: A Validity Report," *NASSP Bulletin* 66 (September): 134–142.

Schnake, Melvin E. (1978). "The Performance Evaluation as Motivating Tools," *Supervisory Management* 23 (July): 29–32.

Schneider, Frank (1983). "Merit Pay for Teachers." Mobile, AL: Division of General Services, Research and Evaluation, Mobile County Public Schools. June. Mimeographed.

Scriven, Michael (1967). "The Methodology of Evaluation," in *Perspectives of Curriculum Evaluation*. Ralph Tyler, R. Gagne and M. Scriven, editors. *Curriculum Evaluation*. AERA Monograph Series on Curriculum Evaluation, No. 1, Chicago, IL: Rand McNally.

Scriven, Michael (1980). "The Evaluation of College Teaching," *Professional Development Occasional Paper #3*. Syracuse, NY: National Council of States on Inservice Education.

Seeley, David S. (1979). "Reducing the Confrontation Over Teacher Accountability," *Phi Delta Kappan* 61 (December): 248–251.

Seldin, Peter (1984). *Changing Practices in Faculty Evaluation: A Critical Assessment and Recommendations for Improvement*. San Francisco, CA: Jossey-Bass.

Semmel, Melvyn I. (1978). "Observer Agreement and Reliability of Classroom Observational Measures," *Review of Educational Research* 48 (Winter):57–84.

Sergiovanni, Thomas J. (1977). "Reforming Teacher Evaluation: Naturalistic Alternatives," *Educational Leadership* 34 (May):602–607.

Shavelson, Richard J. (1976). "Teachers' Decision Making" in *The Psychology of Teaching Method*. Part I, 75th Yearbook, National Society for the Study of Education. Chicago: University of Chicago Press.

Shaplin, J. T., and H. F. Olds, editors (1964). *Team Teaching*. New York: Harper & Row.

Shavelson, Richard, and Nancy Atwood (1977). "Generalizability of Measures of Teaching Process," in *The Appraisal of Teaching: Concepts and Process*. Gary D. Borich and Kathleen S. Fenton. Reading, MA: Addison-Wesley Publishing Co.

Shearron, Gilbert F. (1976). "Developing and Improving Instruments for Measuring Competence of Pre-Service Teacher Education Students." A paper presented at a Conference on Competency Based Teacher Education in Special Education Assessments, New York: August 11, ED 129 803.

Shoemaker, David M. (1977). "The Contribution of Multiple Matrix Sampling to Evaluating Teacher Effectiveness," in *The Appraisal of Teaching: Concepts and Process*, Gary D. Borich and Kathleen S. Fenton. Reading, MA: Addison-Wesley Publishing Co.

Shulman, Lee S., Editor (1976). *Review of Research in Education*. vol. 4, Itasca, IL: F. E. Peacock Publishers.

Shulman, Lee S., Editor (1977). *Review of Research in Education*. vol. 5, Itasca, IL: F. E. Peacock Publishers.

Shutte, A. J. (1971). "An Exploratory Investigation of Micro-Teaching as Pre-Service Technique and Its Evaluation, Using Flanders' System of Interaction Analysis." Unpublished doctoral dissertation. New York: New York University.

Silverman, Buddy R. S. (1983). "Why the Merit Pay System Failed in the Federal Government," *Personnel Journal* 62 (April):294–297.

Silvern, Leonard C. (1969). *Systems Analysis and Synthesis Applied Quantitatively to Create an Instuctional System*. Los Angeles, CA: Education and Training Consultants Company.

Simon, A. E. (1977). "Analyzing Educational Platforms: A Supervisory Strategy," *Educational Leadership* 34 (May):580–584.

Simon, Anita, and E. Gil Boyer, eds. (1970). *Mirrors for Behavior II: An Anthology of Observation Instruments*. volume A. Philadelphia: Classroom Interaction Newsletter.

Simpson, Roy H. (1966). *Teacher Self-Evaluation*. New York: MacMillan.

Sistrunk, Walter E. *The Supervisory Behavior Description Questionnaire*, Forms 1 and 2. Columbus, MS: West Lowdes Elementary School.

Siv, R. G. H. (1975). *The Tau of Science*. Cambridge, MA: MIT Press.

Smith, B. O. (1980). *A Design for a School of Pedagogy*. Washington, D.C.: U.S. Department of Education.

Smith, Nick L., editor (1982). *Field Assessments of Innovative Evaluation Methods*, Number 13 of New Directions for Program Evaluation, Scarvia B. Anderson, editor-in-chief. San Francisco: Jossey-Bass.

Snyder, K. J. (1981). "Clinical Supervision in the 1980's," *Educational Leadership* 38 (April):521–524.

Soar, Robert, and Soar, R. (1976). "An Attempt to Identify Measures of Teacher Effectiveness from Four Studies," *Journal of Teacher Education* 27 (Fall):261–267.

Soar, R. S. (1977). "An Integration of Findings from Four Studies of Teacher Effectiveness," in *The Appraisal of Teaching: Concepts and Process.* Gary Borich, editor. Reading, MA: Addison-Wesley Publishing Co.

South Carolina (1981). "Act No. 187 of the 1979 Session of the South Carolina General Assembly with 1981 Amendments." Columbia, SC: The South Carolina Educator Improvement Task Force.

Spady, William G. (1977). "Competency Based Education: A Bandwagon in Search of a Definition," *Educational Researcher* 6 (January):9–14.

Stake, Robert (1977). "Formative and Summative Evaluation," in David Hamilton, Barry MacDonald, Christine King, David Jenkins, and Malcolm Parlett, editors. *Beyond the Numbers Game: A Reader in Educational Evaluation.* Berkeley, CA: McCutchan Publishing.

Stake, Robert (1967). "The Countenance of Educational Evaluation", *Teachers College Record* 68:523–540.

Stallings, Jane A. (1977). *Learning To Look: A Handbook on Classroom Observation and Teaching Models.* Belmont, CA: Wadsworth Publishing.

Stallings, Jane (1977). "How Instructional Processes Relate to Child Outcomes," in *The Appraisal of Teaching: Concepts and Process.* Gary D. Borich and Kathleen S. Fenton. Reading, MA: Addison-Wesley Publishing Co.

Stallings, Jane A., and David H. Kaskowitz (1974). *Follow Through Classroom Observation Evaluation, 1972–73.* Menlo Park, CA: Stanford Research Institute.

Steel, Carolyn F., and David R. Stone (1973). *Taxonomy of Teaching Competency: Skill Domain.* Salt Lake City, UT: Utah State University.

Stevens, Romiett (1912). *The Question as a Measure of Efficiency in Instruction.* New York: Teachers College, Contributions to Education, No. 48, Columbia University.

Stipnieks, Anita T. (1981). "A Study of Teacher Evaluation Practices in Selected School Districts in the United States." Ph.D. dissertation. Austin, TX: The University of Texas at Austin.

Stodolsky, Susan S. (1984). "Teacher Evaluation: The Limits of Looking," *Educational Researcher* 13 (November):11–18.

Stow, Shirley B. (1979). "Using Effectiveness Research in Teacher Evaluation," *Educational Leadership* 37 (October): 55–59.

Strotnik, Kenneth A. (1981). "An Inter-Observer Reliability Study of the SRI Observation System as Modified for Use in a Study of Schooling." *A Study of Schooling in the U.S.,* Technical Report #27. Los Angeles, CA: Graduate School of Education, University of California at Los Angeles, ED 214 895.

Stubbs, Michael, and Sara Delamont (1976). *Explorations in Classroom Observation.* London: John Wiley and Sons.

Stufflebeam, Daniel L., and William J. Webster (1980). "An Analysis of Alternative Approaches to Evaluation," *Educational Evaluation and Policy Analysis* 2 (May–June):5–20.

Stufflebeam, Daniel L., Editor (1971). *Educational Evaluation and Decision Making.* P. D. K. National Study Committee on Evaluation. Itasca, IL: F.E.A. Peacock Publishers.

Stufflebeam, Daniel L., Editor (1979). *Standards for Evaluation of Educational Programs, Projects, and Materials.* Western Michigan University, MI.

Stulac, Josef F., et al (1981). *Assessment of Performance in Teaching: Field Study Instrument.* Columbia, SC: South Carolina Educator Improvement Task Force, July.

Sutherland, John W. (1978). *Societal Systems—Methodology, Modeling, and Management*. New York: Elsevier North-Holland.

Sopranovich, Beth B. (1982). "Differentiated Staff. Revisited," *Phi Delta Kappan* 64 (September):20–21.

Sweetland, R. C., and D. J. Keyser, editors (1983). *Tests: A Comprehensive Reference for Assessments in Psychology, Education and Business*. Kansas City: Test Corporation of America.

Taba, Hilda et al. (1972). *Teacher's Handbook for Elementary Social Studies*. 2nd ed. Menlo Park, CA: Addison-Wesley.

Taylor, William (1979). "Contraction or Decline," The Cocking Lecture for 1979, delivered to the National Conference of Professors of Educational Administration, Edmonton, Alberta, Canada, August 13.

Teacher Competence Research Project (no date). "Teacher Practices Observation Record." Gainesville, FL: College of Education, University of Florida.

Teacher Evaluation (1967). Washington, D.C.: Administrative Leadership Service, Educational Service Bureau.

Temple, ISD (1980). "Summary Report: Preliminary Survey of Teachers Using De-TEK for the First Time." Temple, TX: Temple Independent School District. Mimeographed.

Texas Cooperative Committee (1979). *Principles and Guidelines for Teacher Evaluation Systems*. Austin, TX: The Committee, Texas Classroom Teacher's Association.

Thomas, Don R. (1971). "Preliminary Findings on Self-Monitoring for Modifying Teacher Behaviors," in *A New Direction for Education: Behavior Analysis*, vol. 1, Eugene A. Ramp and Bill Hopkins, editors. University of Kansas, Support and Development Center for Follow Through, Department of Human Development.

Thomas, M. Donald (1979). *Performance Evaluation of Educational Personnel* (Fastback 135). Bloomington, IN: Phi Delta Kappa Educational Foundation.

Thomas, M. Donald (1984). "Educational Personnel Evaluation," *Educational Leadership* 42 (December/January):32.

Thompson, Jack M., and William Dewall (1972). "A Teacher Self-Evaluation Program: A Progress Report." Sonoma, CA: Sonoma County Office of Education. Mimeographed.

Tikunoff, William, D. C. Berliner, and R. C. Rist (1975). "An Ethnographic Study of the Forty Classrooms of the Beginning Teacher Evaluation Study Known Sample," Technical Report No. 75-10-5. San Francisco, CA: Far West Laboratory for Educational Research and Development.

Tillman, Murray (1982). *Trouble-Shooting Classroom Problems*. Glenview, IL: Scott, Foresman.

Tracy, Saundra J., and Robert MacNaughton (1984). "New Wine for Old Bottles: Refurbishing an Existing Teacher Evaluation System," *Thresholds in Education* 10 (May):30–32. DeKalb, IL: Northern Illinois University.

Trang, Myron L., and Owen L. Caskey (1981). *Improving Instructor Effectiveness Through Videotaping Recall*. Palo Alto, CA: R and E Research Associates, Inc.

Travers, Robert M. W. (1981). "Criteria of Good Teaching," in *Handbook of Teacher Evaluation*. Jason Millman, editor. Beverly Hills, CA: Sage Publications.

Tremba, E. A. (1975). "The Effectiveness of Videotape Feedback with Microteaching and Modeling." Unpublished doctoral dissertation, Lehigh University.

Trump, Lloyd, and G. F. Vars (1976). "How Should Learning Be Organized?" *Issues in Secondary Education.* National Society for the Study of Education, 75th Yearbook, Part 2. Chicago: University of Chicago Press.

Tuckman, Bruce Wayne (1979). *Evaluating Instructional Programs.* Boston, MA: Allyn and Bacon.

Tuckman, Bruce, J. Stebor, and R. Hyman (1979). "Judging the Effectiveness of Teaching Styles: The Perceptions of Principals," *Educational Administration Quarterly* 15 (Winter):104–115.

Turney, Mildred I. (1969). "A Comparison of Varied Time Periods of Microteaching in the Development of Interpersonal Relationships in Teaching. Final Report." Stevens Point, WI: Wisconsin State Universities Consortium of Research and Development. ED 054 078.

Tyler Independent School District (1980). "Overview of Clinical Supervision Techniques as a Method of Principal-Staff Evaluation," in the *Policy Manual,* Tyler Independent School District, Tyler, TX.

Valverde, Leonard A. (1982). "The Self-Evolving Supervisor," in *Supervision of Teaching.* Thomas J. Sergiovanni, editor. Alexandria, VA: Association for Supervision and Curriculum Development.

Veldman, Donald J. (1970). *Student Evaluation of Teaching.* Research Methodology Monograph No. 10, Research and Development Center for Teacher Evaluation. Austin, TX: The University of Texas at Austin (Spring).

Veldman, D. J., and R. F. Peck (nd). *Comprehensive Personal Assessment System: Student Evaluations of Teachers Set I.* Austin, TX: Research and Development Center for Teacher Education, The University of Texas at Austin.

Von Fange, Theodore and Sterling Benson (1978). *Competency Assessment Model: Development and Verification.* Lindsborg, KS: Department of Education, Bethany College, ED 180 934.

Walberg, Herbert (1974). *Evaluating Educational Performance.* Berkeley, CA: McCutchan Publishing.

Walberg, H. J., D. Schiller, and G. D. Haertel (1979). "The Quiet Revolution in Educational Research," *Phi Delta Kappan* 61 (November):179–183.

Walker, Hill M., and Hyman Hops (1977). "Use of Normative Peer Data as a Standard for Evaluating Classroom Treatment Effects," in *Evaluation Studies: Review Annuals.* volume 2, 1977. Edited by Marcia Guttentag with Shalom Saar. Beverly Hills, CA: Sage Publications.

Warner, Allen R. (1981). "Conferencing: The Heart of the (Supervisory) Matter," in *Improving Classroom Practice Through Supervision.* Robert H. Anderson, editor. Dallas: Texas Association for Supervision and Curriculum Development.

Webster, William J. (1983). "Perspectives on Evaluation: A Retrospective and Perspective View." Unpublished paper presented at the American Educational Research Association meeting, Montreal, Canada, April.

Weise, Kay, and Carl Harris (1984). "To Test, or Not To Test . . . Begging the Question?" *Teacher Education and Practice* 1 (Spring):17–19.

Weiss, Carol H. (1972). *Evaluation Research: Methods for Assessing Program Effectiveness.* Englewood Cliffs, NJ: Prentice-Hall.

West, Ed L. (1979). "Quality Through Evaluation," *Points.* 12 (September):1–3.

White, Alvin M. (1981). *Interdisciplinary Teaching.* New Directions for Teaching and Learning. Number 8, December 1981. San Francisco, CA: Jossey-Bass.

Wise, Arthur E., et al. (1984). *Case Studies for Teacher Evaluation (N-2133-NIE).* Santa Monica: The Rand Corporation.

Wise, Arthur E., and Linda Darling-Hammond (1984). "Teacher Evaluation and Teacher Professionalism," *Educational Leadership* 42 (December–January):28–33.

Wise, Arthur E., et al. (1984). *Teacher Evaluation: A Study of Effective Practices* (R-3139-NIE). Santa Monica: The Rand Corporation.

Withall, J., and F. H. Wood (1979). "Taking the Threat Out of Classroom Observation and Feedback," *Journal of Teacher Education* 30 (January–February):55–58.

Wolf, Robert L. (1979). "The Use of Judicial Evaluation Methods in the Formation of Educational Policy" *Educational Evaluation and Policy Analysis* 1 (May–June):29–38.

Wolf, Richard M. (1979). *Evaluation in Education. Foundations of Competency Assessment and Program Review.* NY: Praeger Publishers.

Wolff, Theodore F. (1984). "The Critic's Role: To Encourage Talent, Never to Dictate to It," *The Christian Science Monitor (December 24):21–22.*

Wood, C. J., and P. A. Pohland (1983). "Teacher Evaluation and the 'Hand of History'," *The Journal of Educational Administration* 21 (Summer):169–181.

Yamamoto, Kaoru (1977). "Vulnerability in College Teaching," *Proceedings of the 4th Annual Conference on Higher Education.* College of Education, Texas Technological University, Lubbock, Texas.

Yelland, Robert C. (1968). "The Rating Game," *Personnel Journal* 47:865–67.

Yankelovich, Daniel (1979). "Executive Newsline," *Flightime Magazine,* Continental Airlines, February.

Yulo, R. J. (1967). "An Exploration of the Flanders' System of Interaction Analysis as a Supervisory Device with Science Interns." Unpublished doctoral dissertation, Harvard University, Cambridge, MA.

Zumwalt, Karen K. (1982). "Research on Teaching: Policy Implications for Teacher Education," in *Policy Making in Education,* Part I, 81st Yearbook, National Society for the Study of Education. Ann Lieberman and M. W. McLaughlin, editors. Chicago, IL: The University of Chicago Press.

Index

DATE DUE

2 11 '87	
12 25 '87	
3 25 87	
4-15	
8 05 '87	
AM 23 '91	
JUN 1 5 94	

BRODART, INC.   Cat. No. 23-221